Zen Skin, Zen Marrow

Zen Skin,
Zen Marrow

Will the Real Zen Buddhism
Please Stand Up?

STEVEN HEINE

OXFORD
UNIVERSITY PRESS

2008

OXFORD
UNIVERSITY PRESS

Oxford University Press, Inc., publishes works that further
Oxford University's objective of excellence
in research, scholarship, and education.

Oxford   New York
Auckland   Cape Town   Dar es Salaam   Hong Kong   Karachi
Kuala Lumpur   Madrid   Melbourne   Mexico City   Nairobi
New Delhi   Shanghai   Taipei   Toronto

With offices in
Argentina   Austria   Brazil   Chile   Czech Republic   France   Greece
Guatemala   Hungary   Italy   Japan   Poland   Portugal   Singapore
South Korea   Switzerland   Thailand   Turkey   Ukraine   Vietnam

Copyright © 2008 by Oxford University Press, Inc.

Published by Oxford University Press, Inc.
198 Madison Avenue, New York, New York 10016

www.oup.com

Oxford is a registered trademark of Oxford University Press

Library of Congress Cataloging-in-Publication Data
Heine, Steven, 1950–
Zen skin, Zen marrow: Will the real Zen Buddhism please stand up? / Steven Heine.
    p. cm.
Includes bibliographical references and index.
ISBN 978-0-19-532677-2
1. Zen Buddhism.   I. Title.
BQ9265.4.H45 2007
294.3'927—dc22   2007010408

9 8 7 6 5 4 3 2 1

Printed in the United States of America
on acid-free paper

Preface

The idea and inspiration for this book came to me while I was presiding at a panel at a national conference dealing with applications of Zen Buddhist and other forms of East Asian thought to the realm of ethics. As the presider, my role was simply to announce and to keep time for the presenters and to moderate the discussion part of the session. The panelists gave outstanding presentations on how traditional Zen thought was highly appropriate and adaptable to the relativism of the postmodern world and to environmentalism in an era experiencing the threat of global warming, etc. After a little over two hours of lectures and response by the discussant, I opened up the panel for questions from the floor after observing a very attentive and patient audience, most of whom had stayed in the room for the entire session (rather than the usual coming and going).

The first question came from a scholar known as a harsh critic of the behavior of some aspects of the Zen institution, who challenged just about everything the main speakers had been saying. Here, I thought, was a moment either of great intellectual challenge and debate or of embarrassment in that one side of the argument, representing a defense of Zen, or the other side, representing a critique, would easily put away the other party's claims. However, I was quickly surprised to see that neither of these options was actually the case. Instead, the conversation deteriorated into an instance of two parties talking past each other. A couple of speakers responded by denying the validity of the question by maintaining that they were focusing on theory rather than practice, and to be fair to them it became clear that the inquirer was repeating verbiage used in other contexts and had not tried to adjust his query to what had been presented during the panel. In short, neither side tried to engage the other in a stimulating, thought-provoking roundtable. Instead, there was a problematic, partisan refusal on both sides of the debate to acknowledge that there are some harsh realities and difficult choices confronting us in understanding the history of Zen as well as in contemplating its future path. What could have been a grand opportunity for long-term thinking about the role of Zen Buddhism in the twenty-first century faded into a brief exercise in disappointment.

The aim of this book is to begin to move past the vicious cycle of having apologists and detractors continue to ignore the opposing view by presenting the different positions with studied neutrality, while juxtaposing and forcing into interplay and constructive exchange both sides of the story. To paraphrase what I say in the fourth chapter, we must recognize that what seems to traditionalists/apologists as the strong suit desperately needed for the recovery of a world plagued by the threat of environmental disaster and nuclear holocaust is precisely the weakest link, according to the critics/detractors, which reflects an ethical morass lying at the root of many of today's social problems.

Following an introductory chapter that explains the significance of the book's title and subtitle by introducing the historical background of the images of skin and marrow (in contrast to flesh and bones) in the context of trying to discern the "real" Zen, the next chapters each examine how the debate takes place on a particular issue. Chapter 2 focuses on whether Zen's literary production represents a contradiction with the ideology of silence. The next chapter considers the question of the extent to which rituals and devotional practices, which are pervasive at many Zen temples, jeopardize the traditional emphasis on meditation. Chapter 4 deals with assessments of Zen's role in relation to modern sociopolitical and human rights issues. Finally, the epilogue highlights the importance of repentance as a traditional rite in contemporary contexts, as a means of discerning a middle way between apologetic and critical standpoints.

Acknowledgments

I thank Oxford University Press editor Cynthia Read for her ongoing support, and I also thank a host of colleagues who discussed some of the concepts of the book with me, including Roger Ames, Paula Arai, William Bodiford, Victor Forte, Griffith Foulk, Ashok Gangadean, Victor Hori, Chris Ives, Richard Jaffe, Hans-Rudolf Kantor, Gereon Kopf, Ken Kraft, Dan Leighton, Dan Lusthaus, Michel Mohr, Steve Odin, Jin Park, Linda Penkower, Mario Poceski, Charles Prebish, David Riggs, Karen Smyers, Jackie Stone, John Tucker, Youru Wang, Albert Welter, Duncan Williams, Pamela Winfield, and Dale Wright, among others. I also thank the several assistants who helped to proofread and edit the manuscript, particularly Aviva Menashe along with Maria Cubau and Jessica Reyes.

Contents

1. Fore Play:
   The Relativity of Truth and Uncertainty of Method, 3

2. Zen Writes:
   Fun and Games with Words and Letters, 37

3. Zen Rites:
   The Eclipse of Buddha, 73

4. Zen Rights:
   A Series of (Un)fortunate Social Events, 115

Epilogue. The Real Zen Buddhism:
   Engaged, Enraged, or Disengaged? 155

Notes, 173

Bibliography, 201

Index, 213

Zen Skin, Zen Marrow

I

Fore Play

The Relativity of Truth and Uncertainty of Method

War: What Is It Good For?

In recent years, the history and thought of Zen Buddhism has been examined and dissected from critical perspectives which use a variety of methodologies to probe and undermine the traditional self-definition and thereby create significant discussion and debate about what constitutes the "real" Zen. In the current environment of controversy and contest, it is fair to say that nearly everyone agrees that Zen is generally rather sorely misunderstood and is in desperate need of clarification, although this situation is not necessarily unusual or surprising, given the problematic field of studies of the Orient. Because of the legacies of colonialism and Romanticism that affect diverse Western intellectual endeavors, various forms of Buddhism along with more general cultural arenas in the East have been misappropriated repeatedly, and from different angles, as part of the phenomenon of Orientalism.[1]

The Battle over Orientalism

From the standpoint of identifying and deconstructing the roots and effects of Orientalism as initiated by Edward Said and carried out in diverse permutations by dozens of other scholars, Western discourse is often criticized for stereotyping Oriental culture based on thinly disguised imperialist, hegemonic agendas.[2] The colonial

West has portrayed the East as a Hades on earth, an inferior and fearsome realm of moral decay and a degree of social degeneracy reaching nearly apocalyptic proportions, or as a yellow peril badly in need of being dominated by a more rational and ethical civilization.[3] Conversely, a product of Romanticism is the seemingly opposite pattern of thought known as reverse Orientalism (or Occidentalism), whereby the stereotyping is inverted to assert the superiority of the Orient.[4] From this standpoint, Asia is depicted as a blissful Shangri-la, or a serene and beatific land of transcendental lotus eaters dwelling in a romanticized image of perfection and offering solace and a possible cure for the world's problems.[5] Or, as in the case of Puccini's *Madame Butterfly*, based on a story by Pierre Loti, and its many variations, there seems to be a bit of the worst of both elements. In a land of charming, graceful—yet complacent and compliant—women, an exotic and erotic, but subservient and wholly submissive Japanese bride is led to a tragic suicide when she discovers that she has been betrayed by her coarse, indifferent, and patronizing American husband.

As part of the vacillation between the extreme views of condemnation and praise, which share an unwillingness to deal realistically or forthrightly with the East and a propensity to view it in monolithic, black-and-white fashion without nuance, Buddhism also is viewed in skewed fashion. It is seen either as a sublime and quaint form of meditative mysticism, based on mind purification and self-transformation, unburdened by the theological baggage plaguing other world religions, or as the hollow shell of a sequestered ancient cult that broods on death and decay yet thrives on monastic political intrigue.[6]

Proponents of Zen may well be considered reverse Orientalists, who immunize themselves by arguing that criticisms reveal that only insiders—or, further, natives—can properly understand and experience Buddhist truth; in other words, the Orient is only for Orientals, and others, try as they might to comprehend, need not apply. For example, Eugen Herrigel, who became renowned for the book *Zen in the Art of Archery*, which tracks his six-year journey to penetrate the "insurmountable barriers" of Zen's relation to the martial art form, writes, "Wrapped in impenetrable darkness, Zen must seem the strangest riddle which the spiritual life of the East has ever devised: insoluble and yet irresistibly attractive."[7] While "for us [Zen teachings] are completely bewildering," he goes on to remark, "[f]or Orientals these mysterious formulae are clear and familiar truths."[8] Reverse Orientalism, which rejects comparisons with Western spirituality as being somehow beneath the pale of Zen, tends to view Eastern mysticism in a way that inverts—or converts—European Romantic fantasies of an idyllic realm, or at least builds on conceptions of religious experience initially developed by the West (although this also has roots in Asian expressions of utopian ideals).[9]

The conflict between attitudes based on stigmatization/condescension and on romanticization/idealization toward Asian society has been playing out in an increasingly polarized fashion. One may read a scholarly tome that skillfully debunks the notion of invariable cultural differences between East and West as so much Orientalist—or, in a perspective such as Herrigel's, reverse Orientalist—"mumbo jumbo" or "hocus pocus," to cite the phrasing in *The Lotus and the Robot* by Arthur Koestler, a primary critic of Herrigel and of Zen more generally.[10] This criticism might seem to evoke an untenable theory of universalism, which implies that all cultures should be held to one standard of evaluation, but in Koestler's case, his book's epilogue expresses an unabashed Judeo-Christian agenda that undermines his critique that he can find nothing that offers "significant advice" in Zen or in "any other Asian form of mysticism."[11] At the other end of the spectrum, *The Geography of Thought: How Asians and Westerners Think Differently . . . and Why* argues in a kind of post-Orientalist manner for there being irreconcilable differences in the ways of perceiving the world by East and West.[12] According to this work, with its reverse Orientalist implications, the cultures are blessed with variant cognitive processes, resulting in distinct social structures and belief systems, as if communities (or ethnicities) were hardwired for a particular set of impulses and responses.

Each of these approaches, when given consideration in and of itself, may be seen as worthwhile or even brilliantly insightful in offering a significant contribution to comparative cultural history. The problem is that the respective outlooks, when weighed against one another, tend to come across as reactive and partial, or biased and one-sided, as in the Jain proverb of the six blind men inspecting the elephant and mislabeling each part they touch as the whole. Each approach rests on a theory of knowledge that is not necessarily aiming for a mutuality of understanding nor arriving at a common sense of what is true, something that can only be derived from constructive interaction and dialogue between views. Therefore, the juxtaposition of approaches, unless tempered by a self-reflective, self-critical methodology, does not enable them to become more open-ended and balanced in relation to the other. Rather, it reinforces the stiffening effect of opposition and polarization, which are the results of Orientalism and which cannot help but be Eurocentric, and of reverse Orientalism, which in Japan is known as *Nihonjinron*, or the nativist position of cultural exceptionalism.

In the case of Zen, there remain fundamental disagreements about the root causes of misappropriations. According to a lyric by singer/songwriter

Leonard Cohen, "There is a war between the ones who say there is a war, / And the ones who say there isn't."[13] Indeed, there seems to be a war in the sense of a conceptual and verbal exchange of conflict and hostilities regarding what constitutes and who gets to explicate Zen, whereby different factions unproductively talk at or past—but not constructively with—one other, whether intentionally or not. The main debate is between two factions. One faction involves traditionalists, referred to here as supporters of the TZN, who continue to articulate and reinforce their view of the "traditional Zen narrative" and may come off as apologists and/or reverse Orientalists (even if they are Westerners like Herrigel). The other faction includes critics and reformers referred to here as supporters of HCC, who attempt to carry out historical and cultural criticism and may appear, like Koestler, hypercritical in their judgments and evaluations, which evoke shades of Orientalism.

Traditional Zen Narrative (TZN) versus Historical and Cultural Criticism (HCC)

On one side of the argument there stand exponents of TZN, which argues that Zen is an idealistic, utopian vision of nondual experience that by its very nature continually stands beyond the fray and is free from contestation because it cannot be defined and resists any attempt at explication. Its own means of expression are merely heuristic devices or skillful means that form part of an indirect communication through paradox and other literary techniques pointing the way to silence as the ultimate truth. To think otherwise is simply to misrepresent Zen, which has traditionally promoted itself as a religious standpoint based on three main pillars:

1. Ineffability, or adhering to a process of a "special transmission outside the scriptures" (C. *chia-wai pieh-ch'üan*, J. *kyōge betsuden*) undertaken "without relying on words and letters" (C. *pu-li wen-tzu*, J. *furyū monji*). This is epitomized by legends of Mahakasyapa receiving transmission via a flower when Sakyamuni gave a silent sermon; of second patriarch Hui-k'o attaining his status in receiving Bodhidharma's "marrow" by remaining silent while the three other contestants, who responded with words, received his "skin, flesh, and bones"; and of Hui-neng's ripping and Te-shan's burning of the sutras. It is also shown in the emphasis on "swallowing the red-hot iron ball" of the *Mu* (no or nothingness) kōan in the first case of the *Wu-men kuan* (J. *Mumonkan*) collection of 1228,[14] as well as in countless cases that defy conventional language by demanding, for example, that a

disciple say what an object, e.g., a water pitcher is, without calling it a water pitcher and without not calling it a water pitcher.

2. Nonduality, or the espousing of a philosophy based on a direct, unmediated experience of reality beyond the realm of conditioning, which does not require intercession through the conventional use of objects of worship, such as images, symbols, or representations of deities. The nondual philosophy is epitomized by Bodhidharma's response of "no merit" to the imperial query about the value of good works; by Lin-chi's dictum "kill the Buddha"; by T'ien-jan's burning of a wooden image of the Buddha on a cold night when he needed firewood; and by the saying "Wash out your mouth every time you utter the word Buddha." It is also shown in the minimalist architectural style of the prototypical seven-hall monastery (*shichidō garan*) and in the saying often cited by Zeami that "moonlight is cast on snow falling on the white heron standing by the silver bowl," as well as in the monochromatic rock gardens at Ryōanji and other temples, which resonate with the simplicity of the empty circle (*ensō*) that appears at the conclusion of the original set of Ten Oxherding Pictures.

3. Societal harmony, or embracing the equality of all beings by virtue of their possessing the common endowment of original enlightenment (C. *pen-hsüeh*, J. *hongaku*) or innate Buddha-nature (C. *fo-hsing*, J. *busshō*). The approach to maintaining strict institutional hierarchy founded on the essential, underlying unity of all members of the samgha is reflected in the requirement for communal labor as expressed in the (no doubt) apocryphal set of monastic codes attributed to Pai-chang, which stress the virtues of poverty, humility, and self-sacrifice, in addition to the detailed instructions governing behavior in the Monks Hall in the seminal *Ch'an-yüan ch'ing-kuei* (J. *Zen'en shingi*) of 1103 and other examples of rules and regulations.[15] The Zen emphasis on group harmony is also represented by the traditional role of the chief cook (*tenzo*) at the monastery, who is judged by whether or not he can prepare the proper amount of rice, such that by the end of a meal, especially during a period of intensive meditation (*sesshin*), not a single grain is either left over or wanted by a hungry monk.

To be fair to the standpoint of TZN that stresses the ineffable, iconoclastic, and irrational qualities of the Zen experience, we probably should invert the Cohen lyric, for the sake of emphasis, to read: "There is a war between the ones who say there is no war, / And the ones who say there is." For TZN, there is not a war, and there can never be conflict about what Zen really means, which defies explanation or analysis. The appearance of war is itself a product of a hopeless misunderstanding on the part of those who think there is a war, that is, by the kind of people who would foolishly try to eat a bowl of ramen noodles or a serving of sushi with a Western knife and fork. But given that, despite protests, the war seems to be raging nevertheless, TZN has redoubled its resolute efforts at opposing critics who, out of frustration and futility, use their metaphorical silverware to carve up their opponents by criticizing without comprehending traditional Zen.

At the other end of the spectrum, the standpoint of HCC argues that apologists deliberately cloak Zen in a shield of opaqueness. This is done to avoid or to claim immunity from the careful scrutiny of historical examination, which would disclose inconsistencies, contradictions, and even basic flaws in the character of Zen as a social institution conditioned by the flux of everyday events and the turmoil of worldly affairs. HCC shows that proclaiming "Zen and the art of archery (or flower arrangement, etc.)"[16] in triumphal fashion should really become sustained criticism of Zen and the art of the funeral (or religious prejudice, to cite recent studies). From the standpoint of HCC, which emphasizes the need to analyze the causes and consequences of the development of Zen in the context of East Asian history and society, there can and must be a war of ideas that challenges what is often the cynical obfuscation and hypocrisy inherent in traditional Zen.

HCC is composed of diverse methods for trying to construct a self-critical (or deconstructive) approach to appropriations of Zen by the West or its critics (Orientalism) and to presentations by the East or its sympathizers (reverse Orientalism). HCC defeats stereotypes by showing the myriad of factors that do not fit neatly into or that defy the pillars of TZN.[17] In contrast to the slant of the traditional self-definition and the way Zen generally portrays itself, modern scholarship has been pointing out that Zen is actually characterized by:

1. Speech, or the extensive use of language in the voluminous records produced in the Sung Chinese and Kamakura Japanese eras, which raise questions about why Zen seems to be slapping itself in the face in fervently denying, yet at the same time utilizing, the efficacy of language in both oral and written communications. Recent literary criticism of Zen texts, in some cases following the lead of biblical criticism or of scholarship on other types of sacred writings, have analyzed the variety of styles, including poetry, historical (or pseudohistorical) records, kōan commentaries (in prose, verse, and capping phrase, or *jakugo*, form), formal and informal sermons, and monastic rules. These studies are carried out in terms of current theories on genre,

orality, and narratology at both the atomic level of syntax and speech parts and the meta level of discourse and ideology.[18] Other HCC approaches question in Koestlerian fashion whether Zen opaqueness and obscurity make any sense.

2. Mediation, or the widespread use of rituals and supernaturalism in the spread of the school throughout East Asia, particularly in ceremonies for lay believers and converts from other sects seeking practical worldly benefits (*genze riyaku*) through rites and symbols for healing or for gaining prosperity or longevity.[19] Showing the pervasive function of the ritual element in institutional history, as well as the assimilation of esoteric Buddhism along with Taoist/Shinto and folk religious elements, makes traditional claims for the priority of iconoclasm seem like little more than idle rhetorical flourishes.

3. Discrimination, or the unfortunate contributions of Zen to problems of gender and class conflict, such as intolerance toward the outcast community (*burakumin*), nationalism, and militarism especially in colonial and prewar Japan. A main example is the use of posthumous ordination names (*kaimyō*) during funeral services as part of the widespread Japanese phenomenon of funerary Buddhism (*sōshiki Bukkyō*); these names are coded to indicate the social status—or lack of it, in the case of outcasts—of the deceased. This gives rise to accusations that, like many other forms of spirituality, unfortunately, while Zen says it espouses peace and harmony, in actuality it has acceded to being a part of social injustice and military aggression.

When we juxtapose the three pillars of TZN with the three rebuttals of HCC, we find a kind of continuum that starts with a sense of compatibility and cooperation between the two viewpoints yet extends to polarization involving hostility and mutual negation. On the first issue, regarding the role of language, HCC concurs and in some ways amplifies the message of TZN by showing the richness and creativity of the Zen literary tradition in its diverse manifestations, even if there is disagreement about whether silence is the culminating truth beyond discourse. Sounding a contrary note that sets the stage for more vehement criticisms on the other two issues, especially matters of social responsibility, for Koestler the contradictory quality in Zen rhetoric is an example of "double-think" put forth by the "only school which has made a philosophy out of [inarticulateness], whose exponents burst into verbal diarrhea to prove constipation."[20]

In dealing with the second issue, regarding the role of religious practice, the HCC approach begins by pointing out that TZN represses its origins in overlooking the extent to which Zen has assimilated folklore and popular religiosity associated with rituals for pacifying demonic spirits and venerating the power of local deities. An analogy to the TZN attitude would be a nouveau riche family that deliberately conceals its true lineage by tampering with family records or that claims to be blissfully unaware of what might be considered an embarrassment in its background. A study by Duncan Williams, *The Other Side of Zen: A Social History of Sōtō Zen in Tokugawa Japan*, which deals with pilgrimages and healing rites in the early modern Sōtō sect particularly associated with certain prayer temples (*kitō jiin*), suggests that it is time to recognize that the neglected roots of Zen practice have remained crucial throughout history.[21] By examining "temple logbooks, prayer and funerary manuals, letters to and from village officials as well as the government's Office of Temples and Shrines, death registries, miracle tales of popular Buddhist deities, secret initiation papers, villagers' diaries, fund-raising donor lists, and sales records of talismans," Williams joins other scholars seeking to locate "Buddhism on the ground."[22] This refers to the lived form of Buddhism rather than what is portrayed in texts, whether primarily theoretical/philosophical or hagiographical/mythological. The question arises about the relation between this other side and the unnamed first side (presumably, the elitist, iconoclastic view based on textual abstraction rather than concrete reality)—in other words, are these complementary or conflictive? For Williams, at least, the popular religious side of Zen is something endlessly fascinating, and adherents should not be ashamed of it. However, for many on the side of criticism, the HCC rebuttal on the issue of ritual practice punctures the image of irreverence or blasphemy and compounds the Koestlerian implication that there is no small degree of hypocrisy and bad faith embedded in the TZN position.

In the debate regarding the third pillar, this contentious outlook is carried further. For HCC, unmasking the deficiencies in the TZN approach necessitates an assault on the citadel to penetrate what turns out to be the thin veneer of arguments for transcendence. The HCC critique of the second issue indicates that Zen was never a purely reclusive tradition because its survival as an institution was always connected with imperial governance, patterns of patronage, and other means of attracting lay support. On matters of transgression in the social sphere, Zen's deficiencies cannot be blamed on an indifferent or unresponsive attitude, for in some cases it has been actively pursuing a reprehensible agenda. Perhaps part of the problem is Zen's apparent lack of a sense of good versus evil on a metaphysical level in stressing that all phenomena are interconnected and interpenetrating. This suggests a radically relativist position that opens the door to antinomian tendencies, as in

Ikkyū's motto "Entering the realm of the Buddha is easy, entering the realm of the demon is difficult," which could be interpreted as giving license to demonic activity. HCC's criticism reaches a level of rejection, and even revulsion, toward the traditional self-definition, as found in works such as *Rude Awakenings*, *Pruning the Bodhi Tree*, and *Zen at War* (and its sequel, *Zen War Stories*).[23] This seems to leave the respective approaches at antithetical vantage points and in an immovable stalemate.

The continuum, when extended to its logical conclusion, does seem to escalate to war, which TZN regrets and denies and HCC approves and abets. For TZN, HCC's sense of aggressiveness reflects an all-too-human attempt to avoid a genuine effort to appropriate a higher level of truth in which petty debates and conflicts are surpassed. The TZN rejoinder, in some cases absorbing and responding to criticism from HCC and in other cases remaining oblivious to it, defends and promotes Zen's role in terms of social ethics by portraying it as a guiding light and potential leader of environmentalism and peace issues (such as nuclear nonproliferation).[24] Far from being deficient and outdated, Zen is the most enlightened and progressive standpoint on the world scene today.

While acknowledging that HCC creates a challenge that contributes to an overall understanding of the tradition, for TZN the tendency toward hypercriticism and an unproductively dismissive tone fails to comprehend true Zen, whereas for HCC it is the triumphal assertions of self-surpassing truth in TZN's often hyperbolic apologetics that blocks an appreciation of how Zen functions. This requires a deliberately rude, in-your-face hermeneutics to deconstruct and dislodge stubbornly false claims.[25] But, is HCC a correction or just one more viewpoint, another side of Zen that is presumptive and stiffening in its own problematic way? While HCC asks, "Which side are you on?" TZN wonders, "War, what is it good for?" One cannot escape the sad irony that, for HCC, war is not something metaphorical but involves Zen's complicity in imperial aggression and atrocities.

How is it possible to penetrate the morass of views and discern the real Zen, if any? Would it be the traditional view of a utopian, self-sustaining community of dedicated monks who rise above the world of strife yet have solutions for current problems? Or would there be a very different picture derived from critical studies that help to expose Zen as at least a bewildered and indifferent, and perhaps even hypocritical and corrupt, monastic system rife with inconsistencies and injustice? Which view is the distortion, and which the disguise?

We may ask, "Will the real Zen please stand up?" à la the old TV series *To Tell the Truth*, in which at the climactic moment near the end of every show, the announcer intoned, "Will the real so-and-so please stand up?" (as part command and part query). The fundamental flaw in that analogy, however, is that in the show, after a series of questions by the panelists addressed to three contestants, two of whom were pretending or playacting at the identity that the third person really had, there is one and only one correct answer: the real so-and-so. This is also the case in similar kinds of contests that rely on the use of decoys or teasers. For example, a museum display may have a piece of porcelain from some medieval object and may list three possible uses that visitors are to guess from, but only one of these is accurate and the other two are simply plausible "coulda' beens."

Another model to consider in trying to reconcile the disparities and come to terms with the actuality of the situation is the game theory of James P. Carse's *Finite and Infinite Games*, in which he argues, "Finite players play within boundaries; infinite players play with boundaries."[26] Perhaps this discrepancy can be applied to HCC's dealing with concrete issues and playing a finite game within social-historical boundaries and to TZN's dealing with timeless truths and playing an infinite game outside the boundaries of language and social structure. Therefore, the reason that the two sides have difficulty communicating is that they do not play by or even comprehend each other's rules, aims, and methods. In terms of history of religions methodology, this issue is parallel to a debate between the cosmological view of sacred space as universal and unrestricted and the locative view of it as particular and local.[27] We can also evoke the so-called two-tiered model of the intersection of a religion's great tradition (literary, clerical, universal, and institutional) and little tradition (oral, charismatic, local, and diffuse).

The Buddhist version of this kind of analysis is the distinction between the level of absolute or ultimate truth, which involves the realm of unconditioned reality or emptiness, and the level of relative or conventional truth, which involves the realm of conditioned reality or form. At times, the two levels harmoniously intersect and complement—as in the *Heart Sutra* dictum "form is emptiness, emptiness is form"—and at other times, they contradict and mutually negate one another as in the *Lotus Sutra* parable of the illusory city as a decoy for nirvana. However, the problem with both game theory and the two levels of truth model is that this kind of approach may leave one satisfied with the notion that the TZN and HCC approaches are simply different or coexistent levels which do not need to be reconciled in terms of their contrasts and oppositions.

Meanwhile, if there is a sense of compatibility between these approaches, this seems to enable TZN to emerge relatively unscathed, whereas the HCC position arguing for contrast and difference seems to be on the defensive. To quote a popular song, "So let's leave it alone / 'Cause we can't see eye-to-eye / ... There ain't no good guy, there ain't no bad guy / There's only you and me, and we just disagree" (Dave Mason, "We Just Disagree," 1977). However, since neither side would be happy with that conclusion, it would seem just as appropriate to consider a Dr. Jekyll and Mr. Hyde model that sees Zen projecting one bright side to the public (TZN) while being barely able to bottle up and conceal its inevitable underside (according to HCC). On the other hand, it seems the better literary reference may be to the Lewis Carroll characters Tweedledum and his look-alike partner Tweedledee, who always insists "contrariwise."

As disinterested observer/participants, we need to be able to stand back and dislodge from fixed perspectives as the arguments fly back and forth and to ask two main questions. The first question is intellectual/historical: How and why has such a degree of polarization managed to infiltrate and settle into the world of Zen studies? Answering this question takes us back to the complexity of the Eugen Herrigel–Arthur Koestler controversy and how and why the latter spent considerable time attacking Herrigel and his supporter D. T. Suzuki. Now, half a century old and seemingly passé, this debate, and its implications for the state of Zen studies, is still very much alive based on the enduring popularity of *Zen in the Art of Archery* as a vehicle for expressing TZN that has had a tremendous impact on all parties, including its critics. Koestler is also intriguing for the way he at once, unfortunately, echoes seemingly obsolete Orientalist deficiencies yet anticipates much of the twenty-first century's cultural criticism.

The second question is methodological: What are the possibilities for developing a balanced and nuanced middle-way approach that avoids the excesses of triumphal self-congratulation and the dismissive tone of hypercriticism? The challenge is to craft a model that is open-ended and flexible enough to encompass the extremes of polarization and to create the interactive give-and-take of constructive dialogue that acknowledges the contributions yet, without forcing the respective views to withdraw or collapse, compels them to adjust to one another through the dialectical process of the encounter of ideas.

Here, I will consider a Zen model based on Dōgen's interpretations of the record of Bodhidharma awarding his "skin, flesh, bones, marrow" to the four disciples in competition to become his heir. Conventional interpretations see this in the context of a *To Tell the Truth*–style correct-versus-incorrect outlook, with skin as the most superficial level, reflecting the incorrect response or the loser, and marrow (awarded to second patriarch Hui-k'o for keeping silent) as the deepest level, reflecting the correct response or the winner in the contest. Dōgen, on the other hand, advocates the equality of the respective views reflecting "neither superficiality nor depth." Skin and marrow are considered to be of the same value but with the distinctions held intact, and so function like bookends seen in a horizontal or side-by-side rather than a vertical or top-down fashion.

Which Side Are You On?

Historical Overview of the Battleground

The current debate about what constitutes the real nature of Zen is traceable to the formative and classical periods during the T'ang and Sung dynasties that saw the rise to prominence of the so-called Meditation school in the highly competitive environment of Chinese religions. There were internal dissensions between Ch'an factions, which were splintered in the early days and remained contentious, as well as discussions with external figures, including monks and thinkers representing other Buddhist and Taoist schools, and lay scholar/officials or civil servants affiliated with Confucianism (or neo-Confucianism). The debates generally revolved around the issues of the efficacy of language in relation to maintaining a noble silence, the role of ritual practices vis-à-vis meditation as means of cultivating self-discipline, and whether the contemplative state should be considered passive and renunciative, or dynamic and active, in relation to mainstream society. Even at the early stages of history, there was a sense of tension in that, "[f]or all of its talk about 'not setting up scriptures,' the Ch'an school...valued the written word and prized the sutras as the ultimate source of authority in historical evidence."[28]

In the ninth century, Tsung-mi, as part of a process of doctrinal classification, examined and evaluated the relative merits of divergent Zen standpoints. Unlike some of his more irreverent Ch'an contemporaries associated with the iconoclastic Southern school, Tsung-mi was a meticulous scholar who wrote extensive critical analyses of the various Ch'an and scholastic sects, along with numerous scriptural exegeses. Tsung-mi was deeply interested in both the practical and doctrinal aspects of Buddhism and was especially concerned with exposing antinomian tendencies in the Hung-chou stream of the Southern school. This movement, represented by eminent masters Ma-tsu, Pai-chang, Huang-po, and Lin-chi, which became the mainstream Ch'an branch, was based on the radically nondual view of the "interpenetration of phenomenon and phenomenon" (C. shih-shih wu-ai, J. jiji muge) philosophy of the Hua-yen school that was set in contrast by Tsung-mi to the dualism of the defunct Northern Ch'an school.[29]

In addition to Tsung-mi's Buddhist critique, Confucianists and even some Taoists lambasted iconoclastic practices at reclusive Zen monasteries for being parasitic and failing to contribute to the well-being of ordinary society. Indeed, Zen and other Buddhist schools and foreign cults (e.g., Christianity, Judaism, Islam, Zoroastrianism, and Manichaeanism) were proscribed in the 840s, although the ban on Buddhism was lifted shortly thereafter.[30] Following several centuries of decline, by the twelfth century, Ch'an had reemerged as the dominant sect among religious movements in China based in large part on imperial support that was a trade-off for supervision and regulation of its temples.

During the Sung, Lin-chi school master Ta-hui, who advocated exclusive contemplation of the *Mu* case in an approach known as "introspecting the kōan" (C. *kan-hua Ch'an*, J. *kanna Zen*), became involved in a heated debate with Ts'ao-tung school master Hung-chih's advocacy of "silent illumination" (C. *mo-chao Ch'an*, J. *mokushō Zen*). Ta-hui accused his rival of leading disciples to a state of becoming like "dead wood" or "dried ashes," that is, of being hopelessly escapist and world denying in cutting off rather than transmuting attachments and distractions.[31] As another premodern example of the internal debates and dissensions within Zen, during Tokugawa era Japan, in a wide-ranging social critique, Tominaga Nakamoto's *Emerging from Meditation* (*Shutsujo kōgo*) attacked a false sense of transcendence found in a variety of Buddhist approaches.[32]

"Sukiyaki" Invasion

In the modern period, Zen became a global movement after being introduced to the West from the time of the 1893 World Parliament of Religions and through the efforts of thinker/translator/commentator D. T. Suzuki, in addition to the early Japanese immigrant communities, especially in Hawaii, the West Coast of the United States, and Brazil. The rapid rise of Zen inevitably generated the TZN-HCC debates, which became heated in the post–World War II period, beginning in the 1950s when the impact of Zen was felt on multiple levels in worldwide scholarship and cultural influences. This was the time of the rapid dissemination of Zen ideas and applications in a variety of ways. The main vehicles were the expository writings of Suzuki, Alan Watts, and Christmas Humphreys; the literature of Beat poets and novelists dealing with Buddhist themes, including Allen Ginsberg, Gary Snyder, and Jack Kerouac; and the works of other religious thinkers and writers affected by Zen, such as Thomas Merton, J. D. Salinger, and Norman Mailer. Popular cultural expressions highlighting Buddhist mysticism and an Asian mystique more generally were found in a variety of popular films and television shows, ranging from *Sayonara, World of Suzie Wong, A Girl Named Tamiko*, and *Auntie Mame* to *I Love Lucy*. For example, in one *Lucy* sequence, a send-up of the film *My Geisha* starring Shirley MacLaine, which was itself a spoof of some of the films listed above, the Ricardos and Mertzes travel to Japan, with Lucy and Ethel dressing up like geishas in order to fool their husbands, whom they suspect of flirting with real Japanese geishas. The show was produced around the time the song "Sukiyaki," imported from Japan, became the number one hit on American charts.

Meanwhile, among Japanese writers and filmmakers gaining an international reputation, novelists Kawabata Yasunari and Tanizaki Jun'ichiro, perhaps influenced by the Kyoto school of philosophy, evoked classical Zen themes in explicating traditional Japanese cultural values, and film director Kurosawa Akira portrayed a Zen samurai in *Yojimbo*. However, the equally prominent though far more controversial author Mishima Yukio wrote a devastating critique of corruption at the heart of the Zen monastic institution in the novel *Temple of the Golden Pavilion* (*Kinkakuji*), which is based on a real-life incident in which an acolyte burned down one of the most famous Rinzai temples in Kyoto.[33] Also, director Mizoguchi Kenji offered an oblique but forceful criticism of Buddhism in *Life of Oharu* (*Saikaku ichidai onna*).[34]

The early postwar period also saw several other important developments. One was the burgeoning of Zen practice sites in the United States, and eventually the opening of centers run by prominent East Asian teachers like Maezumi Taizan and Sasaki Joshu and by Americans trained by Japanese masters, including Robert Aitken, Philip Kapleau, and John Loori. The new centers could not help but be affected by the shifting economic conditions and gender roles in the American context. Another development was in the world of scholarly studies, covering academic research and curriculum development, in which works by Jacques Gernet, Paul Demieville, Heinrich Dumoulin, and Walter Liebenthal made impressive strides with translations and historical interpretations of textual materials.[35] Also at this time, Zen texts began reaching a vast audience through a small volume, *Zen Flesh, Zen Bones*, edited by the first great American haiku poet, Paul Reps, along with Nyogen Senzaki. Originally compiled from three smaller books—*101 Zen Stories, The Gateless Gate* (*Wu-men kuan*), and *The Ten Bulls*, or Ten Oxherding Pictures—and first published in the 1930s by Doubleday, the book with the addition of a fourth item, *Centering*, was widely distributed under the Tuttle imprint in 1957, and has remained a fixture.[36]

At that time, Alan Watts noted the multiplicity of approaches involved in studying and practicing Zen. A famous short essay from 1957 provided a threefold typology: "Beat Zen," which refers to the literary approach that pursues the dharma in a hip, unconventional manner; "Square Zen," which tries to emulate the practice style of Japanese temples; and "Zen" (by which he meant classical Zen). The classical Zen of the T'ang through Sung and Ka-makura eras in China and Japan (eighth through fourteenth centuries) could best be appropriated, Watts felt, through historical studies in order to correct the extremes and excesses of the lifestyle orientations of the first two ap-proaches. However, an answer to the question of how best to carry out his-toriography in order to properly access the classical period remained elusive. As Robert Sharf notes, studies of Zen generally follow one of two methods. The first is buddhology (which could be called "desk work"), that is, philology or textual criticism mainly dealing with the history of ideas expressed in kōan collections and transmission of the lamp records. The other method is social science (or "fieldwork"), which uses an anthropological approach to the cultish side of ritual practices at temples and festivals in order to understand the social history of Zen as a religious movement.[37]

Amid the waxing and waning of approaches, the initial sense of there being a sharp and bitter division within the ranks of Zen scholars was framed in the January 1953 issue of *Philosophy East and West*. The debate emerged between positivist historicism, examining the historical development of the school in medieval times, which was undertaken by Chinese scholar Hu Shih, an advocate of historiographical methodology, and the philosophical psy-chology of D. T. Suzuki, highlighting Zen as a path of interior experience transcending history. Each claimed the other could not understand the real Zen, with Hu Shih saying, "I emphatically refuse to accept [Suzuki's view]."[38] Bernard Faure notes:

> The positions of the two protagonists were deeply entrenched: ac-cording to Hu Shi, Chan is merely one religious movement among others, and its development was an integral part of the political his-tory of the Tang. According to Suzuki, however, Zen transcends history, and historians are by definition reductionists.[39]

For Suzuki, there are "two types of mentality: the one which can understand Zen and, therefore, has the right to say something about it, and another which is utterly unable to grasp what Zen is ... [for] Zen belongs in a realm alto-gether transcending." Suzuki, an international sensation by then who also declared, "Hu Shih fails to understand this [distinction]," seemed to gain the upper hand. This meant that the attitude rejecting the notion of there being a war between factions prevailed for a time—just as the war was really about to begin.

While the positions of Hu Shih and Suzuki may seem opposite and irreconcilable, from another perspective, the participants in this "rather sterile antimony," according to Faure's estimation, can be grouped together as apologists who accepted uncritically the traditional self-definition, thereby practicing neither good history nor good philosophy.[40] This group is then contrasted by Faure with the more viable historical approach of Japanese scholar Yanagida Seizan, who helped to train a generation of Western scholars. In his seminal study of early Zen history, *Shoki zenshū shisho no kenkyū*, published in 1967 (the same year that Philip Yampolsky's monumental translation with historical introduction of the *Platform Sutra* was released), Yanagida sought to create a balance between traditional Zen hagiography, which cannot claim the status of truthful narrative but neither can it be dismissed as empty fabrication, and modern historiography.[41] As innovative and groundbreaking as the works by Yanagida and Yampolsky are, however, these scholars have been lumped together and labeled by their critics as being unable to extricate themselves (and Zen) from outmoded assumptions and misappropriated materials in buying into the traditional self-definition.[42]

Much Ado about "It"

In this context of continually shifting priorities and perspectives about the real Zen, where apparent opponents end up making strange bedfellows by being cast in alliance, willingly or intentionally or not, the Herrigel-Koestler controversy came forth by the early 1960s and in many ways remains front and center nearly a half century later. It is difficult to overstate the impact (though not necessarily, from a strict standpoint, the merit) of their relatively thin works. Herrigel's slim volume, based on the experiences of a German mystic who lived and taught in Japan in the 1920s before returning to his homeland, was first published in Germany in 1948 as an updated version of an earlier publication from 1936. It was translated into English five years later, two years before his death, and eventually came full circle by being translated into Japanese in 1982; it has remained at the top of the reading list of nearly everyone who becomes interested in Zen, a perpetual trendsetter that has spawned countless imitations, take-offs, and send-ups, too numerous to begin naming.[43]

The *Lotus and the Robot* was released two years after the English publication of Herrigel's work by a controversial, side-changing intellectual who was a Marxist and then a critic of the Soviets, a Zionist, and a critic of Judaica. The book was based on Koestler's observations while traveling in Asia in search of a mystical response to the problems of modern Europe. The sense of disillusionment and disgust in Koestler's book, his only major work dealing with Zen,[44] seems like a throwback to unrepentant Orientalists whose agenda it was to turn Asian religious thought into disreputable clichés. But at the same time, to his credit, Koestler presciently anticipated and articulated nearly all of the main rebuttals to TZN provided by HCC on the issues of language, ritualism, and societal affairs, even raising the issue of possible Nazi affiliations on the part of Herrigel and not letting Suzuki off the hook for ignoring this.[45]

Fascination with Herrigel's account of his training in archery, which presages the participant-ethnography of Carlos Castaneda's series of books on practicing with a shaman in Mexico, revolves around the emphasis he puts on the syllable "It" in the instructive phrase used repeatedly by his Japanese mentor Awa Kenzō, "'It' shoots."[46] According to Herrigel, Awa—whose method of joining archery and religion was apparently considered uninformed and controversial by his contemporaries—insisted that the key to success is to realize that from the standpoint of all-encompassing emptiness, nobody in particular lets loose the arrow, because "It" does the shooting in and of itself. Herrigel struggled with this conundrum for a while until he unconsciously had a breakthrough one day that was acknowledged by Awa, who "made a deep bow and broke off the lesson. 'Just then "It" shot' he cried, as I stared at him bewildered. And when I at last understood what he meant I couldn't suppress a sudden whoop of delight."[47]

There quickly developed opposition to Herrigel's approach from different angles. By the time *Zen in the Art of Archery* was well known in America, the insider Mishima had written an insightful and devastating attack on Zen monastic life based on an incident of temple arson, although the sharpness of the criticism was somewhat blunted by his well-known loyalty to imperial Shinto and his public ritual suicide (*hara-kiri*) in 1970. From a very different angle, another German in the field, the Jesuit missionary Heinrich Dumoulin, completed his first comprehensive study of the history of Zen by, in the final sentences of the book, calling the satori experience "imperfect," for it is "only the eternal Logos," he insists, that "can ever lead to the perfect truth."[48]

The work of Koestler, a German-speaking Hungarian Jew, shows that at this period European intellectuals still dominated debates about Zen. Koestler goes right after Herrigel's claims of "'It' shoots," perhaps making this the biggest deal ever about a single two-letter syllable aside from Bill Clinton's notorious "It depends on what the meaning of the word 'is' is." According to Koestler:

> The main emphasis in "applied" Zen training is on complete indif-
> ference towards success and failure. The "It" will only enter into
> action when straining and striving have ceased and the action be-
> comes "effortless" and automatic. The formula is, of course, quite
> misleading... [because] the contestant must be hypnotized into the
> belief that he does not care about the outcome, that he is not com-
> peting but performing a mystic ritual.

Koestler dismisses Herrigel's book, "which manages to combine the more ponderous kind of Germanic mysticism with the more obvious kind of Zen hocus-pocus," and comments on how "distressing" it is that such a work "is taken seriously by the public in the West."[49] However, it must be noted that Koestler, who claimed to be a lifelong atheist, manages to combine Dumou-lin's assertion of the supreme value of the "Logos incarnate"—although nei-ther one names Jesus—with a broad attack on nearly every feature of traditional and modern Japan from sumo wrestling and haiku poetry to de-partment stores and the high-tech industry. He has a field day with Japan bashing, although he also notes a fascination with the way East Asian society integrates "Confucius and Zen, rigid perfectionism and elastic ambiguity."[50]

The unreliability factor cuts both ways if we probe beneath the surface of how these authors are defined in relation to their messages. It turns out that Herrigel *was* a Nazi sympathizer who probably had certain political reasons for promoting Zen and Japanese culture to a German audience in the 1930s, as pointed out by Koestler, who refers to his adversary a couple of times as "Herr Herrigel." However, Koestler, who was partly Jewish, also had an erratic career as a writer/intellectual that culminated in an oddly anti-Jewish tract (*The Thirteenth Tribe*, 1976) about the Khazars,[51] and he may well have had at least a quasi-political motive for the pro-Christian concluding section of *The Lotus and the Robot*.

A more systematic yet respectful critique of Herrigel was provided four decades after the fact by Yamada Shōji,[52] who questions by means of a so-phisticated historical and language analysis whether the experience of "'It' shoots" could have ever taken place. Yamada's analysis covers the following factors: (1) the history and typology of Japanese archery, which has no sub-stantial connection to Zen; (2) the eccentric and eclectic teachings of Awa Kenzō who, inspired by Zen mottos and phrases, tried to turn archery into a kind of religious experience, although he lacked any formal background or training in Zen; (3) the limitations of the interpreter Komachiya Sōzō, who was admittedly loose in his translations (perhaps resembling the scene in the film *Lost in Translation* where Bill Murray receives instruction in filming an ad for Suntory whiskey and keeps asking the interpreter whether the overbearing director did not in fact say much more than the little bits of information she either chooses or is able to reveal);[53] (4) Awa's own disclaimers about his recollection of the conversations, which took place without the presence of Komachiya; and (5) how this episode was portrayed by Herrigel.

Yamada also points out that in the twelve-year gap between his original work and its reissue in German, Herrigel apparently rather drastically changed the description of the key event, as the "It" reference was not nearly of the same order of significance in the first version (and, interestingly, by the time this gets translated into Japanese, it is completely absent). Drawing on ideas proffered by Japanese and Germans involved in archery lessons concerning whether this term would be possible in Japanese syntax or represents the intrusion of German locution, Yamada speculates that Herrigel simply misheard or mistook the innocuous Japanese phrase *sore deshita*, which means "that's it."[54] Perhaps Awa meant, "That was a good shot," without suggesting that an extraneous force was responsible. Therefore, despite Herrigel's claim that his "book contains not a single word that was not said directly by my teacher,"[55] the essence of what he portrays that has had such a tremendous impact on the way millions of readers have understood Zen may rest on mere fabrication and fantasy.

Minority Report

Is there a middle way between the TZN and HCC standpoints? In considering the " 'It' shoots" controversy, for example, is there an approach that avoids the triumphal, ahistorical reification of "It" as some kind of *Star Wars*–like supernatural force and the debunking trivialization that devalues and denies the author's experience altogether? The debate over "It" is not an isolated focus on a single syllable, but is emblematic of much larger issues in the juxtaposition and jostling of opposing viewpoints. The first of John McRae's "Rules of Zen Studies," which consist of four ironic principles, is "It's not true, and therefore it's more important." Unfortunately, for some, the converse is taken for granted, that is, importance must be equated with alleged truth or untruth.[56]

The aim of this book is not so much to look for ways of reconciling and resolving the conflict or ending the so-called war, as to explore different aspects and multiple layers of the disagreements regarding the three main issues, where inconsistencies between what Zen says and what Zen does— or is, on the ground—become apparent. The approach here strives for a descriptive, nonjudgmental tone in carrying out a careful historical assessment that avoids the extremes of apology and excessive criticism and that enables diverse facets and factors of Zen to reveal themselves and be assessed appropriately.

I support a model for understanding the relation between the TZN and HCC viewpoints that is derived in part from Dōgen's minority-opinion reading of the kōan case in which skin, flesh, bones, and marrow were awarded respectively to four finalists by Bodhidharma in the competition to select his successor, who would become the second patriarch. This outlook, which represents traditional Zen, albeit in somewhat unconventional fashion, will be balanced with current historical scholarship that calls into question some of the mythology that has built up around the tradition's account.

The following translation of the kōan is based on the slightly different versions included in Dōgen's *Kana Shōbōgenzō*, the "Kattō" fascicle, and *Mana Shōbōgenzō* (case 201), texts that are, in turn, culled from the *Ching-te chuan-teng lu* transmission of the lamp record from 1004:

> The twenty-eighth patriarch [the venerable Bodhidharma, who was about to go back to India] said to his disciples, "As the time is drawing near [for me to transmit the dharma to my successor], please tell me how you express your understanding."
>
> One of the students, T'ou-fu said, "My present view is that we should neither be attached to words and letters nor abandon words and letters, but use them as an instrument of the Tao." Bodhidharma responded, "You express my Skin."
>
> Then nun Tsung-chih said, "As I now see it, [the dharma] is like Ananda's viewing Akshobhya Buddha's land just once and never again." Bodhidharma said, "You express my Flesh."
>
> Tao-yü said, "The four great elements are originally empty and the five aggregates do not exist. Therefore, I see not a single thing to be expressed." Bodhidharma said, "You express my Bones."
>
> Finally, Hui-k'o came forward and prostrated himself three times, and stood silently in his place. Bodhidharma said, "You express my Marrow." Thus, he transmitted the Dharma and robe to [second patriarch] Hui-k'o.[57]

As several scholars, including Ishii Shūdō and T. Griffith Foulk, have shown, this case like so many other examples in the Zen records did not spring forth in a pristine way but evolved slowly over several centuries of refinement.[58] In the early days of Zen studies, which means prior to the Yanagida Seizan era, it was usually taken at face value that kōans preserved in the

Ching-te chuan-teng lu and subsequent collections were valid historical documents that reflected what pre-T'ang and T'ang masters, including the early patriarchs, actually said.[59] Now, it is clear that almost invariably, the *Ching-te chuan-teng lu* along with other frequently cited texts from the Sung dynasty came toward the beginning, rather than at the end, of a long process of culling and editing the records that came to be known as kōans. Therefore, the contents of Sung texts are not only unreliable as historical documents, but even their hagiographical value is limited by the fact that the *Ching-te chuan-teng lu* version represents only one of several different ways the tradition has portrayed itself in this and other dialogues.

The aim of the historian is to piece together the puzzle of self-definition or identity, which is by no means monolithic. In the case of the record of Bodhidharma and his four disciples, there is a pattern similar to what Yamada has exposed with regard to *Zen in the Art of Archery*. What is generally considered to be the most important aspect of the kōan, the emphasis on silence associated with Hui-k'o attaining the marrow, did not even appear during the more than two centuries of textual development leading up to the *Ching-te chuan-teng lu*. Throughout this period, there were discrepancies about (1) the number of disciples, with several examples including only three; (2) whether there is any dialogue included or just a list of the awards bestowed; (3) the significance of the nun's role and whether she is the most superficial or second in the sequence; and (4) whether the sequence starts with the skin or with the marrow (also, in at least one instance, blood is substituted for skin as the most superficial level). In any case, there is no indication of the crucial role that silence plays in selecting the second patriarch prior to the *Ching-te chuan-teng lu* version.

According to Table 1.1, in the first record of the case, from the *Li-tai fa-pao chi* of 774, there were three disciples but no dialogue, with the marrow awarded first to Hui-k'o (it never varies that he is the recipient), then the bones to Tao-yü, and the flesh to Tsung-chih.[60] In the *Pao-lin chuan* version of 801, there are four contestants and there is also a double sequence. Bodhidharma first says to the four disciples that one will receive the marrow, another the bones, a third the flesh, and a fourth the blood, and then he mentions that the blood goes first to T'ou-fu, followed by the flesh to Tsung-chih, the bones to Tao-yü, and the marrow to Hui-k'o.

Moreover, there is still no dialogue, so the reader does not know the basis for making the awards (although at the time, this may have been passed down as an oral tradition). In the next text, the *Nei-cheng fo-fa hsüeh-mo pu* of 819, the case starts with the marrow and has three contestants with no dialogue, as in the *Li-tai fa-pao chi*.

TABLE 1.1. The Evolution of the Skin, Flesh, Bones, Marrow Narrative.

Text (Year)	No.	Sequence of Elements
Li-tai fa-pao chi (774)	3	marrow, bones, flesh
Pao-lin chuan (801)	4	blood, flesh, bones, marrow
Nei-cheng fo-fa hsüeh-mo pu (819)	3	marrow, bones, flesh
Tsung-mi's *Ch'an-men shih-tzu* (841)	3	flesh, bones, marrow
Tsu-t'ang chi (952)	3	marrow, bones, flesh
Ching-te chuan-teng lu (1004)	4	skin, flesh, bones, marrow (= silence)
T'ien-sheng kuang-teng lu (1036)	3	flesh, bones, marrow
Ch'uan-fa cheng-tsung chi (1061)	4	skin, flesh, bones, marrow

Tsung-mi's version in 841 in the *Chung-hua ch'uan-hsin-ti ch'an-men shih-tzu ch'eng-hsi t'u* for the first time contains dialogue, but it is quite different from the standard *Ching-te chuan-teng lu* version a century and a half later in making no reference to the skin and with the marrow awarded last, although not for silence. According to this version, nun Tsung-chih received the flesh for saying, "When afflictions are cut off, one realizes bodhi," and Tao-yü received the bones for saying, "When deluded there are afflictions, when awakened there is bodhi." Hui-k'o received the marrow for saying, in a manner that resembles the famed *gatha* verse of sixth patriarch Hui-neng, "Fundamentally, there are no afflictions, and the original state is bodhi." Furthermore, Tsung-mi's commentary was unorthodox in preferring the supposedly inferior positions and disputing the supremacy of Hui-k'o's comments.

There were several more variations, including the *Tsu-t'ang chi* of 952, which is similar to the original version but also mentioned that Hui-k'o gained the dharma seal to denote the interiority of awakening and the robe to establish the authority of the lineage. Then, the 1004 *Ching-te chuan-teng lu* version included four disciples, with the skin being awarded first, the nun coming second in the sequence, and silence as the correct final answer. Some of the subsequent versions, including the next major one in the *T'ien-sheng kuang-teng lu* of 1036, reverted back to mentioning three contestants and some contained other variations as well.

While the standard interpretation indicates that Hui-k'o's standing in his place suggests that "the way of verbal expression was cut off and the basis of mental activity was destroyed," an alternative view was provided by prominent T'ien-t'ai exegete Chih-li, whose version and understanding of the dialogue was similar to Tsung-mi's (with the contestants gaining skin, flesh, and marrow). Chih-li notes that Tsung-mi's position is closer to the skin and flesh views of Bodhidharma's lesser disciples, that is, he does not approve of Hui-k'o's statement about the original state and prefers to highlight the struggle with overcoming affliction, especially in the middle response. Chih-li, however, agrees with defenders of the orthodox position that Hui-k'o's view represents the supreme dharma.

As for the *Ching-te chuan-teng lu*'s emphasis on the second patriarch's silence, the reticence is sometimes absolutized as a stark rejection of all oral and written words, particularly those of the sutras, which are alluded to or cited by his three unsuccessful rivals. But in other interpretations, silence is seen not as a literal and total rejection of speech but as a superior ability to penetrate to the deepest meaning of the sutras, or a probing analysis that follows words as far as they can go and then, at the extreme limit of conceptualization, leaves them behind.[61]

The heart of Dōgen's interpretation, cited at length below, is unique in arguing against the conventional view of the superiority of silence, and it is quite useful as a model for understanding dissensions and debates between the TZN and HCC perspectives:

> You must study the first patriarch's saying, "You express my
> Skin, Flesh, Bones, and Marrow," as the way of the patriarchs. All
> four disciples heard and realized this saying all at once. Hearing and
> learning from it, they realized the Skin, Flesh, Bones and Marrow of
> the liberated body-mind, or the Skin, Flesh, Bones and Marrow of
> casting off body-mind [*shinjin datsuraku*]. You should not interpret
> the teachings of the patriarchs and masters from a single specific
> viewpoint. It is a complete manifestation without partiality.
>
> However, those who do not fully understand the true transmis-
> sion think that "because the four disciples had different levels of
> insight, the first patriarch's saying concerning the 'Skin, Flesh, Bones
> and Marrow' represents different degrees in recognizing the super-
> ficiality or depth [of understanding]. The Skin and Flesh are further
> [from the truth] than the Bones and Marrow." Thus, they say that
> [Bodhidharma told Hui-k'o] that he "expressed the Marrow because
> the second patriarch's understanding was superior." But interpreting
> the anecdote in this manner is not the result of studying the buddhas
> and patriarchs or of realizing the true patriarchal transmission.
>
> You should realize that the first patriarch's expression "Skin,
> Flesh, Bones and Marrow" does not refer to the superficiality or depth
> [of understanding]. Although there may remain a [provisional] dis-
> tinction between superior and inferior understanding, [each of the
> four disciples] expressed the first patriarch in his entirety. When
> Bodhidharma says, "You express my Marrow" or "You express my

Bones," he is using various pedagogical devices that are pertinent to particular people, or methods of instruction that may or may not apply to particular levels of understanding.

It is the same as Sakyamuni's holding up an *udambara* flower [to Mahakasyapa], or the transmitting of the sacred robe. What Bodhidharma said to the four disciples is fundamentally the selfsame expression, but since there are necessarily four ways of understanding it, he did not express it in one way alone. Even though each of the four ways of understanding is partial or one-sided, the way of the patriarchs ever remains the way of the patriarchs.[62]

The following principles are enunciated in this approach:

1. There is no winner or loser, depth or superficiality, top or bottom, as each view expresses a degree of understanding yet is incomplete, as in Heidegger's saying, "There is truth in errancy, and errancy in truth."
2. The appropriate interpretive style is, therefore, horizontal and non-evaluative or uncommitted to a preference for a particular view.
3. This allows for a focus on particular perspectives in terms of their unique and distinctive characteristics without a reduction to a one-size-fits-all theory, while also enabling an overall view of a broad spectrum of multiple standpoints—not losing the forest for the trees, and not losing the trees for the forest.
4. The goal, therefore, is to let a hundred blossoms bloom and allow them to constructively encounter, rather than remain polarized against, each other.
5. This compels, rather than constrains, a constructively critical outlook that, in exposing deficiencies, highlights areas for revision and reform.

Around the time of the English publication of Herrigel's book, Reps and Senzaki were capturing the imaginations of many readers by titling their small, simple, appealing book *Zen Flesh, Zen Bones*. Perhaps this was done to suggest the irony that these were the in-between levels considered inferior to the marrow—which is "never found in words," according to Reps[63]—yet superior to the skin, and therefore functioning within the realm of challenge and turmoil as one struggles to attain insight by grappling with kōan cases. In any case, the Reps-Senzaki book came at the beginning of a long historical curve when Zen was still being introduced to the West. Now, after a lengthy process that has seen Zen become nearly commonplace in commanding a high level of interest and intrigue among specialists in scholarship and practice yet remain exotic in some quarters and problematic for others, I offer the title of this book to further depolarize the sense of depth versus superficiality. This helps to enhance our sense of disentangling the entangled vines (of misimpression and misappropriation) by means of working constructively and creatively through the vines.

We can now consider how a *Zen Skin, Zen Marrow* approach can be applied to the case of Herrigel's "It." On the one hand, it seems likely, based on historical criticism, that he mistook or somehow misrepresented his mentor's statement, perhaps turning a mere congratulatory comment into a reified exclamation. Herrigel was prone to exaggeration in his handling of the relation between archery and Zen, and in the cycle of translations, perhaps an appropriate understanding got lost and further removed from what actually transpired in his interactions with Awa. On the other hand, the experience he depicts is by no means altogether dismissible based on the enduring popularity of the book and its impact on admirers and critics alike, so that the refutations, like any bad press, may only serve to keep inspiring curiosity and interest.

The question is, how far-fetched is it to imagine that Awa told Herrigel something that was translatable as " 'It' shoots"?[64] To find a nonjudgmental interpretation, let us consider the meaning of the phrase in terms of syntax and context. The use of the reified "It" in a way seems implausible, yet may be well suited to typical Japanese syntax, which emphasizes the predicate and leaves vague, suppressed, or unspoken the identity of the subject. The meaning is to be determined by tone of voice or another communicative indicator, as in the assertion "Feeling hungry" instead of "I am hungry," or the query "Healthy?" instead of "How are you feeling?" What is really going on with " 'It' shoots," it can be argued, is just the opposite of the reification of a subject, but rather a Western way of capturing the dynamic, action-oriented Japanese syntax. The expression replaces the typical personal subject with an impersonal one in a way that paradoxically removes the barrier between subject and predicate, or displaces subjectivity from the spotlight by emphasizing the act of shooting in and of itself.

Despite the objections of Koestler and Yamada, there are numerous precedents for Herrigel's phrase in traditional Zen sayings. These include the prose comment on case 16 of the *Wu-men kuan*, "The Sound of the Bell," which asks rhetorically, "Does the sound come to the ear, or does the ear go to the sound?" In other words, there is no "I hear" but rather "hearing" or " 'It' hears." Another example is Dōgen's remark in *Shōbōgenzō* "Immo" that the sound of the bell is not a matter of the clapper striking the bell nor the bell resounding from the clapper, but the "ringing of the ringing." Dōgen also comments on the saying "When the donkey sees the well, the well sees the donkey" by suggesting, "The donkey sees the donkey, and the well sees the well," with the common ingredient of all these factors being the act of "seeing" that is subject-free.[65] Herrigel's expression is also echoed in Martin Heidegger's emphasis on activity beyond subject-predicate distinctions in his oft-cited dictums "Language speaks" and "The Event happens."

The context of " 'It' shoots" can be further understood by considering the following scenario. Suppose that one day someone tells an old friend of difficulties in her relationship with her spouse. Then, as several weeks go by, the conflicts are resolved. The next time the friend is seen, a response to the question "How's your marriage?" is the proclamation "It works." This "It" refers to the dynamic interactions at the root of the experience of the relationship as a kind of third party or triangulation, not in the literal sense of constituting another, separate entity but metaphorically as a sum (the relationship) that is greater than the parts (the two spouses). "It" thus refers to the indivisibility of partner and partner, as well as concrete persons and the abstraction of their relationship. Or, in the case of Herrigel, "It" refers to the unity of shooter and bow, or of arrow and target, such that there is no particular (independent or autonomous) shooter, no particular arrow, and no particular target, in the sense of there being separable entities distanced from the holistic act of shooting.

There still may not be an equivalent to Herrigel's phrase in Japanese syntax, but at least this discussion makes his account plausible without eliminating a healthy skepticism or the need to dig further into historical criticism of his training and conversations with his mentor, guided or not by an interpreter. There are, no doubt, many readers of *Zen in the Art of Archery* who are unaware of the criticisms and would not be familiar with how to locate the sources, or perhaps would remain indifferent and unshaken in their commitment to the author's message if they did learn of this. The result of the encounter between Herrigel and his critics is a constructive exchange that helps to clarify and invigorate the TZN standpoint, which no longer seems isolated, oblivious, and defensive, while also deepening the need for HCC to investigate the sources and implications of Zen theory and practice without going to the excesses of wholesale denial and negation of TZN. Both standpoints can benefit from undergoing, through the creative juxtaposition, a sense of what Zen refers to as the great doubt, which leads to a greater degree of clarity. Evaluating neither the TZN nor the HCC approaches as representing exclusively the skin or the marrow enables us to select appropriate elements from the respective sides in order to reach a better understanding of the overall significance of Zen.

Zen Writes, Zen Rites, Zen Rights

This section provides a methodological anchor and framework for the constructive juxtaposition that enables a creative interaction and dialogue instead of opposition and polarization between the TZN and HCC positions, by orienting the discussion in terms of the main ingredients of Zen's original self-definition and how in early sources Zen portrayed itself as a unique and distinctive tradition. After we have established a basis for analyzing and evaluating the exchange of ideas concerning the real meaning of Zen theory and practice, the following chapters carry out an examination of the three main topics that have been at the heart of recent debates, with each section focusing on particular case studies that illuminate broader themes in the controversy.

The first issue to be discussed in chapter 2, "Zen Writes: Fun and Games with Words and Letters," is ineffability versus speech, which concerns the role of language and discourse in a tradition that has produced voluminous texts despite an emphasis on being a special transmission without reliance on words and letters. This chapter considers the question of whether Zen literature is primarily used as a heuristic device, as claimed by TZN, or represents some kind of gibberish, as charged by HCC's harshest skeptics, by comparing the wordplay and allusions in Zen commentaries to the "nonsense" writing in Lewis Carroll's *Alice in Wonderland* and the free-floating surrealism of T. S. Eliot's *The Waste Land*. By focusing on several specific kōan case records, the chapter argues that Zen literature is the product of carefully constructed narratives. The narratives are not nonsense in the conventional use of the term, but show the role of bizarre or outrageous personal interactions between masters and disciples that establish the value of radical antistructural behavior within the otherwise conservative setting of monastic institutions.

The next area of debate, nonduality versus mediation, examined in chapter 3 on "Zen Rites: The Eclipse of Buddha," involves the function of rituals and other mediating elements of practice, such as objects of worship, in what is supposedly an iconoclastic tradition founded on direct, unmediated experience realized through meditation conducted in the Monks Hall on the seven-hall monastery grounds (*shichidō garan*). By looking at key examples of how prayer temples (*kitō jiin*) evolved in relation to monastic training centers, this chapter argues that TZN must acknowledge that Zen encompasses a wide variety of compound layouts. Temples that put an emphasis on aesthetic contemplation for monks may incorporate rock gardens or teahouses, for example, while those emphasizing the pursuit of worldly benefits for lay followers generally have a prominent shrine dedicated to an indigenous or esoteric deity that has been assimilated as an avatar (*gongen* or *myōjin*) or bodhisattva.

The third topic, dealt with in chapter 4 on "Zen Rights: A Series of (Un)fortunate Social Events?" societal harmony versus discrimination, is the most hotly contested area between the TZN and HCC standpoints. It involves the impact of Zen, which espouses peace and tolerance, on a variety of social issues, including class and gender discrimination, and nationalism and imperialism in Japan. The chapter traces the roots of antinomianism and how this tendency has led to apparently compromised values and a static status quo in the context of the ethical concerns of modern society to a lack of regard in Zen practice for the role of confessions.

The epilogue, "The Real Zen Buddhism: Engaged, Enraged, or Disengaged?" sums up the arguments and explores ways of trying to break through the sets of polarized antinomies, so that the TZN and HCC positions can be reinvigorated in light—rather than by suppression—of their differences. In considering recent movements, such as Critical Buddhism, which criticizes Zen for not fulfilling its role in modern society, and engaged Buddhism, which advocates Zen as a remedy for the contemporary world, the conclusion reflects on debates between defenders and detractors about whether Zen can and should be engaged or cannot help but be disengaged from social issues. It explores the extent to which Zen allows, or causes, a sense of being enraged by instances of injustice and intolerance by retrieving repentance as a means to create reform. It also discusses the possibility for recapturing a genuine sense of repentance (*Zangedō*) and of what is referred to in modern Japan as self-criticism (*jiko hihan*), in the Zen outlook.

On Establishing a Methodological Basis for Analysis

In order to ensure that the juxtaposition between opposing views is mutually constructive and does not deteriorate into mere name calling, it is necessary to establish a basis for discussion by discerning how Zen traditionally has defined what it is supposed to represent. This allows us to determine the extent to which the tradition seems to live up to and fulfill its stated aims, as well as the merit of social and historical criticisms. Taking the first step of finding a methodological anchor is particularly challenging because, according to TZN, the real meaning of Zen is elusive and indescribable, and according to HCC, the sources are unavailable or unreliable. Forcing the issue might create an artificial litmus test that neither side accepts, but failing to develop this leaves

the debate unframed and possibly falling into an endless sense of disconnection. Therefore, establishing an anchor must begin with a disclaimer that
acknowledges discursive limitations while forging opportunities for exchange
and dialogue.

With the constraints understood, it is possible to put forward two main
sources that provide what a majority of informed people would agree constitutes an authoritative idea of what Zen has claimed that it is supposed to be.
Therefore, the validity of the TZN and HCC standpoints can be assessed in
relation to how they appropriate and interpret this standard. The first source is
a brief text attributed to T'ang dynasty master Pai-chang known as the *Ch'an-
men kuei-shih* (hereafter CMK), which is said to be the first attempt to define
Zen's temple layout in comparison with other Chinese Buddhist schools and
to offer behavioral guidelines for adherents.[66] The second source is the *Gozan
jissatsu zu* (hereafter GJZ), a collection of drawings and diagrams depicting
the ground plans for the layout of Zen temples that were originally developed
and used in Sung China and then transmitted to Kamakura Japan.[67] Taken
together, these texts—the first a manifesto regarding the school's ideals, and
the second a practical application of what apparently took place—tell the story
of how Zen was formed by making subtle yet profound changes in the way the
monasteries were built and religious life conducted.

The main temple structures are shown in the schema in Figure 1.1 (with
several important secondary buildings listed in brackets); the full significance of their functions will be described over the course of several chapters.
Each of the buildings, according to Tokugawa era sources, especially the renowned Rinzai scholar of monastic history and organization Mujaku Dōchū, is

(12) [Abbot's Quarters]

(3) Dharma Hall (head)

(10) [Patriarchs Hall]   **(11) [Earth Deity Hall]**

(2) Buddha Hall (heart)

(6) Samgha Hall (left arm)   **(7) Kitchen (right arm)**

(8) [Reading Room]   **(9) [Bell Tower]**

(4) Latrines (left leg)   **(1) Mountain Gate (groin)**   **(5) Bathhouse (right leg)**

FIGURE 1.1. The seven-hall style of Zen monasteries with additional chambers.
Brackets indicate buildings not officially part of the seven-hall layout.

associated with a part of the Buddha's body, so that entering the temple grounds can be considered the equivalent of communing directly with Buddha himself and occupying his domain on a regular basis. The halls include, on the main north-south axis, the mountain gate or entrance (associated with the groin), the Buddha Hall (*butsudō* or *butsuden*) for displaying icons and hosting banquets (heart), and the Dharma Hall (*hattō*) for sermons before the assembly (head). On the east-west axis, the right leg is associated with the bathhouse (*yokushitsu*) and the right arm with the kitchen (*kuin*), whereas the left leg is associated with the latrines (*tōsu*) and the left arm with the Samgha (or Monks) Hall (*sōdō*). The anthropomorphic symbolism suggests that the Buddha is not an external icon but the expanse of the mini-universe of the temple grounds covalent with the attributes of the real persons who enter the gates.[68] Yet, this emphasis—or perhaps overemphasis—on the majestic quality of temple occupants may open the door to an attitude that the head of the temple, or abbot, can do no wrong since he equals or surpasses the historical Buddha; this has important consequences for social issues, or Zen rights, to be discussed in subsequent chapters.

To put the significance of the CMK and GJZ in historical perspective, the origins of Zen are traced back to the mid-sixth-century arrival in China of first patriarch Bodhidharma, who supposedly established the first temple and principles of theory and practice. Following sixth patriarch Hui-neng in the eighth century, whose life and teachings are recorded in the *Platform Sutra*, the Hung-chou branch of the Southern school, encompassing four main patriarchs Ma-tsu, Pai-chang, Huang-po, and Lin-chi, became the dominant approach through the mid-ninth century and beyond. In 845, the Chinese government persecuted and proscribed Buddhism, along with other foreign religions, but the ban on Buddhism was lifted quickly. By the end of the next century, the Zen school had reemerged as the major religious force in China, primarily by espousing Hung-chou principles based on the spontaneity and antistructural approach found in encounter dialogues. Ready to proclaim its independence and distinctiveness, Zen monks began producing an extraordinarily high volume of texts at an increasingly accelerated pace. The first main set of texts was the transmission of the lamp records, which are pseudohistorical accounts of the dialogues held by eminent masters with their disciples that were later incorporated into the recorded sayings of individual teachers and into collections of kōan cases with prose and verse commentaries.

As part of this textual production, by the end of the tenth and the beginning of the eleventh century, the CMK began being featured in the transmission of the lamp accounts of the life of Pai-chang, one of the main figures in the Hung-chou branch. The CMK, which may have been circulating for decades but was first published in 988 and 1004, a century and a half after the master's death in 849, is considered by TZN to have monumental significance. It served as the basis for a comprehensive set of monastic rules used in all Zen monasteries, the *Ch'an-yüan ch'ing-kuei* produced in 1103.[69] But HCC has shown that the links among the three points of reference separated by time and circumstance—the life of Pai-chang in the ninth century and the production of the two texts a couple of centuries later—are speculative at best.

Even if the HCC view is accepted, the CMK remains the primary source that defines the meaning of Zen. It emphasizes the crucial role of the abbot as a charismatic teacher who is considered a living Buddha, thus superseding conventional objects of veneration, including Sakyamuni, and is seen in relation to the function of the main buildings and types of practice in the monastic institution. The CMK opens by pointing out that even after the time of the first and sixth patriarchs, Zen monks for the most part resided in Lü (J. *Ritsu*) school monasteries. The Lü school may seem to refer to the Chinese version of the Vinaya school imported from Indian Buddhism, but this term actually designates a much broader category of private monasteries. At some point during the T'ang but surely by the early Sung dynasty, the Zen school came to be independent of the Lü school and formed the main component of the public or state-regulated monastery network, which eventually was known as the Five Mountains (C. *wu-shan*, J. *gozan*) system that included Ten Directions (C. *shih-sha*, J. *jissatsu*) temples.

The CMK is quite short but filled with important details about the special features of Zen. What makes the CMK so intriguing is its explanation of the rationale for the break from earlier forms of Buddhism in China, which provides an anchor for our understanding of what Zen says it is supposed to be. The first principle in declaring independence from the Lü school is that Zen regulations at once represent an admixture and a transcendence of Hinayana and Mahayana precepts, with both sets of vows being required to become a Zen monk in China and, for the most part, in the Rinzai sect in Japan. The rules attributed to Pai-chang further advocate rituals revolving around the deeds and words of "a spiritually insightful and morally superior" abbot, or elder, who guides his disciples by exemplary behavior and a variety of instructional methods. The master conducts different kinds of open debates, performed in the Dharma Hall, along with individual instruction, conducted in the Abbot's Quarters, while also leading the monks in communal meditation, conducted in the Samgha Hall, and labor.[70]

The basic layout in which the "seven halls constitute no more than the essential minimum skeleton of the Zen monastery," or "irreducible core"[71] of the monastic compound in the GJZ, reveals a sparse, Spartan approach to temple design that contains the essential structures conducive to communal training and instruction by the abbot. For TZN, the design reflects a disdain for worldly concerns and embodies the school's main principles of simplicity and directness in cultivating spiritual discipline, without interference or mediation by extraneous rituals or supernatural elements. It is a concrete manifestation of Bodhidharma's "no merit" expressed in response to an imperial question about the importance of good deeds, including construction projects, in the first case of the *Blue Cliff Record* kōan collection, as well as Lin-chi's becoming a "true man of no rank" or Dōgen's "forgetting the self" through casting off body-mind. However, HCC has shown the flaw in an overreliance on the layout design as an indisputable model. The whole notion that there are a fixed number of temple buildings is not specified in the GJZ and was probably invented in the Tokugawa era and retrospectively applied to the earlier periods, and the ritual functions of the buildings are probably also often at variance with what is depicted.

The approach to defining the religious lifestyle of Zen in the CMK is both supported and contradicted by the second source, the GJZ. Whereas the CMK appeared around the year 1000 and described in a somewhat idealized fashion what had taken place in Zen during the T'ang dynasty, the GJZ, which was brought to Japan in the mid-thirteenth century, showed the way Zen temples were already being constructed during the intervening years. The CMK looked back to the classical period, and the GJZ was forward-looking in serving as the model for producing Japanese monasteries.

Despite differences in interpretation and application, both parties in the debates about the real Zen would agree on the importance and underlying validity and value of the two sources that developed at the peak of the school's prominence in China in the eleventh and twelfth centuries as the closest available proximity to an *Ur* approach. The CMK and GJZ agree on the importance of the Samgha Hall as the center of the monastery where monks sleep, eat, and meditate in a group with a set of administrators assigned specific oversight functions. However, a seemingly minor but extremely interesting and important discrepancy between the two sources concerns the role of a couple of the other main buildings, especially the Buddha Hall. The CMK deems this structure to be unnecessary because the master's teaching takes place exclusively in the Dharma Hall and Abbot's Quarters. However, the GJZ, which does not include the Abbot's Quarters as one of the primary buildings, does include the Buddha Hall, which was invariably used in Zen temples in China and Japan. In other words, TZN stresses the ascendancy of the Dharma Hall and Samgha Hall based on the charisma and wisdom of the abbot as a genuine innovation depicted in the CMK, whereas HCC highlights that, regardless of this rhetoric, the GJZ shows that the Buddha Hall and objects of devotion reasserted their dominance in nearly all Zen temples.

It will be shown in the following chapters that this discrepancy opens the door to vigorous disputes about the role and meaning of Zen writes, rites, and rights. The three main topics currently under debate can be understood through associations—or lack thereof—with the three major temple buildings (which are in turn linked to the three jewels in which followers take refuge, according to the teachings of Sakyamuni, that is, the dharma, the Buddha, and the samgha). First, the role of language—which involves the sense of hearing, or instruction listened to—in relation to Zen writes is connected to the function of the Dharma Hall (and also to the closely related Abbot's Quarters), where the master gave oral sermons and other instructions that were eventually transcribed and made part of the permanent record of the Buddhist canon. The second topic of mediation—or the sense of seeing, or objects seen—in relation to Zen rites is linked to the role of the Buddha Hall and its icons, which were never eliminated from the temple grounds and in many cases were worshiped as the main ingredient of religious practice. Finally, social issues—affecting the community, or those whose needs are met—involving Zen rights are connected to the Samgha Hall and the matter of ethical relations within the community of monks and in their relations with the lay and secular communities.

It is also important to recognize the chronological significance of the three topics and of how they are related to historical periods. The topic of language, and the emerging of the records of Zen discourse, is primarily connected to the T'ang and Sung dynasties in China and Kamakura Japan, especially in the eighth through early fourteenth centuries. The transmission records, recorded sayings, and kōan collections were created in the Sung and Kamakura periods from Dharma Hall discourses, with many of these attributed or referenced back to T'ang masters. The role of mediation is linked to the late medieval (Muromachi) and early modern (Tokugawa or Edo) periods of Japan, covering the second half of the fourteenth century to the middle of the nineteenth century, when Zen, especially the Sōtō sect, spread as a popular religious movement and modified the role of the Buddha Hall. The results of these amalgamations are also evident and very significant for understanding the network of Zen temples and their impact on society today. The topic of societal issues, which builds on the legacy of previous developments, is centered on the transition from early modern to modern (Meiji and post-Meiji eras), when Zen monks and their Samgha Hall have played a role in an increasingly secularized contemporary world.

TABLE 1.2. Relation among Main Topics, Temple Halls, Activity, and Chronology.

Topic	Issue	Main Hall	Activity	Period
Writes (language) silence vs. discourse	sense or nonsense	Dharma	hearing	T'ang/Sung China and Kamakura Japan
Rites (mediation) nonduality vs. assimilation	syncretism and worldly benefits	Buddha	seeing	late medieval and early modern Japan
Rights (social issues) harmony vs. discrimination	militarism and injustice	Samgha	meeting	modern Japan

Therefore, understanding the significance of the discrepancy between the CMK and GJZ regarding the Buddha Hall and its relation to the other two main structures is crucial for dealing with the question of how faithful has Zen been to its own definition. For TZN, Zen has never really strayed, and any apparent wavering is the mere skin of historical development that does not impede the marrow of a timeless paradigm. For HCC, the paradigm is not timeless but is rooted in a particular historical era and constantly evolving, so that timelessness is the skin that covers and conceals the marrow of contingency and variability. The reason that TZN falls short, according to HCC, is that it conflates the sect's own mythology and hagiography with history and historiography, which is the basic drawback found in many traditional religious standpoints.

2

Zen Writes

*Fun and Games with Words
and Letters*

What Do We Hear at Zen Temples?

What should we expect to hear at a Zen temple? Given the emphasis
on Zen as a special transmission outside the scriptures, without reliance on words and letters, perhaps we would hear the sounds of
silence as in, for example, the murmur of rustling leaves or whispering pines, the hush of falling snow, or the gurgle of rushing
streams that are considered to evoke the voice of Sakyamuni.[1] In
addition to these natural resonances, temple life would encompass
nonverbal sounds generated by monks, such as sweeping floors,
cooking, and doing other chores; the ritual ringing of the temple bell
at key intervals during the daily round of activities; and reciting or
chanting (though not necessarily delivering exegesis on) the sutras.
But what happens when it comes to light that in Zen there has always
been a large and fundamental role for verbal communication and
that, indeed, Zen masters have produced a tremendous volume of
writings that originally were based on oral teachings (while the claim
for the priority of orality has itself been questioned)? Does this point
to a basic contradiction or hypocrisy in Zen, or would the prevalence
of literary production mean that our understanding of what constitutes Zen transmission in relation to oral and written discourse must
be reconfigured?

The main controversy regarding the issue of writes involves
the value of various sorts of literary pursuits in connection with the

aims of religious practice, with the traditional Zen narrative (TZN) emphasizing the role of ineffability and going beyond language, whereas historical
and cultural criticism (HCC) stresses that expression and speech have been
central to the Zen approach. It has been said that nobody writes or talks more
about the need to refrain and desist from writing or talking than mystics. In
advocating the path of silence as key to realizing an ultimately interior and
inexpressible truth, they produce, often at an accelerated or even feverish
pace, voluminous texts filled with poetic and prose compositions, as well as
the records of oral discourse.[2] Are mystics violating their sacred principles? Is
this issue a product of some basic confusion or inconsistency in the mystical
viewpoint? Or, should we instead focus on the positive side, that is, the elo-
quence of mystical literature that is very much celebrated, ranging from the
exalted verse of the Song of Songs and the creativity of the Sufi and Taoist
poetic traditions to the metaphysical musings of neo-Platonic, Kabbalistic, and
Advaita Vedantic thinkers.

According to TZN, the Zen outlook is consistent, and through devices
such as the *Mu* kōan and the image of a master ripping the sutras, it helps to
bring to a culmination a basic trend in Buddhist thought toward a grave
suspicion and transcendence of words. This is indicated in the Buddha's
refusal to respond to questions about the afterlife or eternity that "tend not to
edification," the Madhyamika refutation of partial viewpoints (e.g., Chi-tsang's
"the denial of all false views is the correct view"), and the *Vimalakirti Sutra*'s
highlighting the significance of "no words about no words." Zen also borrows
heavily from Taoist critiques of the limitations of conventional language and
logic, as in Lao-tzu's opening line, "The Tao that can be talked about is not the
real Tao," or Chuang-tzu's emphasis on "forgetting" ordinary patterns of
thought in order to achieve a higher level of spiritual realization.

The Zen approach to reticence was perhaps given its first forceful assertion in the early transmission of the lamp text from around 710, the *Chuan
fa-pao chi* (J. *Den hōbōki*), which argues, "This transcendent enlightenment is
transmitted by the mind [in a process that] cannot be described. What spoken
or written words could possibly apply?"[3] This outlook is extended by Lin-chi's
proclamation that he "discarded" all the texts he had studied after having
"realized that they were medicine for curing illness that otherwise displayed
[one-sided] opinions,"[4] and by similar examples of disdain for the written
word in Zen sayings and anecdotes far too numerous to mention. However,
Zen is perhaps best known not so much for the negation of speech, which
would represent an extreme view, but for inventing a creative new style of
expression that uses language in unusual and ingenious fashions to surpass a
reliance on everyday words and letters.

Zen "encounter dialogues" (C. *chi-yüan wen-ta*, J. *kien-mondō*) and kōans demonstrate radical irreverence and iconoclasm in evoking "extraordinary words and strange deeds" (*kigen kikō*), a phrase used to characterize the T'ang dynasty Hung-chou school, which includes such luminaries as Ma-tsu, the founder, and disciples Pai-chang, Huang-po, and Lin-chi. In this style, paradox, irony, non sequitur, and absurdity mingled with sarcastic put-downs and devastating one-upmanship are linked to extreme physical gestures and body language, including grunts and shouts, or striking and slapping, as ways of moving beyond conventional speech. Moreover, Tung-shan Shou-ch'u, a disciple of Yün-men, makes the distinction between living words, which surpass reason, and dead words, which are limited in that they reflect a reliance on logical thinking that results in "speaking all day long without having said a thing." For TZN, living words have usefulness in that they are deployed to expose the futility of and to bring to an end the use of dead words, or as a poison to counteract poison or as an example of fighting fire with fire.

The HCC position questions what it sees as TZN's tendency to overemphasize silence as the exclusive rationale for Zen discourse. HCC highlights how a wide variety of conditioning factors contributed to the creation of the voluminous body of Zen writings during the classical periods of the T'ang and Sung dynasties in China and to the establishment of Zen in medieval Japan. HCC points out that the historical study of Zen has been infected by the presuppositions of sectarian advocates and has built up a series of stereotypes and clichés that must be defeated before genuine access to the tradition can be launched. For example, William Bodiford argues that some Sōtō sect scholars have done an "injustice" in applying a view that was generated in the Tokugawa era, when the sect was generally opposed to the use of kōans, in contrast to the Rinzai Zen approach in the Kamakura and Muromachi eras, for which nothing, he argues, could be further from the truth. Medieval Sōtō masters developed many kinds of oral and written commentaries that have come to be known collectively as *shōmono* literature, which was for the most part neglected or suppressed until recent studies reversed this trend.[5]

HCC further undermines TZN assumptions by showing that many of the notions with which Zen is most closely associated and which are attributed to the formative days of the tradition, especially the so-called radical iconoclasm of the early patriarchs and the Hung-chou lineage, were likely Sung inventions applied retrospectively. These sectarian assumptions have now become deeply ingrained as a kind of modern scholastic orthodoxy, so that it is a difficult challenge to dislodge and disrupt them. This is an unfortunate irony for a tradition seemingly hell-bent on overturning misguided presuppositions of all sorts, but perhaps it is a case of self-criticism being delayed or deflected or, to put it more crudely, of a religious group that is capable of dishing out criticism but not taking it (i.e., self-reflection).

It is now clear that the kōan about Mahakasyapa's receiving the flower after Sakyamuni's wordless sermon, as well as slogans like "special transmission outside the teaching" and "no reliance on words and letters"—originally separate items that came to be linked in a famous Zen motto attributed to Bodhidharma—were created in the Sung dynasty.[6] First making their appearance in eleventh-century transmissions of the lamp texts, including the *Ching-te chuan-teng lu* (1004) and the *T'ien-sheng kuang-teng lu* (1036), these rhetorical devices were designed to support the autonomous identity of Zen in an era of competition with neo-Confucianism and are not to be regarded as accurate expressions of the period they are said to represent.[7] A close examination of sources reveals that T'ang masters with a reputation for irreverence and blasphemy were often quite conservative in their approach to doctrine by citing (rather than rejecting) Mahayana sutras in support of teachings that were not so distinct from, and were actually very much in accord with, contemporary Buddhist schools.[8]

Deconstructing from a historical standpoint many of the deep-seated misunderstandings has led to two very different cultural critical evaluations regarding the aims and significance of Zen writings. Opinion is divided among HCC critics about the impact of this deconstruction and whether, underneath the Zen love of paradox and absurdity in an endless series of quixotic, enigmatic utterances—regardless of when they were composed—there lies either an empty shell of discourse that makes no sense or a creative form of nonsense that represents a higher level of communication. One wing of HCC, which can be referred to as the "dissolution thesis," suggests that what gets revealed is a hopeless inconsistency and a kind of rhetorical cover-up for a tradition devoid of meaning. The views of Koestler and Mishima discussed in chapter 1 are not alone in questioning the validity of Zen writes. In this chapter, I argue against the dissolution thesis view of Zen as meaningless, idle word games and gibberish by pointing in two directions, that is, to Taoist roots and to comparisons with various modes of modern Western literature and thought. I briefly consider Carroll's *Alice in Wonderland* and T. S. Eliot's *The Waste Land*.[9]

This chapter argues for the validity of the other wing of HCC, which can be referred to as the "realization thesis," based on the view that Zen writings are fully expressive of spiritual attainment, rather than merely a prelude to the abandonment of language. Recent literary critical studies of Zen texts, in some cases following the lead of biblical criticism, have analyzed the richness and variety of styles. In this approach, clarifying historical trends opens up diverse and complex aspects of literary production, so that the real target of criticism is not Zen itself, as in the case of the dissolution thesis, but TZN's unfortunate one-size-fits-all approach, for which strained claims of a special quality actually leave the genuine distinctiveness of the tradition somewhat concealed.

For TZN, the emphasis on silence conveyed in numerous slogans and kōans is the essence or marrow, while the skin, flesh, and bones are represented by the different kinds of speaking and writing that point deliberately yet evocatively beyond words and letters. But for HCC, this relation is reversed, so that the marrow is the variety and variability of expressions, with silence as one among several possible techniques that are constituted on more superficial levels. Yet, TZN and the realization thesis of HCC concur in a focus on the creative ingenuity evident in the vast storehouses of Zen literature attributed to eccentric, blasphemous, and irreverent patriarchs. Kōans, which are enigmatic dialogues culled from longer transmissions of the lamp texts, became the subject in the major collections of extensive, multilayered prose and verse commentaries containing philosophical and biographical elements replete with complex wordplay and allusions. According to Heinrich Dumoulin's assessment of the prominent *Pi-yen lu* (J. *Hekiganroku*), or *Blue Cliff Record*, kōan collection compiled in the twelfth century, "The selection of one hundred cases is exquisite. In the rich variety of their content and expression the [kōan cases] present the essence of Zen," making this text rank as "one of the foremost examples of religious world literature."[10]

However, I will argue that the mainstream of the HCC realization thesis also falls short in failing to recognize that a crucial component of kōan literature is its focus on monastic ritualism. By examining several kōan records, especially "Te-shan Carries His Bowl," which is included in the *Wu-men kuan* (case 13) and *Tsung-jung lu* (case 55, called there "Hsüeh-feng, the Rice Cook") collections, this chapter shows that Zen carefully constructs narratives about the role of interpersonal relations and interactions between masters and disciples or rivals in the setting of monastic institutional structures.[11] The monastic setting—and the intrigues and contests taking place therein—is not only the location, but also the ritual and conceptual basis for much of the discourse in a way that links the matter of Zen writes to Zen rites.

Of the three main topics treated in this book, the area of writes is perhaps the least controversial in that both TZN and a major wing of HCC are to a large extent in accord. However, by interpreting kōan literature as being based primarily on the monastic element, it is possible to show a link between writes and the topic of rights whereby a greater degree of discord becomes evident. In Zen dialogical exchanges, masters test the limits of the social structure with displays of antistructural behavior, which are deliberately eccentric and transgressive, such as cutting off fingers or limbs, jumping off poles, turning over dinner tables, or shouting, striking, or slapping. This radical behavior, even if an exaggerated image in Zen writes rather than a record of actual deeds, leaves the door open to the criticism that Zen rites are antinomian and therefore deficient with regard to the matter of Zen rights.

Zen's Shift to the Dharma Hall

The debate concerning ineffability versus speech, or the role of language and discourse in a tradition that has produced voluminous texts despite an emphasis on being a silent transmission independent of words and letters, needs to be oriented in terms of the origins and historical context for the articulation of Zen teachings. As indicated in chapter 1, one of the main ideas of the *Ch'an-men kuei-shih* (CMK), the first Zen monastic code attributed to Pai-chang, is that a spiritually insightful and morally superior abbot becomes the center of religious life as the living representative of the Buddha. Thus, the development of Zen writes is directly linked to the ascendancy and authority, the charisma and wisdom of the abbot as a substitute or replacement for Sakyamuni, and to his manner and content of expression, or the who, when, where, and what of how he spoke and wrote.

As Griffith Foulk notes, "In effect, Zen patriarchs *were* Buddhas." Furthermore, whereas the teachers in other Buddhist schools at the time had only secondhand, hearsay knowledge of awakening, Zen masters "derived their spiritual authority from a direct experience of the Buddha-mind." Therefore, "their words and deeds [of each generation of living buddhas] were at least equivalent to the sutras, which recorded the words and deeds of Sakyamuni and the other Indian Buddhas, and perhaps even superior in that they were the records of native Chinese Buddhas."[12]

Several well-known literary conventions quickly emanated from the distinguished masters, including refined poetry commemorating transmission and death experiences and the dialogical style of interaction, including seemingly absurd, nonsensical remarks considered revelatory of the enlightened state beyond reason.[13] These discourses were recorded in the hagiographical transmission of the lamp texts. From that set of materials, arranged according to the sequence of masters in a lineage, there were created two additional genres with different arrangements: recorded sayings texts, which contained all relevant biographical anecdotes and utterances of an individual master, and kōan collections, or extensive prose and verse commentaries on prominent encounter dialogues.

The CMK also specifies that a primary requirement for the abbot is the delivery of public sermons, and furthermore, this innovation is related to the function of the temple halls:

> The entire assembly meets in the Dharma Hall twice a day for morning and evening convocations. On these occasions, the Abbot enters the hall [C. *shang-t'ang*, J. *jōdō*] and ascends [to] the high seat. The head monks and rank-and-file disciples line up on either side of the hall to listen attentively to the Abbot's sermon. The sermon is followed by an opportunity for a stimulating debate about the essential meaning of Zen doctrines, which discloses how one must live in accord with the Dharma.

This passage indicates that twice-daily sermons were delivered by the abbot who "enters the hall" as a demonstration of his wisdom and guidance. Dale Wright remarks of T'ang master Huang-po, "Like other Zen masters of his time, he was perhaps first and foremost a skilled speaker, both on the lecture dais and in personal encounter."[14] Wright also points out that Zen "priests of this time either gained fame, or failed to do so, primarily based upon their mastery in these domains. The master spoke from the position in the Dharma Hall traditionally given to the image of the Buddha and, therefore, spoke as an instantiation of enlightenment."[15]

The style of sermon known as "entering the hall" became synonymous with the location of the Dharma Hall, which was generally a two-story structure that had an aura of grandeur much like the Buddha Hall, which it was supposed to replace. One of the innovations of Zen was that this building became the central site on the compound:

> Dharma halls in Sung Zen monasteries were large structures with architectural features and appointments identical to Buddha halls, with the exception that their Sumeru altars had no Buddha images on them. Instead, dharma hall altars bore high lecture seats that were used by abbots for preaching the dharma, engaging the assembled monks and laity in debate, and other services. The association of an abbot with the Buddhas in this context was unmistakable.[16]

The CMK mentions another key aspect of the style of discourse provided by Zen masters, which is also associated with one of the temple halls: "Monks may request or be invited for personal interviews or instruction by entering into the Abbot's Quarters. Otherwise, each disciple is primarily responsible for regulating his own diligence or indolence [in making an effort at meditation], whether he is of senior or junior status." According to this passage, the practice of meditation is less important—or at least less organized and regularized— than the individual, private teachings provided by the abbot to motivated disciples. The procedures required for requesting permission to "enter the [abbot's] room" (C. *ju-shih*, J. *nyūshitsu*) are prescribed in later texts, especially the *Ch'an-yüan ch'ing-kuei*, which mentions how the master is to give informal private sermons known as "small convocation[s]" (C. *hsiao-ts'an*, J. *shōsan*) in his room, which are distinguished from the formal public sermons provided in the Dharma Hall, which are known as "large convocation[s]" (C. *ta-ts'an*, J. *daisan*). However, exact requirements and methods of implementation probably varied with the particular temple and its abbot.

Although technically not a part of the seven-hall temple layout, according to the *Gozan jissatsu zu* (GJZ), the Abbot's Quarters was generally of great importance in the rituals of the compound, and it was usually situated above (north) and a little to the left (western) side of the Dharma Hall, hence, off center from the central axis. The chamber is a central area of the compound where the master gives oral sermons and other instructions, some of which have been transcribed and made part of the Buddhist canon. One of the main reasons that Dōgen admired his Chinese mentor at Mt. T'ien-t'ung was that frequently Ju-ching spontaneously initiated the entering-the-room ceremony, sometimes even by waking up the assembly during the night to call a special session.[17]

For the most part in China, however, the informal sermons of Zen masters were not recorded, whereas careful records were kept of the formal sermons, although these records do not generally contain the open discussions and sometimes freewheeling debates held during the public sessions. Perhaps inspired by his teacher, Dōgen collected his own informal sermons, some of which were later heavily edited, in the *Shōbōgenzō*, which is one of the few texts in the history of the tradition that captures a master's entering-the-room style of sermon. The appeal of the *Shōbōgenzō* is largely due to this unusual quality, but the collection of Dōgen's formal sermons, the *Eihei kōroku*, while often overlooked, is equally important for an understanding of his complete writings.[18]

The Abbot's Quarters is known as the "ten-foot square hut" (C. *feng-chang*, J. *hōjō*), following a passage in the *Vimalakirti Sutra* in which an informed layman holding forth in a humble abode demonstrates the ability to outsmart bodhisattvas. This chamber also seems to have roots in the layout of Taoist temples, which did not have the equivalent of a Dharma Hall or Buddha Hall and where the room for the abbot was more of an all-purpose area used not only for residential and instructional purposes, but also for administration and cultural demonstrations. As time went by, the function of the Abbot's Quarters as a center of cultural activities began developing in Zen as well. Also, for both Taoist and Chinese Zen temples, the term *fang-chang* was used to refer to both the facility and the person residing therein, much as Zen masters often took their monikers from the name of the mountains where they abided (or vice versa).[19]

This basic pattern of linking the two structures (Dharma Hall and Abbot's Quarters) with the two styles of sermons (entering the hall by the master and entering the room of the master), initiated in Sung dynasty Chinese Zen temples, is also found in Japanese temples established in the mid-thirteenth century when Zen was being imported from the mainland. These include such prominent examples as Tōfukuji founded in Kyoto by Enni Ben'en, Eiheiji founded in Echizen province by Dōgen, and Kenchōji founded in Kamakura by Lan-hsi. Enni and Dōgen both traveled and trained at temples in the Chinese Five Mountains monastic system, including Mt. Ching, the lead temple in the system where Enni spent six years, and Mt. T'ien-t'ung, where Dōgen studied for a few years and from which he brought back the Sung style. Lan-hsi came to Japan from Mt. Ching at the invitation of the shogun. However, the scale of the Chinese temples was considerably larger and grander, with the monastery becoming a sizable administrative unit with many divisions and departments, whereas Japanese temples functioned on a more minimalist and simplified scale. The diagram from a temple brochure highlighted in Figure 2.1 shows the close proximity and affinity of the Dharma Hall and Abbot's Quarters at Kenchōji, which are separated by a special gate (*karamon*). According to the anthropomorphic model formulated in Tokugawa era Japan, the head of the Buddha consists of both structures, with the Dharma Hall representing his voice and the Abbot's Quarters his mind.

HCC scholars have noted several problems with the traditional account of the Dharma Hall and Abbot's Quarters. First, Pai-chang's text, traditionally referred to as the original Zen monastic code and attributed to the mid-ninth century but first appearing in the early eleventh century, is of questionable provenance. Also, Zen temples in both China and Japan were much more complex and diverse in their practices than indicated in the CMK, so that the presence of relics, the act of repentance, chanting, and incense burning, among many other functions, led to the establishment of multiple structures for administration, ceremonies, labor, and outreach, as indicated in the GJZ. Indeed, Zen temples "had spacious compounds encompassing over fifty major and minor structures, facilities for a rich variety of religious practices and ceremonies, and sometimes more than a thousand persons in residence,

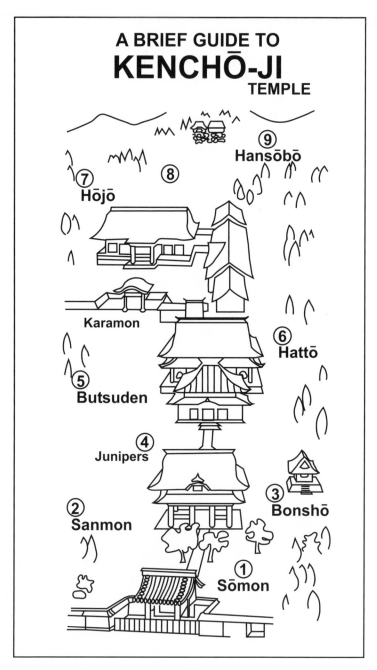

FIGURE 2.1. Kenchōji temple layout. From temple promotional materials.

including monastic officers, ordinary monks and nuns, lay postulants and laborers."[20] Furthermore, it is difficult for modern researchers to recreate what transpired in the medieval period, since so many structures in China were destroyed over the centuries by war and the elements, and then again by modern events, including the Cultural Revolution, and the same is true in Japan due to fires, wars, and other disasters. For example, Eiheiji temple's buildings have been repeatedly rebuilt, so that the oldest structure on today's compound, which is located on a different peak than was the original temple, is less than two hundred years old.

According to the CMK, the emphasis on the abbot's public functions in the Dharma Hall obviates the need for a Buddha Hall, which was the centerpiece of the temples of other schools as a place to enshrine and display images and icons as objects of worship. Even though the Zen approach to temple design is said to be unique compared to that of other Buddhist schools, HCC argues that the main halls in Zen compounds were actually more or less the same as other temples from the era, including the Lü (or Vinaya) and T'ien-t'ai schools in China and the Japanese Tendai sect.[21] On the one hand, these schools similarly emphasized the role of lectures, and at the same time, the Dharma Hall in Zen was not necessarily used in the way described by the CMK. The Dharma Hall was in fact more like the Buddha Hall, and even though eliminated in theory, it is clear from the GJZ that this structure was never abandoned. Perhaps the two structures were used somewhat interchangeably as the grand, ceremonial hall that was the jewel of the compound. Another common feature of Zen temples was the Reading Room (shuryō) for the study of sutras, which were often chanted aloud in the Samgha Hall but not studied for pedagogical purposes.

Nevertheless, there were significant differences between Zen and Buddhism more generally and between Zen and Taoism, reflecting a divergent ideological emphasis. Whether or not directly related to the Dharma Hall, Zen masters created a distinctive and lasting form of discourse. Other Chinese Buddhist schools did not create kōans or commentaries nor did they develop the kind of creativity in using words and letters to defeat words and letters that Zen masters consistently demonstrated over the course of several peak centuries (especially the eleventh through fourteenth centuries) of continuing innovation. Zen masters had a particular style, for example, in using the ceremonial fly whisk as a rhetorical element by drawing a circle in the air to convey ultimate nonbeing, throwing it down to show disgust with a disciple's comment, or claiming it turned into a dragon or flogged a thousand wild foxes as an ironic expression of magical beliefs. However, once the tremendous literary productivity of Zen masters is acknowledged, the question remains whether their profusion of words and countless instances of contradictory and absurd utterances and gestures make any sense.

Sense or Nonsense?

Zen discourse is deliberately opaque and mysterious, sphinx-like and perplexing, elusive and enigmatic. Ambiguity, incongruity, and contradiction are blended with tautology and assertions of the obvious in order to throw the disciples/readers off guard or catch them by surprise so as to overturn idle assumptions and preoccupations. Who can say for sure what any of this really means, or if it means anything at all? The image of an inkblot spilled on calligraphy, which appears on the cover of a translation of one of the major kōan collections, *The Book of Serenity*[22] (C. *Tsung-jung lu*, J. *Shōyōroku*), as shown in Figure 2.2 highlights the Rorschach quality of Zen writings, into which one can read as much or as little as one likes.

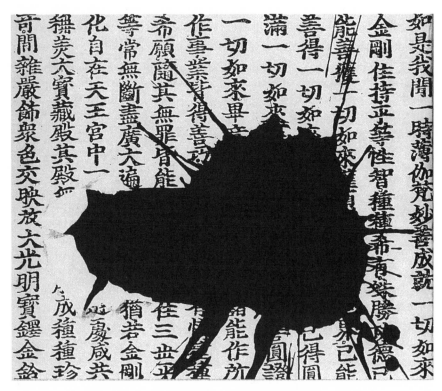

FIGURE 2.2. From the cover of *The Book of Serenity*.

Dale Wright comments on a quixotic event in which Huang-po drove monks away from the Dharma Hall with his staff, and when they were leaving he called to them, "The crescent is like a bent bow, very little rain but only strong winds." Wright wonders about the relevance of the master's seemingly random remark, "Perhaps, like us, no one [in the audience at the time] had the slightest idea what Huang Po was talking about. Or perhaps there were clues, present only in that immediate context or decipherable only to an exclusive few."[23]

In a way, both TZN and what would seem to be its nemesis, the dissolution thesis wing of HCC, agree that Zen discourse is nonsensical, but they come to this conclusion for nearly opposite reasons. For TZN, nonsense in Zen is understood in the most positive of terms on a metaphysical level rising above and standing beyond the contrast and conflict between sense and senselessness. Nonsense is a tool skillfully used to help put an end to seeking a path of reason and to point to an enlightened state unbound by the polarity of logic or illogic. For the dissolution thesis, on the other hand, the endless wordplay in Zen literature represents an infantile stammering and the willful abandonment of meaning, and is a kind of verbal cunning and trickery that harbors risky ethical (i.e., antinomian) consequences. Here we find clearly the roots of the critique of Zen's failure to negotiate human rights issues, which seems to rest on a tendency toward deceptive, duplicitous rhetoric that avoids being pinned down or committed to any particular view or decision.

A prime example of the dissolution thesis is the comment by the Jesuit Leon Wieger, who wrote in 1927 that the "immense literature" of the Zen school was

a quantity of folios filled with incoherent, meaningless answers, made to any kind of question, and carefully registered, without any commentary or explanation. They are not, as has been supposed, allusions to interior affairs of the convent unknown to us. They are exclamations which escaped from the stultified ones, momentarily drawn from their coma.[24]

This type of critique, which suggests that monks in meditation are nothing but zombies, cannot avoid being considered Orientalist in its one-sided, dismissive disregard of trying to understand Zen sympathetically and on its own terms.

What happens when forceful criticism comes not from the West but from the Orient itself? In an example of what can be referred to as inverted Orientalism, Mishima Yukio ponders the question, if Zen dialogues are so open-ended as to allow for constant shifting between multiple perspectives, on what basis can standards of evaluation and guidance be established without self-contradiction or hypocrisy? In *Temple of the Golden Pavilion*, a scathing critique of Zen monastic life in postwar Japan by an author known for his pro-imperial and anti-Buddhist political leanings, Mishima exposes a potentially fatal flaw of kōan cases used in Zen training when they are given idiosyncratic and seemingly capricious, distorted readings by key characters to justify their questionable motives.

In a novelization based on a true incident in which a disturbed acolyte torched one of the famous Zen temples, the father superior of the temple uses the "Nan-ch'üan Kills the Cat" kōan to explain away the tragedy of war as well as his own lack of leadership during times of hardship. Also, the disabled social misfit Kashiwagi evokes the same case to defend his exploitation of beautiful women. Mishima further contrasts Father Zenkai, who exhibits "the gentleness of the harsh roots of some great tree that grows outside a village and gives shelter to the passing traveler," with more typical Zen priests. These are depicted as being

> apt to fall into the sin of never giving a positive judgment on anything for fear of being laughed at later in case they have been wrong. [They are] the type of Zen priest who will instantly hand down his arbitrary decision on anything that is discussed, but who will be careful to phrase his reply in such a way that it can be taken to mean two opposite things.[25]

A contemporary Western scholar, Alan Cole, takes Mishima's view a few steps further regarding what Cole refers to as the deficient manner of thinking, "I'm sure the Master knows." He denounces the way Zen rhetoric hedges its bets or dodges commitment to a set standpoint for the sake of concocting what he regards as an obfuscation (i.e., that Zen is all things to all people, or whatever it is imagined to be). This approach probably helped to expand the sect's base of appeal in an environment where it competed with rival ideologies in Buddhism, Taoism, and Confucianism.

Cole examines one of the earliest transmissions of the lamp texts, the *Chuan fa-pao chi* attributed to the Northern school (interestingly, this text contains no reference to sixth patriarch Hui-neng, who is generally portrayed by supporter/evangelist Shen-hui as the sharpest critic of the Northern school in founding the Southern school). In discussing the problematics of interpreting the text, he compares the creation of Zen writings to the historical formation of the violin. Both Zen and the violin "underwent a gradual development in which its place at the meeting place between performer and audience was refined to maximize that exchange." "However," Cole argues:

the key difference between the evolution of Chan rhetoric and the violin is that Chan doesn't have a tangible product. The knowledges at play in Chan discourse produce "music-like" discourse effects that are as real as anything else, it is just that they aren't secured to anything substantial, and instead derive from subjects thinking in a certain way about other subjects (the perfect masters), and then re-conceiving their own subjecthood in a new form as a consequence of that fantasy being taken as real. Moreover, because there is nothing here other than this circle of self-reference, the music can stop at any moment.[26]

For Cole, Zen rhetoric is a sham that uses enigmatic expressions as a smoke-screen to conceal its empty shell, and there is not even a(n albeit fictional) Father Zenkai–like figure to resuscitate the tradition through a wholesome and healing outlook.

While Cole provides a probing and detailed study of the formative period, the limitation here is that the advances of HCC scholarship seem to have led full circle to the reintroduction of Orientalism now disguised as sophisticated scholarship. One counterattack offered by TZN is to show that Zen rhetorical strategies did not represent an unstable and arbitrary attack on reason, but had deep roots in Chinese thought and were influenced by the inexpressibility of the Tao, as evoked in Lao-tzu's polysemous verse, Chuang-tzu's puzzling narratives, and Tao Yuan-ming's utopian parables. Chuang-tzu offers the example of a fish trap to demonstrate the instrumental function of language, which is quite similar to the Buddha's discardable raft and Wittgenstein's image of a ladder that is no longer used when one reaches the roof: "The fish trap exists because of the fish; once you've gotten the fish, you can forget the snare. Words exist because of meaning; once you've gotten the meaning, you can forget the words."[27] In a similar vein, Tao Yuan-ming's philosophy of life is epitomized by his house or hut as a central metaphor for the unity of self and nature gained while living contemplatively amid the dusty world:

> I built my hut within the world of men,
> But there is no noise of carriages and horses.
> You may ask how this is possible:
> When the heart is subdued, solitude comes.
> Picking chrysanthemums by the eastern fence,
> Unawares I catch a glimpse of the southern mountains
>   in the distance.
> The mountain air is fresh during the lovely sunset.
> And flocks of birds are returning to their nests.

There is a great meaning in all of these things,
But when I try to express it, I cannot find [forget] my words.[28]

Other influences on the style of Zen writings derive from a variety of East Asian literary games, which have the effect of making discourse seem mysterious or even pointless as uninitiated readers grasp in vain to discern unidentified resonances. Typical techniques include (1) the extensive use of allusions, which create a feeling of disconnection with the main theme; (2) indirect references, such as titling a poem with one topic and composing a verse that seems on the surface to be totally unrelated; (3) inventive wordplay based on the fact that kanji (Chinese characters) are homophonic and convey multiple, often complementary or contradictory meanings; and (4) linking the verses in a sustained string based on hidden points of connection or continuity, such as seasonal imagery or references to myths and legends. As Victor Hori points out:

> In Chinese literature the generally dominant place given to allusion
> and analogy means that language is often used to say one thing
> and mean another. Indeed, the game is at its best when the oppo-
> nent-partners are so well matched that each understands the other's
> use of images, allusions, or turns of phrase without requiring any-
> thing to be explained or deciphered.[29]

In addition to showing various influences from other Eastern traditions, an argument in support of TZN's emphasis on the idea that Zen masters make sense beyond the dichotomy of sense and nonsense is that Zen has had a great affinity with, and in some cases a direct impact on, a variety of intellectual, artistic, and literary movements in the modern West. These range from American transcendentalism and French impressionism in the nineteenth century, when America and Europe were first being exposed to Asian thought, to phenomenology, dadaism, expressionism, surrealism, stream of consciousness, Beat poetry, and postmodernism in the twentieth century, as well as the zany comedy of the Marx Brothers and the experimental music and writings of John Cage. In these examples, we find thinkers, writers, and artists moving away from factual discussions or realistic portrayals toward a form of expression that allows the inner truth of subjectivity to prevail in a decentered universe in which the lines separating subject and object, reality and illusion, or truth and untruth, have broken down.

To put it another way, the trend has been away from language used for the sake of signification, assertion, and insistence on logical argumentation, which is invariably partial and one-sided, toward endlessly playful uses of words and an interplay with silence. Contemporary philosophical, literary, and other kinds of artistic works may not seem to make much sense, but harbor other levels of meaning. As Mark Taylor suggests, Western discourse recognizes presence pervaded by absence, and evokes notions of liminality, marginality, transgression, or the carnivalesque to cause the disappearance of fixed notions and presuppositions and the erasure of differences between falsely imposed categories.[30] This bears a striking resemblance to Tung-shan's living words, which may appear senseless or disruptive of common sense, but in revealing that all words have only relative validity and are therefore ultimately meaningless, actually point to a higher truth or uncommon sense beyond speech and silence.

One of the most aggressively anti-logocentric movements at the beginning of the twentieth century was dadaism, which sought an overturning of logic and reason brought about by eccentric expressions of poetry and art. At the first public soiree at a cabaret on July 14, 1916, the manifesto for the dada movement was recited, calling for a reading of poems meant to dispense with conventional language. Dadaists claimed to have lost confidence in modern culture and wanted to do the unexpected and shock common sense, as well as public opinion, education, institutions, museums, good taste, and the whole prevailing order.[31]

Another interesting example is Lewis Carroll's two *Alice in Wonderland* books, which raise a series of interesting questions regarding the nature of language, selfhood, and time that challenge conventional views and point toward a Zen-like realm of understanding. Carroll was a don at Oxford who published hundreds of books and pamphlets on mathematics and logic, among other topics, in addition to the parody nonsense epic *The Hunting of the Snark*.[32] Hugh Haughton points out that throughout the two Alice books, there are "persistent puzzles, paradoxes and riddles, which haunt the apparently stable mirror theories of language which have dominated the philosophy of the West."[33]

Logical reasoning is used in Alice's conversations to prove nonsensical assertions, suggesting that conventional logic happens to be upside down or that in snubbing, contradicting, and ordering Alice about quite callously characters who are pseudologicians can prove themselves superior by arguments which are nonsense but nevertheless seem to satisfy them. The effect is to show the innately absurd and futile nature of language and logic. According to Humpty Dumpty, who is called "the most belligerently radical of the many philosophers of language who haunt their pages" and who demonstrates "linguistic aberration and disorder,"[34] "[w]hen I use a word, it means just what I choose it to mean—neither more nor less." He adds, "The question is, which is to be master—that is all."[35] Wordplay in the Alice books includes the deformation of words, such as "We called him Tortoise because he taught us."[36] Time is given similar treatment by the Mad Hatter, who refers to this dimension not as an "it" but a "him," of whom he asks favors like speeding up the clock. Time and how it serves as an instrument for organizing human affairs is not what it seems, and it is pointed out in *Alice* that an "un-birthday" is celebrated much more frequently than a birthday.

In another example, T. S. Eliot's *The Waste Land* is a poem of anguish, desperation, and collapse on both personal and cultural levels amid a "crazy, fragmented" world that is so obtuse it requires a set of notes by the author to illumine some of the more obscure references. Eliot's writing confronts the first-time reader with the question of "how to read the poem: how to assimilate it and make sense of it." The "apparent chaos of the work, the difficulty, the excess," which in a way captures "the dazzling and sometimes incoherent world outside,"[37] discloses not meaninglessness but a multiplicity of layers of meaning and levels of allusion that make it endlessly rich and thought provoking.

Similarly, in a foreword to the 1961 book *Silence: Lectures and Writings*, which collects a variety of works concerning the basis of musical composition and performance from a twenty-year period (1939–1958), John Cage cites influences from Zen and the *Book of Changes* as well as Western mysticism and psychology. Cage is well known for his composition *4:33* (which refers to four minutes and thirty-three seconds of silence), in which the pianist sits at and opens the instrument but makes no sound. The writings in the book experiment with various stylistic features in terms of format, fonts, layout, etc., to show the limits of written discourse and the avenue to understanding the true meaning of the title word. Responding to disparagement by Alan Watts that he had not studied Zen properly, Cage issued the disclaimer, "What I do, I do not wish blamed on Zen, though without my engagement with Zen...I doubt whether I would have done what I have done....I mention this in order to free Zen of any responsibility for my actions."[38] The Zen quality in Cage, regardless of whether he was immersed in studies of the classical Zen tradition (which, HCC scholars would argue, Watts himself knows only superficially), is to continually cast aside conventional notions of what art and literature are supposed to be and continually reinvent uses of language even if seemingly incomprehensible or absurd.

The light shed on Zen writes by making comparisons with examples of modern Western thought and art can be summed up with a paraphrase of a double-edged Bob Dylan lyric, "There's no sense like nonsense, and nonsense makes no sense at all" ("Love Minus Zero/No Limit," 1964). One point is that one must delve between the lines or beneath the surface to appreciate writings that on the surface do not make much sense. But the real point is that there is no point, and isn't that really the point? Or is it? Once sense itself is challenged as a legitimate category, the next question asks, what is the sense of all this nonsense? That is, are words useful as an instrument for surpassing words, as claimed by TZN? Or, is it because nonsensicality opens up a completely new meaning of sense evoked not by the abandonment but rather through the use of words, as asserted by the realization thesis wing of HCC?

Words, Silence, or No Words?

The TZN tendency to emphasize silence as the necessary final solution to the problem of the innate deficiencies of language and logic in conveying ultimate truth has been challenged by the realization thesis, which looks carefully at Buddhist and Taoist influences that often indicate that silence is one of numerous options but not an absolute. While the debate between TZN and the realization thesis begins in disagreement concerning the role of silence, it ends in an apparent accord that enhances the TZN position by stressing the distinctive quality of Zen writings.

Silence has always been highlighted in Zen. But there has also been a long-standing controversy about whether silence should be seen as the goal, with language serving as a means like the finger pointing to the moon or the polishing of glass to make a mirror bright, or whether the inverse is the case and silence is to be seen as a means with creative uses of language understood as the goal. The emperor's preface to the transmission of the lamp text, the *T'ien-sheng kuang-teng lu*, maintains that language is a form of illusion and bondage: "Those who achieve understanding will thereupon dispel illusion. Those with transcendent realization will thereupon discard the cage of scriptural teaching."[39] At best, he suggests, language is an expedient means that enables one to "peacefully dwell on snowy mountains," but only once its use has been transcended. Yet, in contrast to this, many kōan texts such as the *Wu-men kuan* argue that it is false to speak of transmission yet equally false to deny or to refrain from speaking of it.

How do we reconcile these seemingly contradictory approaches and find a resolution to the double bind implied by the *Wu-men kuan*? TZN would argue that true realization of the dharma invariably transcends the words that convey it, and that this process of going beyond is the real meaning of the phrase "a special transmission outside the sutras," which does not imply a literal rejection of scripture or other forms of language. Rather, the phrase refers to a "superior ability to penetrate to the deepest meaning of the sutras, a penetration that follows words as far as they can go and then, at the extreme limit of conceptualization, leaves them behind."[40] According to this outlook, the way of verbal expression is to be cut off (*yen-yü tao tuan*), as exemplified by Hui-k'o's silent bow, and the basis of mental activity thereby destroyed. Therefore, language is detrimental to the attainment of enlightenment, but it can function as a provisional tool and lead beyond itself.

The realization thesis argues for a devaluation of silence, the valorization of which reduces discourse to a mere instrument, along with a corresponding upgrade of the role of language used extensively by Zen masters, such that words and letters are not considered an obstacle but rather a great reservoir of resources for communicating shades of truth.[41] For example, the passage in which Chuang-tzu uses the fish trap analogy ends with the query, "Where can I find a man who has forgotten words so I can have a word with him?" which suggests that once the true value of words is understood, they can be used in an ongoing creative dialogue. In another passage, Chuang-tzu puts an emphasis on using "goblet words" or "no words," which stand in contrast to Tung-shan's dead words. "With words that are no words," Chuang-tzu writes, "you may speak all your life long and you will never have said anything. Or you may go through your whole life *without* speaking them, in which case you will never have stopped speaking."[42]

Kōan as Monastic Narrative: Actions Speak Louder

TZN and the realization thesis wing of HCC agree that the key to understanding the quixotic utterances and pedagogical puzzles that epitomize the remarkable ingenuity and creativity of Zen Buddhism is, in a word, the kōan. Kōan case records, which form the centerpiece of the vast storehouse of Zen literature as well as techniques for training, have been interpreted in numerous ways, some complementary and others conflicting, including psychological, literary, and ritualistic styles of interpretation. These interpretive styles generally have much to contribute, but each on its own, whether aligned with TZN instrumentalism or the HCC realization thesis model, often ends in a one-sided or partial perspective of the complexity of kōan records and the voluminous, richly textured collections that contain and comment on them. If we remain locked into a polarized TZN-versus-HCC debate, other significant aspects of Zen discourse may well be overlooked.

The approach taken here emphasizes a comprehensive analysis that encompasses aspects of diverse interpretive models by focusing on the importance

of the encounter dialogue component in kōan cases, which involves the interaction between a master and a disciple whom he is testing or a rival with whom
he is contesting wits and spiritual prowess. Therefore, the key element is not the
issue of whether language is a means or an end, but the message of the kōan
cases with regard to their role as monastic narratives. In contrast to Leon Wieger's
comment that kōans are not allusions to "interior affairs of the convent unknown
to us," in many instances, that is exactly what they are. But the message is at once
hidden and revealed in a kind of code that provides a metaphor for, and at the
same time obscures, the kinds of conflicts and decisions that take place in a
monastic setting. As Bernard Faure suggests in his performative approach to Zen
writes:

> Perhaps [kōans] do not intend to express a meaning, but to impress
> an interlocutor, to gain the upper hand in a contest where all moves
> are allowed. Like any ritual or language game, they work simulta-
> neously on several levels—the semantic, the syntactic, and, more
> important, the semiotic or pragmatic levels. They are essentially
> performative. Their function is, to use Austin's terminology, illocu-
> tionary (insofar as they create an "event" and necessitate some kind of
> social ceremonial) and perlocutionary (insofar as they produce effects
> that are not always perceived by the interlocutors).[43]

The political factor of contestation—in a twofold sense of turf battles
within the monastic institutional system set against the background of the
larger sociopolitical context of Chinese society—is quite evident in the literature of encounter dialogues depicting the interpersonal exchanges of Zen
masters. Although often appearing in the guise of presenting a historical
account, Zen writings do not stick to the task of precise historiography. This is
partly because they were products of the premodern Chinese world view,
which was mythological and fanciful in taking magic seriously, but it is also
because their aim was not factuality but persuading the selected audience of
the significance of master-disciple relations in terms of legitimating lineages
and establishing the authority and hierarchy of transmission. From the perspective of seeing the political factor (in the above sense) as the marrow, the
debates between TZN and both wings of HCC (dissolution thesis and realization thesis) seem relegated to the level of skin, flesh, and bones.

We can consider how the enigmatic concluding line of *Pi-yen lu* case 73 on
"Ma-tsu's Four Affirmations and Hundred Negations" underscores the merit
of a comprehensive interpretation of kōan literature that includes the element
of monastic politics.[44] The final line of the case at first seems to epitomize
nonsensicality in bearing no logical relation to the main narrative, but in the

final analysis, it highlights the monastic model of interpretation. The case record's pointer opens with characteristic paradox:

> In explaining the Dharma, there is neither explanation nor teaching; in listening to the Dharma, there is neither hearing nor attainment. Since explanation neither explains nor teaches, how can it compare to not explaining? Since listening neither hears nor attains, how can it compare to not listening? Still, not explaining and not listening will amount to something.

The pointer sets up the question, Where does one go from the double bind regarding sense and nonsense evoked here, other than to an even greater sense of senselessness?

In the main case narrative, a disciple asks Ma-tsu, "Beyond the four assertions and hundred denials, what is the meaning of Bodhidharma coming from the west?" Saying that he is too tired to explain, Ma-tsu directs the disciple to see Tsang (or Hsi-t'ang, one of his primary followers), who says he has a headache and cannot explain it and recommends that the disciple visit Hai (or Pai-chang, Ma-tsu's most famous follower, who carries on the Hung-chou school lineage). Pai-chang also bows out by saying that he does not understand the question. The frustrated disciple returns and tells what happened to the teacher, who declares, "Tsang's head is white, Hai's head is black."

In this case, the disciple prefaces an unanswerable question used in many Zen dialogues with a reference to transcending the polarity of assertion and denial. After getting the runaround from Ma-tsu and his important followers, he receives the teacher's final statement, which could be interpreted as a non sequitur that does away once and for all with the question-answer process. The disciple, who did not get the message the first three times, is informed in no uncertain terms that it is time to cease and desist his pestering. Or perhaps the last line is an ironic affirmation of everyday existence akin to the sayings, "Willows are green, flowers are red," or "My eyes lie horizontally and my nose is vertical."[45] This arbitrariness of the actual words makes the statement seem nonsensical, but it makes sense on a meta level by pointing beyond verbiage to a higher truth. Either reading of the final line, as a thorough negation of the inquiry or as a deceptively simple affirmation of everyday reality, would seem to support the TZN instrumentalist interpretation of the kōan as a kind of verbal stop sign to the questioner, and this method of analysis appears complete and without the need for exploring other levels of meaning.

However, further probing of the concluding line indicates a more complex pattern that tends to support the realization thesis. Ōgawa Takashi shows that in Chinese pronunciation at the time (Sung dynasty), the character for "head" was pronounced in the same way as the character for "marquis."[46] Ōgawa suggests that a reading of the final sentence should be seen in light of *Tsung-jung lu* case 40, Yün-men's "White and Black," which uses the character for marquis in evoking an old story of two robbers. According to the case, Yün-men responds to a monk who outsmarts him by saying, "I thought I was Marquis White, but I find that here is Marquise Black." Marquis White and Marquise Black are noted thieves in Chinese folklore. Marquise Black, a female robber, seems to have been the cleverer of the two, who by a foxy ruse took away everything the male thief had gained in his efforts.

This apparently is why John Wu translates the line in *Pi-yen lu* case 73 as "Chih-ts'ang [or Tsang] wears a white cap, while Huai-hai [or Hai] wears a black cap." By combining the allusion to the thieves with the reference in the case to the word "head," he comes up with a hybrid rendering. Wu remarks that in the legend, the black-capped thief (or perhaps it should be Marquise Black) was "more ruthless and radical than" the white-capped thief (or Marquis White). For Wu, this shows that Pai-chang was more "ruthless" in the sense of being more unsparing in his treatment of the junior figure's irrelevant query than was Hsi-t'ang. While both monks dismissed the disciple, the former's put-down carried a greater sense of authority and finality.[47]

So far, we have not moved beyond the realization thesis, which would find a creative use of literary game-style allusions to be a key to understanding the kōan but would also agree with TZN that the point of the case refers to spiritual attainment, with Ma-tsu giving praise to one of his main disciples for evoking silence. However, without denying this interpretation, a crucial factor to be added to the analysis is that the compilers of Zen encounter dialogues were trying to make a case for the superiority of Pai-chang, who became the heir to Ma-tsu's lineage, over the other two followers, Hsi-t'ang and the inquirer. This interpretation, which stresses the politics of lineage transmission, is reinforced by the *Pi-yen lu*'s capping phrase comment on the concluding line: "Within the realm the emperor rules, but past the gates it is the general who gives orders." This implies that the masters and monks resemble warlords in establishing their domains of hegemony and battling over protected terrain.

By making a rather bold declaration comparing his followers to thieves (and, by extending the theme of combat, to generals), Ma-tsu demonstrates the kind of attitude exhibited in many kōan dialogues that combines elements of a conventional, regulation-based adherence to institutional structure with an unconventional line-crossing and tables-turning antistructuralism. The antistructure evident in such extreme acts as "killing the Buddha" or "jumping from a 100-foot pole," to cite a couple of prominent cases, is transgressive in challenging any and all levels of the status quo. Exchanges in dialogues featuring role reversals and one-upmanship, violent outbursts and physical blows, insults and the undermining of authority show that truth is revealed through the process of contest and confrontation. This is the basis for Zen's seeking to go beyond conventional words and letters, which is not the same as an exclusive focus on silence.

Kuei-shan's "Kicking over the Water Pitcher"

Kōan records were first preserved in dozens of collections created from the eleventh through the fourteenth centuries. At that time, many brilliant though eccentric and unpredictable Zen masters emerged alongside widespread belief in the power of supernatural entities, like magical animals and ghosts, to control sacred domains. This period also saw the proliferation of art-of-war strategies for warriors based on the virtues of attentiveness, alertness, and daring derived from an advanced spiritual awareness. The Zen dialogue is a process of spiritual polishing, or taking a mind that is rough around the edges and making it smooth and attentive to bring out its maximum capability and utility. The dialogues express an orchestration of rituals using symbols, both verbal and physical, interacting with the social order of medieval East Asia that can be applied to today's cultural environment.[48]

Zen masters played off the context of Chinese culture, at once to prove themselves and to seek approval through spiritual competitions or "dharma combats." These are a special form of encounter dialogue between teachers and their disciples, as well as rivals and trainees. The aim of the encounter dialogue is to pit mind against mind, with no holds barred and may the best person win! Some examples were often composed to resemble ritual contests that shamans or wizards held with gods and demons. They were also often couched in an atmosphere of military intrigue, as Zen masters were compared to generals mapping their plans of battle.

Kōan records capture the conversations and nonverbal exchanges that show how masters sought to break through the barriers of language and hierarchy imposed by social and religious structures. It is in this sense that the encounter dialogue represents "extraordinary words and strange deeds" (kigen kikō). Genuine creativity that derives from pure contemplative awareness cannot be contained by the standard use of words that are regulated to reflect mainstream organizational structures. Originality explodes in ways that transgress and disrupt the conventional and ordinary. The point of the master's

FIGURE 2.3. A traditional drawing of Te-shan approaching the hall with his bowl in hand. From Akizuki Ryūmin, *Zen mondō* (Tokyo: Sōbunsha, 1976), p. 168.

approach is to challenge prospective followers and adversaries alike to the core of their being, in order to test their innermost essence. Truth is not confined by words, but demands a breaking out of all borders and boundaries. The master is unwilling to make any concession or to budge an inch. He demands that everybody be a contestant in a match of spiritual wits.

In the course of the dialogues, the Zen masters use words to challenge the conventional institutional hierarchy, which is reinforced by symbols and rituals. When words, even extraordinary (paradoxical or ironic) ones, fail to make the point effectively, the masters then move beyond language to non-verbal forms of communication or strange deeds while pursuing a true vision that resides outside the limits of any framework. During the moment of dialogue, rank or status is thrown out the window, and all that matters is the person's ability to have a personal realization of truth. Yet Zen masters did not remain in the realm of antistructure as an end in itself. They remedied the excesses of violating rules by returning from the outer limits of transgression to occupy their proper place in the monastic system. The pattern of speaking and not speaking, and of behaving and misbehaving in order to cross back and forth over conceptual borders and boundaries, and in and out of structures, is illuminative and instructive for navigating the routes of organizational activity.

Generally, at a critical point in Zen encounter dialogues, the person questioned or doing the questioning expresses antistructural behavior that breaks with convention. The masters tear or burn a sutra or draw a circle in the air while making an offhand, cryptic comment. Or, there may be a dramatic denouement with the master slapping the disciple, or being slapped by him depending on the context, since in the moment there is an overcoming of divisions based on rank, status, or other extraneous criteria. The aim of the slap is not to reprimand or punish but to awaken and inspire the two parties, both the one doing the slapping and the other being slapped. In some cases, the student strikes the teacher to challenge his authority in asking absurd questions in the first place. In other cases, the physical demonstration is more extreme with masters cutting a cat in two, or chopping off the finger of a disciple, or the disciple removing his own arm. These stories were recorded during a premodern period when self-mutilation as a sign of self-sacrifice was a not-uncommon Buddhist ascetic practice.

According to Zen encounter dialogues, the successful way of handling a dilemma is to prove yourself not in words alone, but through some action, demonstration, or gesture that shows a profound understanding. Words intersect with no words, and structure with antistructure, to place personal realization rather than ideas as the highest truth. Silence can easily be misunderstood. There are various kinds of unsaying, whether based on an inability to speak or a purposeful refraining from trying to express what cannot be put in words. It is necessary to determine the basis for keeping quiet. Silence evoked in kōans generally reflects not ignorance and evasiveness but a level of insight based on a lofty transcendental realm, although there are times when it represents someone left speechless or unable to utter a response to a query or command.

Case 40 of the *Wu-men kuan* collection features the way that kōans express a heightening of, as well as a resolution for, the challenge or conflict of an encounter between competing Zen monks.[49] Master Pai-chang requires that his two leading followers tell him about a water pitcher in order to determine the winner of the contest, who will be awarded the abbacy of a new mountain temple. The disciples are put in a double bind of having to describe the object "without calling it a pitcher and without not calling it a pitcher." In a similar case record, whenever a monk passed by a secluded forest hermitage, the master residing there would charge upon him with his pitchfork in hand and demand, "Tell me what this is without calling it a pitchfork, and without not calling it a pitchfork. Now tell me, what it is!"[50] Then, no matter what response he got, he would say, "It is clear that you are a Demon!" or, "So says an enemy of the Dharma (or Buddhist doctrine)!" Either way "gets you thirty blows of the staff!"

The monk declared the victor in the water pitcher case, Kuei-shan, starts the competition as the underdog competing against the monastery's head monk, who makes an indirect verbal response that tries to dodge the question: "It can't be called a wooden clog." Following this, Kuei-shan's response of kicking over the pitcher and simply walking away from the scene is at once more indirect by avoiding the issue altogether and more direct by making a physical assault on the object and, by extension, the questioner. His demonstrative gesture prevails over the adversary, whose answer relied on words, albeit in an inscrutable way. Kuei-shan is praised by Pai-chang, and goes on to become the founder of the new monastery.

A TZN instrumental interpretation sees the kōan as a way of releasing the mind from its reliance on ordinary logic, thus compelling and completing a spiritual breakthrough to a new level of consciousness unbound by conventional limitations. By accentuating the anxiety of the double bind, or the "darned if you do and darned if you don't" condition, the master forces a disciple or rival to go beyond words yet communicate in a spontaneous and convincing fashion. In order to deal with this challenge, the successful monk must react immediately because any trace of undue hesitation or deliberation only interferes with a successful response. While trying to convey insight without relying on words or reason, the disciple also recognizes that failing to react by maintaining a diffident silence or refraining from divulging his inner thoughts would prove ineffective. Performing in this high-pressure atmosphere is the main method for determining the relative merits of contestants. Generally, no one outdoes the master, yet he is the first to admit defeat if and when bested.

A realization thesis interpretation reinforces the TZN approach in stressing an overcoming and transcendence of ordinary ways of thought and expression. However, it also puts a special emphasis on how kōans use language to defeat a reliance on words or speech in order to create a shock effect that stimulates the mind to awaken from its philosophical slumber. Despite discrepancies and inconsistencies, the instrumental and realization interpretations agree that the key point of the kōan is Kuei-shan's turning and walking away from the scene, which demonstrates the inexpressible truth in a way that words and no words are unable to accomplish. Both interpretations stress that in the final analysis speech and silence, as well as kicking and not kicking the pitcher, are ultimately irrelevant. What is crucial is to attain a fundamental level of nonduality that is altogether free of dichotomization or polarization. Therefore, the instrumental approach, which sees the kōan as a heuristic device or a means to the end of attaining the transcendence of worldly ignorance and attachment to reason and language, is not so distant from the realization approach. This approach emphasizes an immanent awareness functioning within the mundane realm, as symbolized by Kuei-shan's kick, rather than the act of going beyond ordinary consciousness, as represented by his departure.

However, the instrumental and realization styles of interpretation may seem limited in neglecting the sociohistorical elements of interpretation. According to a comprehensive interpretive approach, an emphasis on a sudden arising of insight triggered by the kōan that conquers unenlightenment is not necessarily what Zen discourse intended to communicate. Rather, the aim was to construct a broader ideology that would win the favor of government officials and other patrons as well as the masses and that includes a literary component. An overwhelming concern of Zen masters was to develop the rules and regulations of monastic routine, including the transmission of the lineage pedigree and the transfer and inheritance of the mantle of authority and leadership.[51] Therefore, the impact of the kōan is not based simply on Kuei-shan maintaining silence in contrast to the other monk's use of speech nor on the act of kicking, but the way the overall narrative about the contest to gain the abbacy of a new temple in the fledgling Zen school creates an appropriate context for dramatizing the final episode.

From this perspective, the key aspect of the case is the awarding of the abbacy of the new monastery. Although Zen eventually thrived in a competitive religious environment controlled by imperial decrees, Buddhism as a foreign religion was subject to periods of suppression and proscription, especially in the eighth and ninth centuries. A comprehensive interpretation also deemphasizes the iconoclastic rebelliousness of Kuei-shan by pointing out the importance of the background legend for understanding the kōan case that is contained in the transmission of the lamp records, which include folklore and shamanistic elements. According to the fuller narrative in the transmission sources, prior to the contest regarding the water pitcher, Pai-chang had been consulting with the geomancer/wizard Ssu-ma, one of the more intriguing irregular practitioners in Zen lore, about who should take over the new temple. Ssu-ma summoned his occult, supernatural powers to select Kuei-shan as the most appropriate monk, so that the competition in the main case was actually a staged affair with a foregone conclusion based on ritual rather than a spontaneous display of psychological insight or literary flourish. This approach to interpretation combines the emphasis on a spiritual breakthrough in the instrumental and realization interpretations with a focus on the struggle for power in the dialogue's social and historical setting.

Kuei-shan's act is one of the most renowned cases of an antistructural expression in Zen annals because it breaks abruptly with the conventional hierarchy and patterns of discourse. The message seems to be that to stand out one cannot do the same as everyone else. You need to have the courage to try new approaches, which might be perceived as offbeat or "crazy." This is a risk taken to be innovative, which is effective not as an end in itself but only so long as individuality is integrated with eccentricity and an overall commitment to the completion of group goals. Failing to take the opportunity to be uniquely inventive will in the long run stymie communal achievements. Yet, the *Wu-men kuan* commentary makes it clear that we should not just take it at face value that Kuei-shan had an unqualified success, by charging, "He never fully catapulted himself out of the trap cleverly set by Pai-chang."

Breaking down structures, which gains Kuei-shan a leadership role in the monastic system, only works successfully if it takes place at the appropriate time and context, where it communicates persuasively without seeming arbitrary or counterproductive. The narrative about Kuei-shan, who does not appear as a rogue or renegade, symbolizes that when words fail or fall short of getting the point across effectively, a genuine sense of self-confidence and innovativeness beyond speaking that is based on integrity and inner discipline allows for deftness at breaking out of the mold of hierarchical structure. Before doing things this way, it is necessary to have exhausted other avenues of communication and to be certain about the merits and reasonability of an approach intended to abet a productive reforming of structure.

"Te-shan Carries His Bowl"

The effectiveness of a comprehensive approach to interpreting kōans that express a delicate balance between structure and antistructure, or following and breaking the rules, is seen in the case "Te-shan Carries His Bowl," which is included in the *Tsung-jung lu* and *Wu-men kuan* collections.[52] The case involves the story of master Te-shan, who seems to commit a rather serious faux pas in terms of monastic etiquette and is reprimanded by one of his disciples, Yen-t'ou, who accuses him of not understanding the "last word." After a private exchange with Yen-t'ou, Te-shan redeems himself by giving an unusual sermon, and he receives the disciple's high praise.

The TZN and HCC interpretations both focus on the meaning of the last word, as featured in the *Wu-men kuan* verse commentary, and its significance for understanding the role of language, which is highly ambiguous and inconclusive in typical Zen fashion. A comprehensive interpretation, on the other hand, highlights the significance of the case for understanding the establishment of authority in the process of lineage transmission by taking the lead from the capping phrases used in the *Tsung-jung lu* commentary. These evoke the master-disciple relation of Te-shan and Yen-t'ou in terms of the familial model of parent and child and in terms of art-of-war strategizing concerning commanders and soldiers facing opponents on the field of battle.

The following translation is from the *Tsung-jung lu* version, with the main case record appearing in boldface and the capping phrases provided by editor/commentator Hung-chih in italics. The narrative is nearly identical in the two versions, but there is an important difference in the opening lines, which will be explained in detail below. The division of the case into five sections, each accompanied by a discussion of its symbolism, is not a part of the original record or traditional commentaries, and represents my way of organizing the material.

1. Te-shan's Faux Pas

When Hsüeh-feng was at Te-shan's temple working as rice cook—*If you don't work when young*...**one day the meal was late, and Te-shan came to the Dharma Hall carrying his bowl.**—...*you won't have peace of mind when old.* **Hsüeh-feng said, "Old man, the bell hasn't rung yet and the drum hasn't sounded—where are you going with your bowl?"**—*He makes the baby able to scold its mother.*

As shown in Figure 2.3, the narrative takes place at the temple of Te-shan, who at the time was apparently eighty years old and near the end of his life, but who early on had been one of the brashest of Zen figures. He was originally known for his intensive interest in the *Diamond Sutra* and referred to himself as "King of the Sutra." But after getting his comeuppance at the hands of an elderly laywoman who made an ingenious philosophical wordplay, as discussed in the prose commentary on *Pi-yen lu* case 4, Te-shan began to relent and see the wisdom of the Zen approach to transmission outside the scriptures. Following a successful challenge to master Kuei-shan, as discussed in the main record of *Pi-yen lu* case 4, and then gaining enlightenment under master Lung-t'an, as described in case 28 of the *Wu-men kuan*, Te-shan had a lengthy and productive span leading his own temple. There, he cultivated disciples, including Hsüeh-feng, who was one of the most famous chief cooks in the early history of Chinese Zen, so that many aspiring monastic cooks who saw him as a role model took his name.

As an accomplished abbot, Te-shan should have been well aware and helping to enforce the strictness of monastic rules regarding attendance at meals and sermons required for abbots, rectors, attendants, monks, and novices, which forbade entering the hall until the bell had been rung and the drum sounded, regardless of extenuating circumstances. According to the *Ch'an-yüan ch'ing-kuei*:

> Three drum sequences are struck to indicate that the abbot is approaching the hall. The administrators and chief officers bow to the abbot from their positions. After the bell in front of the Samgha hall is rung, the assembly descends from the platforms. The abbot enters the hall, bows to the Holy Monk, and then bows with the assembly simultaneously.[53]

The main difference between the two versions of the case is that the *Wu-men kuan* does not include a reference to the lateness of the meal, which makes Te-shan's blunder seem all the more serious and inexcusable. Also, the *Wu-men kuan* mentions Te-shan entering a "hall," but not explicitly the Dharma Hall, so one could assume that it refers to the dining hall, one of the seven main temple buildings. This is quite an important difference since the implication of Te-shan going into the Dharma Hall in the *Tsung-jung lu* version is that he had bypassed entering the dining hall, assuming the midday meal was not forthcoming, and was about to begin his afternoon sermon even without the meal. In that case, not only does he have a reason to break the rules and is not necessarily to blame for a gaffe, but he demonstrates an aggressive attitude in showing up the cook who was late in serving the meal.

In any event, this kōan conjures a question also addressed in a couple of other *Wu-men kuan* cases about the need to follow rules of etiquette that seem like arbitrary restrictions without intrinsic value other than to regulate the way some monastic activities are conducted in relation to seasonal cycles and hours of the day. For example, case 26 deals with the raising of bamboo blinds, which marks the change of seasons, and in case 16 Yün-men asks rhetorically, "See how vast and wide the world is! Why do you put on your seven-piece robe at the sound of the bell?" Here, Hsüeh-feng, late meal and all, feels perfectly justified in reprimanding the master for failing to comply.

2. Return to His Quarters
Te-shan immediately returned to the Abbot's Quarters.— *It's all in the not speaking.*

Regardless of who is to blame for the faux pas, Te-shan turns back from the hall. According to Robert Aitken's TZN style of interpretation, this part of the case can be considered "Te-shan's silent teaching," about which there are "many stories," including accounts of his giving thirty blows of the stick.[54]

Aitken suggests that the passage recalls another kōan involving Te-shan that is included as *Tsung-jung lu* case 14,[55] in which a disciple, Huo, asks the master a challenging question, to which he responds, "What? How's that?" and the capping phrase reads, "Swift thunder—you can't cover your ears in time." Huo then proclaims, "The order was for a flying dragon, but only a lame tortoise showed up," and a verse comment reads, "Fooling the enemy army into not thinking ahead." Te-shan says nothing, but the next day, Huo's behavior is deferential and Te-shan again remains silent, not having said a word the whole time. The capping phrase reads, "The tiger's head and the tiger's tail are taken all at once."

However, the passage about Te-shan returning to his quarters in the current case is open-ended, and this act could also be interpreted less positively as perhaps a retreat in shameful recognition of defeat or of the extent of his blunder. Or, it could simply represent a nonconfrontational outlook that takes time to pause and reflect on how to react to his underling, whether out of penitence, ignorance, or indifference to the rebuke.

3. The Last Word

Hsüeh-feng reported this to Yen-t'ou.— *The family rebels, the home is disturbed.* Yen-t'ou said, "Even Te-shan, as great as he is, doesn't understand the last word."— *The father is obscured by the son—the straight is therein.*

In this passage, Yen-t'ou the disciple further passes judgment on master Te-shan. Yen-t'ou and Hsüeh-feng are a playful pair of monks, whose antics are also recorded in *Pi-yen lu* cases 51 and 66. Here, they have fun seemingly at their teacher's expense. Yen-t'ou is the junior partner, but he is considered a man of talent and resolution, who helped to confirm the enlightenment of Hsüeh-feng, who had been recommended to study with Te-shan by Tung-shan Liang-chieh, founder of the Ts'ao-tung school, indicating cross-fertilization among lineages. Hsüeh-feng is known as a man of effort who often faced uncertainty. While Yen-t'ou died at age sixty and left only one disciple, who did not propagate the line which quickly died out, Hsüeh-feng's community of followers gave rise to two prominent lineages, the Fa-yen and the Yün-men schools. The latter included Yün-men and his lineage, known for an emphasis on the "one-word barrier" (e.g., What is Buddha? A shit-stick). Another follower in the Yün-men lineage was Hsüeh-tou, who in the eleventh century collected and wrote verse comments on the 100 cases that later became the *Pi-yen lu* when it was further edited by Yüan-wu in 1163.

It is not clear what the last word is supposed to mean, but one way of understanding this is that it would represent a style of discourse that puts an abrupt end to queries, criticism, and conflict or that can decisively snuff out arbitrary questions and judgments. This is what Te-shan was unable to deliver when rebuffed by his follower; instead, he was stymied by paralysis.

4. Retort

Te-shan had his attendant summon Yen-t'ou, and asked him, "You don't approve of me?"— *He pours oil on the fire.* Yen-t'ou then whispered to him what he really meant.— *Private words among people are heard as loud as thunder by the gods.* Te-shan then dropped the matter.— *He still does not understand.*

Back in his room, Te-shan can apparently tell that something is wrong with Yen-t'ou, who has been informed by Hsüeh-tou, and he inquires about the disciple's perspective on his leadership. Whatever Yen-t'ou says privately to his teacher is not disclosed in the narrative, which indicates that there is some kind of intimate (*mitsu* in the *Wu-men kuan* version) connection and familiarity between master and disciple. A TZN interpretation would see this exchange as a prime example of silent transmission as suggested by the capping phrase image of the thunderclap heard by the gods. The role reversal of having Yen-t'ou initiate the conversation is accommodated by similar examples, such as Pai-chang being slapped by his disciple Huang-po at the conclusion of the "Wild Fox" kōan (*Wu-men kuan* case 2 and *Tsung-jung lu* case 8).[56] While one level of silence is the whispering that takes place between master and disciple, another level is represented by the reticence of Te-shan, who once again does not take the opportunity to put an end to the comments of his followers.

5. Te-shan's Sermon

The next day when Te-shan gave a sermon in the Dharma Hall, it was not the same as the usual one.— *He steers backwards against the wind.* Yen-t'ou clapped and laughed and said, "Happily, the old man does understand the last word.— *The shame of the house is exposed to the outside world.* Hereafter, no one in the world will be able to lay a hand on him."— *Why is his nose in my hands?*

Te-shan apparently has regrouped and is able to deliver a compelling sermon demonstrating to Yen-t'ou that he really does have the last word, after all, although the reader of the case has no idea what was expressed and whether it lived up to expectations. The *Tsung-jung lu* prose commentary, which refers to the master as "a toothless tiger" who "still has claws," is, like the capping phrase above, characteristically dismissive and contradictory of Yen-t'ou's positive assessment in saying, "Yet this too is adding error upon error." The prose comments also indicate that Yen-t'ou says that Te-shan only has "only three years to go," and sure enough, according to tradition, he died three years later. This suggests that Yen-t'ou holds real power regardless of his rank.

The merit of a comprehensive interpretation becomes clear in interpreting this final passage of the case record. The approaches of TZN and the realization thesis would continue to emphasize the significance of the last word seen in terms of the paradoxical relation between the first and last word, as suggested by the *Wu-men kuan* verse comment:

> If you know the first word,
> Then you understand the last word;
> The last and the first—
> Are they not this one word?

The *Wu-men kuan* prose comment suggests in tongue-in-cheek fashion that neither figure really gets the point, as they turn into an idle Punch and Judy or Bert and Ernie partnership of folly: "As far as the last word is concerned, neither Yen-t'ou nor Te-shan has ever seen it in a dream. Examining them, they're much like puppets on a stage." The focus remains on the matter of facility with—as well as the limits of—using words in connection with no words.

Comprehensive Interpretation

A comprehensive interpretation focuses not merely on language but on action, and argues that the meaning of the case narrative's denouement is that conflict and uncertainty are once and for all resolved, in that the central Zen monastic ritual of delivering a sermon in the key temple space of the Dharma Hall is being upheld. Te-shan may or may not have redeemed himself through the power of words, but he clearly was able to reestablish and reassert his authority and his ability to command his troops by the power he wields in the temple system. This interpretation is reinforced by the capping verse's theme of building on the analogy of familial relations and maintaining a house's (or lineage's) reputation. In a traditional prose commentary, You-ke said, "Those who conceal an army to fight by night do not see [Te-shan]. Those who attack occupied territory by day can hardly know [Yen-t'ou]. What they don't realize is that the battle commander picks fights by day, the watch commander patrols the camp by night."[57] According to this, Te-shan the master still rules by night, which has the advantage, and Yen-t'ou the disciple leads by day.

The difference with *Wu-men kuan* case 40 is that the Kuei-shan narrative ends with antistructure, whereas the Te-shan record opens with two examples, one deficient (Te-shan's move to the hall before the ringing of the bell, which disrupts the order of things) and the other surpassing conventional roles (Yen-t'ou's willingness to criticize his mentor in front of others). The Te-shan case ends with a reaffirmation of structure, showing that everyone including the master must follow the rules, but the rules are made to be broken by the master, who is not considered an authentic leader unless he knows the appropriate way of doing this. Te-shan did not, by his own admission through his reticence, do it the right way at first. Rules for Zen are at once everything and nothing, the necessary glue that makes society work and the chains in the dungeon that must be cast aside. They are carefully crafted and invariably arbitrary and capricious.

The weight of the imagery in the case record supplemented by the art-of-war style of the commentary suggest that a new order needs to be created based on the charisma and spontaneity of the leader, but this will not prevail unless there is a careful plan for ritual implementation within the halls of the temple compound. The temple layout is sufficient to leave room open for both the breaking and the reasserting of regulations. The Zen abbot cannot and should not be bound by any system, which is arbitrary, but at the same time, he must epitomize and recognize that he is not above the rules of the system.

Does the master really replace the Buddha, as the CMK indicates? What is the relation of the abbot to other objects of veneration, and how are these commemorated within the monastic system? Exploring these questions connects the matter of Zen writes with Zen rites and rights.

3

Zen Rites

The Eclipse of Buddha

What Do We See at Zen Temples?

What should we expect to see at a Zen temple? Minimalist yet elegant
structures as part of the simple design of the essential seven-hall
layout conducive to long periods of meditation, set against a monochromatic backdrop of rock gardens or other natural features that
help to eliminate distractions and contribute to a life of contemplation? Would the temple compound have almost no objects of veneration, other than the spare statue of Sakyamuni in the Buddha Hall
(conceding that this is present despite the CMK injunction to the
contrary) and the "holy monk" represented by Manjusri in a chamber
of the Samgha Hall? What would be the implications if it were shown
that rock gardens were not created primarily for the purpose of
meditation, and represented a refined, elite culture that only came to
be situated on some temple grounds for historical or social reasons?[1]
Furthermore, how should we explain the profusion of devotional
objects and rites at so many Zen sacred sites, which include a large
percentage of prayer temples (*kitō jiin*)? Does the presence of a diverse and colorful array of icons and other symbols along with ritual
utensils indicate that the "pure" quality of Zen is not so apparent or
has been violated, and does this force us to change or expand our
overall definition of Zen religiosity?

The main conflict between the traditional Zen narrative (TZN)
and historical and cultural criticism (HCC) standpoints on the issue

of rites involves the role of various sorts of intermediary forces in religious training. The TZN position is that the only religious practice of real value is zazen (seated meditation), along with related techniques conducive to the contemplative state, such as kōan exercises and pedagogical interactions with the abbot. Traditional Mahayana Buddhist rituals like sutra chanting are allowed but are seen as limited in significance. TZN points to monastic training centers as exemplary of temples that still maintain a focus on contemplation, including Eiheiji founded by Dōgen and now one of the two headquarters of the Sōtō sect in addition to Sōjiji, and Myōshinji, Daitokuji, and Kenninji, each of which is the head of a subfaction in the Rinzai sect. Training methods, including temple chores such as cooking and cleaning in the kitchen, bathhouse, or latrine, help to regulate daily behavior, discipline the spirit, and enhance meditative awareness. These practices, which highlight an intensive internal experience of self-awakening without any need for mediation or the intervention of symbols or icons, are seen as constituting "rituals" only in the broadest sense of the term as referring to routine behavioral patterns. Otherwise, any trace of ritualism in the conventional meaning of ceremonial activities performed as a means of attaining a pragmatic end from a higher power is obviated or kept to a bare minimum in Zen as a mere accessory function.[2] Or, ritualism is seen as a necessary evil occasionally incorporated in concession to local customs and the need to curry favor with donors or officials or to accommodate the general public's (or lay followers') demand for the delivery of Buddhist teachings in an accessible fashion.

The HCC approach, on the other hand, shows that nearly all temples since the early history of Zen in China are filled with many kinds of rites and symbols. These range from enshrining relics and performing deification ceremonies for deceased masters to the worship of various Buddhist and local gods through iconography, incantations, or talismans, in addition to the exorcism of demons. As Griffith Foulk notes, "[T]here is no validity whatsoever to the notion that Sung Ch'an monastic practice dispensed with literature, images, or rituals."[3] Today, numerous temples feature the veneration of quasi-historical or semi-mythical Zen heroes, including Daruma, who is derived from the first patriarch Bodhidharma and portrayed as a limbless good luck charm (the Asian Humpty Dumpty); Hotei or the Laughing Buddha; Hanshan the poet/recluse; or the arhat Pindola, who is part of the collection of the Five Hundred Rakan (arhats).[4] Furthermore, as will be discussed in the following chapter on social issues, many temples have as a primary function the performance of funerals and observance of mortuary rites for both clerics and the lay community, including abortion rites (mizuko kuyō).

The images of Zen heroes could be justified as expressions or tools to trigger an awareness of the ramifications of the experience of enlightenment. However, HCC points out that many Japanese Zen temples resemble other Buddhist and non-Buddhist sites by incorporating such elements as *torii* gates (generally painted gray, rather than the Shinto vermilion color) in addition to the Mountain Gate (*sanmon*) of the seven-hall design, the ritual washing of hands (*te-mizu*) at the entranceway, burning incense, and selling fortunes in the form of plates (*ema*) and paper (*o-mikuji*). Furthermore, HCC explains that there are numerous dedicated prayer temples in the Zen network, some of them among the most popular and thriving centers especially in the Japanese Sōtō and Rinzai sects. At these sites, zazen takes a decided backseat, if it occurs at all, to the assimilation and nearly exclusive dedication to folk religious and devotional or esoteric Buddhist elements. In addition to—or sometimes combined with—Kannon or Jizō worship, there are many examples of a local demon-turned-deity, or a malevolent spirit (*onryō*) that realizes an underlying and undying wish to serve the dharma. These include the Kitsune (magical fox, also known in its positive manifestation as Inari, the rice fertility deity) and Tengu (mountain goblin), which is sometimes associated with the practice of mountain asceticism (*shūgendō*, or the *yamabushi* cult).[5] Demonic spirits are frequently transformed into avatars or concrete manifestations of Buddha (*gongen* or *myōjin*), at times superseding any other recognizable feature of Zen training or even of traditional, presyncretic Buddhist devotion.

Temples housing such powerful spirits are primarily concerned with delivering to their congregations of lay adherents the power to heal ailments and providing an avenue to achieving worldly benefits (*genze riyaku*), including good fortune (*kaiun*) and prosperity (*shōbai hanjō*).[6] They offer the capacity to achieve commercial success and relief from misfortunes ranging from fires and floods to health problems and infertility. Prominent examples of Sōtō Zen syncretized with esoteric Buddhism and folk religious elements include temples dedicated to Kannon and Jizō, Inari and Tengu. For example, Kōganji temple venerates a statue of the Buddhist goddess Kannon in honor of the magical effect of the bodhisattva Jizō, who once saved the life of a girl in dire straits, and Saijōji temple celebrates a monk who was transmuted into a mountain goblin. Also, the two main branches of Myōgonji temple combine the rice fertility god Inari with the esoteric Buddhist deity Dakini-shinten, as both are symbolized by the image of Kitsune, the shape-shifting fox.

TZN acknowledges aspects of religiosity assimilated from other traditions only as external forms, or a skin that does not disrupt or impede the marrow of using meditation for the attainment of a pure experience, which ultimately casts off and transcends any reliance on mediation in attaining mindfulness. Since the marrow is characterized by pure unmediated spiritual realization, the skin represents the superficiality of superstitions and supernaturalism, which can serve as convenient devices or skillful means in teaching the dharma, a technique used since the origins of Jataka literature about the previous lifetimes of the Buddha. However, HCC reverses this understanding by claiming that the marrow, or real core, of Zen consists of diverse ritual methods, with strained proclamations about the priority of zazen accompanied by disingenuous denials of ritualism often functioning on the level of skin, flesh, and bones.[7] For HCC, this rhetoric of immediacy cloaks the fact that the process of suppressing and converting autochthonic gods was a wide-ranging historical model whereby the advent of Zen overtook and supplanted local shrines and deities associated with esoteric or devotional Buddhism and with indigenous, pre-Buddhist movements (Taoist, Shinto, or amorphous folk traditions). But in many instances, the Zen Buddhist site was itself surpassed or at least accommodated to a non-Zen cult that reemerged from a suppressed state and transformed the focus to the attainment of worldly benefits. This is a key point, often overlooked, about the existence of Zen temples that are unrecognizable as such and are attended by lay believers who assume that they are folk shrines, which will be analyzed more fully below.

However, the HCC position is by no means monolithic. While the analysis of social-historical criticism is largely uniform on this issue in focusing on the prevalence and pervasiveness of popular religiosity in Zen temples, there is a range of interpretive attitudes about the meaning and significance of these phenomena. The attitudes begin, on one end of the spectrum, with admiration and applause for Zen's flexibility and ability to construct a synthesis of enlightened and everyday perspectives by using ritual forms as a skillful means that synthesizes the absolute and relative levels of reality.[8] For example, Duncan Williams refers to the "vitality" and "dynamic" quality of Sōtō rites, especially in the Tokugawa era when they helped lead to the "unprecedented expansion of the sect."[9] In many ways, in its positive assessment of the Zen legacy, this approach is complementary to the TZN view and to the HCC realization thesis regarding the issue of writes. In that sense, HCC contributes a fascination with the diversity of Zen practices to enhance the TZN outlook. However, HCC goes on to include an impartial, nonjudgmental examination of rituals, which opens the door to criticism, as well as the view at the other end of the spectrum of dismay or disdain at the apparent hypocrisy of the Zen institution that is willing to accommodate antithetical elements in a selling out to pragmatism and even crass commercialism. The full range of views attributable to HCC on the matter of rites sets the stage for scathing attacks on Zen's role in terms of social issues or rights, to be discussed in the following chapter.

Where Art Thou, O Buddha Hall?

To understand how such a high degree of variability of practices has come under the banner of Zen—with training monasteries like Eiheiji and Myōshinji tending to support the TZN view and a proliferation of prayer temples supporting the HCC view—it is necessary to look at the early sources, such as the *Ch'an-men kuei-shih* (CMK) and the *Gozan jissatsu zu* (GJZ), in relation to subsequent sectarian developments. Both texts were created in Sung China and may appear less relevant for assessing the expansion of Zen as a popular religious movement in medieval Japan. Nevertheless, the origins and dissemination of Japanese Zen must be traced back to foundational Chinese sources.

As discussed above, one of the main ideas of the CMK is that a spiritually insightful and morally superior abbot becomes the center of religious life. An important corollary is that the abbot as the living representative of the transmission process is celebrated as the "Honored (or Revered) One" (*zon*), rather than the deified images of buddhas and bodhisattvas found in conventional monasteries. The main halls used in Zen compounds were more or less the same as those in other temples from the era, including the Lü and T'ien-t'ai schools, but there were significant differences in usage reflecting a divergent ideological emphasis. For Zen, the emphasis on the abbot's public functions in the Dharma Hall (and Abbot's Quarters) obviated the need for a Buddha Hall, which was the centerpiece of the temples of other schools as a place to enshrine and display images and icons as objects of worship. According to the text attributed to Pai-chang, "There is no need for [a Zen monastery] to construct a Buddha Hall, but only to build a Dharma Hall to revere the Abbot as the legitimate living heir of the transmission of the buddhas and patriarchs."[10] Buttressing this are indications that, in the T'ang era, Pai-chang neglected to build a Buddha Hall in his temple, Lin-chi disparaged the value of this hall, and Te-shan actively dismantled the shrine wherever he served as leader.

The seminal Zen text's focus on the abbot as a replacement for the traditional object of veneration and its shrine provides the basis and framework for what can be referred to as the "eclipse of Buddha" by alternative sources of religious authority and charisma. The process of the overshadowing of Buddha through embodying enlightenment in concrete, contemporaneous living masters rather than historically and theologically distant icons is crucial to

TZN's claim that Zen represents the surpassing of other forms of Buddhist practice, not to mention non-Buddhist methods of spiritual training. Zen takes a middle way between the dichotomies of humanism and theism, existentialism and devotionalism, self-power and other-power.

However, what actually has taken place in eclipsing Buddha is not nearly so clear-cut and straightforward as it may seem in reading the CMK alone. From an analysis of available records, it is clear that Zen never did—and perhaps did not try to—realize the CMK ideal. Although the Pai-chang text theoretically eliminated the need for a Buddha Hall, the GJZ shows that the use of this building derived from the main hall (*kondō* or *hondō*), which contained major veneration images (*honzon*) found in typical Chinese Buddhist temples, "could not be cast aside so easily."[11] Most Zen temples invariably included this chamber, which was used for devotional purposes, for entertaining VIP guests to the grounds, and for lay-follower rites. As Foulk notes, "All Ch'an monasteries had at least one central Buddha hall, sometimes two.... Nor is there any evidence that would indicate that followers of the Ch'an school in the Sung regarded Buddha halls as somehow nonessential or extraneous to 'pure' Ch'an monastic practice."[12]

Furthermore, according to observations during his travels to China in the early thirteenth century, Dōgen, who was a great advocate of the Dharma Hall and Abbot's Quarters as primary sites for instruction, and of the Samgha Hall as the site for communal living, reports that the Buddha Hall was one of the three main buildings found in temple compounds.[13] Period records suggest that over the course of time, events held in the Dharma Hall took place far less frequently and increasingly for ceremonial purposes, as the emphasis beginning in the thirteenth century continued to highlight the role of the Buddha Hall. However, in the fourteenth-century Rinzai school, Daitō founded Daitokuji temple in Kyoto with only a Dharma Hall, while Musō established Nanzenji with an emphasis on the Abbot's Quarters.[14] Still, the gap between the textual model in the CMK and the reality on the ground shown in the GJZ and elsewhere is one of the primary areas leading to discrepancy between the TZN and HCC standpoints.

According to Martin Collcutt, the Buddha Hall "symbolizes the ritualistic, textual, and scholarly aspect of Chinese Buddhism against which early Ch'an had been in revolt. Its acceptance by Ch'an could only mean a loss of independence and dilution of meditation, as Ch'an monasteries, in return for patronage, became vehicles for the satisfaction of secular intentions."[15] As Collcutt's comment suggests, eventually—or perhaps even from the outset— deviation occurred, and temples came to encompass complex and contradictory elements of ritual and supernaturalism, including the Buddha Hall, so that the eclipse may well support the HCC view that Zen is based on a false pretense, or at least on a forgetfulness of its origins.

On the other hand, the prevalence of the Buddha Hall does not mean that it remained the main structure. Rather, it appears that once the eclipsing process was set in motion, the role of the Buddha Hall was itself surpassed, but not necessarily by the Dharma Hall, as the rhetoric of the CMK would indicate. In assessing the debate about Zen rites, one must consider that the basic temple layout has frequently been adjusted to facilitate not only the Buddha Hall, but also additional ritual structures occupying the compound. Indeed, nearly all temple halls from the formative period had tutelary deities, which were conceived of as protecting or encouraging particular activities and "were worshiped and propitiated with regular offerings and appealed to with prayers for assistance."[16] Furthermore, "[i]mages of bodhisattvas, arhats, and Ch'an patriarchs were also enshrined in their own worship halls, where they were the focal point of offering services on a daily, monthly, and annual basis . . . [that] filled the monastic calendar."[17]

Zen temples also incorporated relics and esoteric ritual elements, in addition to lay repentance and ordination ceremonies, thus creating a need for numerous embellishments so that most temple compounds encompassed several dozen or more main buildings for practical, ritual, administrative, and management functions. For example, Mt. A-yü-wang (which is Chinese for Asoka, the Buddhist monarch of India), an important Sung Zen temple near the port city of Ning-po frequently visited by Japanese monks, was known for holding one of three main relics claimed to be Sakyamuni's own, which were supposedly sent to China by King Asoka. Arriving via the Silk Road of the Sea by the early fourth century, the relic has always been the primary focus at Mt. A-yü-wang, which had a seven-century history prior to its conversion to the Zen school in the early eleventh century. The layout, a hodgepodge of diverse styles from different periods of Chinese Buddhist history, remains quite complex and does not resemble the seven-hall style. Eisai went to Mt. A-yü-wang during his journey to China around 1190, and on returning to Japan commented on the miraculous properties of the relic at the temple.

A Tale of Two Halls

As the GJZ illustrates, the core of Zen temple compounds (shown in Figure 3.1) generally had a vertical (north-south) axis extending from the gateway to the meeting halls (Dharma and Buddha halls) and a horizontal (east-west) axis encompassing the everyday functions of the monks (eating, cooking, cleaning, and sleeping). This layout closely resembled Taoist temples of the period, which reflected geomantic principles for channeling energy and warding off demonic spirits and were in turn often based on imperial models of construction.[18] For example, the main figure in a typical Chinese compound (in this case, the Ch'an abbot) faced south with his back to the north, the locus of chaotic spiritual forces, in all activities that took place in the main halls (Dharma Hall or Abbot's Quarters).

Although there is no mention of this in the CMK, the GJZ designs show that to fulfill the function of dispelling evil, most temples had two additional halls on the horizontal axis. The hall to memorialize the deceased patriarchs or ancestors (*soshidō*) of the temple was on the west side, and across the way to the east side there was the hall to commemorate the local earth deity (*dojidō*) associated with protection of the temple grounds. The Earth Deity Hall was frequently supplemented or replaced by halls enshrining other guardian or protector gods.

Both of these halls (whose functions are explained in detail in the *Ch'an-yüan ch'ing-kuei*) contributed to the process of eclipsing the Buddha.[19] Through the Patriarchs Hall, instead of venerating Sakyamuni Buddha or other buddhas and bodhisattvas, it was the major historical leaders of the school, such as first patriarch Bodhidharma, sixth patriarch Hui-neng, and Pai-chang, the initiator of monastic rules, who were enshrined and revered along with the abbots, past and present, of the particular temple. Through the Earth Deity Hall, the local spirits associated with powerful places, beings, and forces of nature received

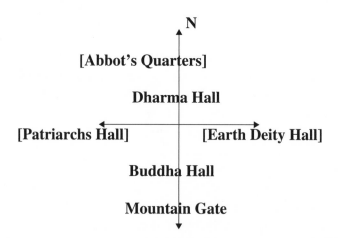

FIGURE 3.1. Axis view of temple layout. Note that the Abbot's Quarters is to the left of the central axis. Brackets indicate structures not part of the seven-hall layout.

attention and often became more of a focal point for worship than the Buddha Hall.

These two halls worked in tandem to provide protection for the temple and the dharma. According to a major study of the role of the portraiture of Zen patriarchs, "the ancestral spirits enshrined in the patriarchal hall and the autochthonous spirits enshrined in the earth spirit hall were associated with each other not only by virtue of their symmetrical placement within the monastic compound, but also by their religious function."[20] Furthermore:

> [T]he spirits of the patriarchs were treated as if they were present long after their physical death. The spirits of Pai-chang and other ancestors enshrined in the Patriarchs hall required daily care—typically offerings of sutras, food, and incense—in order to ensure the continued prosperity of the institution, just as did the earth spirits and protector deities.[21]

In other words, the images housed in both halls were used to evoke guardian forces representing either ancestors or local gods, who came to play a greater role than the Buddha did.

However, in the case of major monastic-training centers, a reverse process often took place whereby the Buddha Hall continued to maintain its high status. At Eiheiji, this hall was originally flanked by two separate buildings. One was the Guardian Deity Hall, which was occupied by spirits, including Daigenshuri, a Chinese dragon deity considered a bodhisattva (bosatsu), who protected travelers to and from Mt. A-yü-wang and assisted Dōgen's return to Japan, especially in crossing the treacherous Japan Sea. In addition, Indian deities such as Bonten or Gohō Myōō (a divine king) were enshrined there. The other was a hall for patriarchs with objects of devotion, such as statues of one or more of the ancestors. At Eiheiji, these were "important buildings in the early medieval monastery, with their own sub-prefects to supervise the various ceremonies. In time, however, both these halls were absorbed into the Buddha hall as altars (dojidan and soshidan) at the back of the hall."[22] Therefore, the Buddha Hall became the site for venerating three representations of the Buddha—Amida representing past vows, Sakyamuni for present enlightenment, and Maitreya for future powers—along with other gods and honored ones, instead of having the alternative spiritual forces enshrined in separate focal points. In another hall, which houses Dōgen's remains, sacred water is offered from a spring at the sacred peak of Mt. Hakusan (the water is known as Hakusan sui), although the claims for the authenticity of the source are sometimes met with skepticism by those attending the ritual, who assume it is piped in locally.

For the majority of temples, the Patriarchs Hall and Earth Deity Hall remained independent sites drawing energy away from and surpassing the significance of the Buddha Hall, thereby contributing to the eclipse of the Buddha. However, as indicated above, this transition was not necessarily directed toward an emphasis on the role of the Dharma Hall. Let us further consider the distinct yet closely related functions of these two subsidiary but crucially important temple halls.

The Patriarchs Hall seems to have evolved out of an emphasis on the sacerdotal duties of the Zen master, who performed ceremonies said to protect the imperial family or affect the weather, which became central components of Zen in China. T'ang legends record the way Zen masters used their supernormal powers (C. *shen-tung*, J. *jinzū*, Skt. *abhijñā*) to overcome spirits and apparitions. In one account, for example, a huge snake confronted Shen-hsiu, who remained seated without fear, and the next day he found a treasure hidden at the foot of a tree, which enabled him to build a temple. "The snake appears in this story as a potentially harmful, yet ultimately beneficent messenger of the invisible world. The spiritual power acquired through meditation allows Shen-hsiu to vanquish fear and obtain the tribute of the local god."[23] There are also examples of masters whose staff or ceremonial fly whisk (*hossu*) has a magical effect, or whose formless appearance is invisible to lesser gods. Or, masters use the power of temple symbols, such as the bell or gate, or indicators of transmission, such as lineage charts or precept scrolls, to evoke multicolored clouds and visions of arhats or to convert local gods and suppress baneful ghosts. However, much of this may be told in narratives in a playful or deliberately disingenuous fashion in relation to the mythological and supernatural elements.

By the Sung dynasty, when the Patriarchs Hall was institutionalized, there was a shift in emphasis from the present (living master or current abbot) to the past (ancestors or patriarchs of the temple), and from life to death, as the commemoration of deceased patriarchs serving as guardian spirits of the temple grounds became commonplace through a nexus of ritual elements. These included highly stylized portraits (C. *ting-hsiang*, J. *chinsō*) of former abbots sitting enthroned in the Dharma Hall while wielding a ceremonial fly whisk or staff, which was either hung on the wall or set posthumously on the high seat or throne, in addition to the preservation of flesh bodies or mummies similarly enthroned.[24] Reflecting the influence of Confucian views on ancestor veneration as well as Taoist images of immortality, the commemoration process involved strict ritual procedures for the funeral, cremation, and burial of deceased abbots. In addition to annual memorial services and offerings, the package of rites included the celebration of the magical effect of relics and objects, such as the robe or transmission certificate of the ancestor (deceased patriarch). The presumption was that the ancestors, who occupied the realm of the dead, would protect the temple from the intrusion of ghosts.

Zen Amalgamations

Zen discourse in China was multivalent. Sung kōan texts make it clear that the native gods remained inferior to the spiritual power attained through meditation by realized Zen masters. According to the commentary in the Tsung-jung lu (J. Shōryōroku) kōan collection on case 10, for example, which follows a passage that cites ironic, quasi-apocryphal comments by Chuang-tzu and Confucius about the powers of divination of a spirit turtle:

> Demons and ghosts become spirits through the power of bewitch-
> ment; spells and medicines become spirits through the power of
> causing [effects]; heavenly beings and dragons become spirits
> through the power of retribution; the wise and sagely become spirits
> through supranormal powers; and buddhas and patriarchs become
> spirits through the power of the Way.[25]

All of these categories possess spiritual power, but the indigenous gods, who surpass the category of ghosts and demons based on their ability to effect rewards and punishments for humans, remain on the third of five levels and cannot be compared to the power of buddhas and patriarchs, who are en-lightened by virtue of their realization of the Tao. Thus, Chinese Ch'an elite or literary discourse kept a distance or remained noncommittal regarding the status of supernatural forces encountered or absorbed from folk religions.

The transmission of Zen from China to Japan was marked by another shift in emphasis from the Patriarchs Hall to the Earth Deity Hall. As much as Sung China had an impact on the formation of Japanese Zen, it is clear that the native religious context was also extremely influential. In an article ex-amining Sōtō amalgamations with various forms of cult belief (or shinkō), including Mt. Hakusan and Inari beliefs, among others, Ishikawa Rikizan notes that Indian Buddhism was syncretized with Hindu deities, who were then transformed into buddhas, and that Chinese Buddhism, especially Zen, was syncretized with Confucian notions of the gentleman (chün-tzu) leading to a veneration of patriarchy.[26] Japanese Buddhism, which absorbed many of these earlier examples of syncretism, was further syncretized with the in-digenous Shinto kami and local spirits (ryūten), resulting in a variety of gods conceived of as avatars of buddhas or protectors (chinju or garanjin) who, on a

TABLE 3.1. Significance of Temple Halls in Relation to Stages of Zen.

Stage	Main Hall	Primary Infleuence
Basic Ch'an	Dharma Hall	T'ang Ch'an, abbot-based
Sung practice	Buddha Hall and Patriarchs Hall	Other Buddhist schools and Neo-Confucianism
Japanese practice	Earth Deity Hall	Indigenous (Shinto/folk)

lesser level of divinity, guard the monastery. Although the protector role was already part of Sung religiosity, it took on an even greater significance in Japan, where the power of the kami maintained a distinct status that was either—or both—embraced or seen as a mischievous force in need of exorcism by the spiritual prowess of evangelical Zen masters. Meanwhile, the role of patriarchy was somewhat diminished and further transmuted into an association with quelling the spirits of the dead.

While the irony of Sung sources such as the *Tsung-jung lu* was preserved in the writings of great Japanese masters such as Eisai, Dōgen, Enni, Daitō, Musō, and others, eventually the eclipse of the Buddha by the local land deities and related gods became the main factor in the rapid expansion of Zen in medieval Japan. This reflected integration with folk religious practices that were evident in Chinese Ch'an but were brought out in new and dramatic ways in Japanese Zen. According to Bodiford, "[T]he incorporation of rural village chapels into formal Buddhist denominations, such as Sōtō, occurred within the context of localized power struggles.... The creation of Sōtō temples necessitated similar accommodations in the spiritual realm, as the new symbols of Zen ideology confronted established beliefs and cultic practices."[27]

It is well known that Sōtō Zen for laypersons since at least the fourteenth century has been quite different than Sōtō training designed for monks or nuns in terms of incorporating popular practices such as divination, pilgrimage, posthumous ordination, and the veneration of indigenous deities in pursuit of healing and the gaining of worldly benefits. Thus, a great number of the approximately 15,000 Sōtō institutions (this number, confirmed in recent surveys, includes a small number of monastic training centers and a very large number of local temples) are designated prayer temples.[28] In the context of popularization, medieval monks who attained spiritual awakening through visions and dreams traditionally made displays of their own meditative powers (*zenjōriki*) for proselytizing, often at the behest or in competition with native gods (as a matter of symbiosis and/or of exorcism), and this reflected a significant degree of syncretism with native rites. In modern times, popular rites continue to be performed at countless prayer temples.

Azuma Ryūshin lists over two dozen local gods or spirits who are typically enshrined as buddha images (*butsuzō*) along with traditional Buddhist deities (buddhas and bodhisattvas), such as Shakuzon (Sakyamuni), Amida (Amitābha), Monju (Manjusri), Miroku (Maitreya), Fugen (Samantabhadra), and Kannon (Avalokitesvara).[29] Some of the most important examples of indigenous gods enshrined in Sōtō temples include Inari, Tengu, and Hakusan Myōjin Daigongen, the god of Mt. Hakusan, which is a *yamabushi* center near Eiheiji, venerated in several temples in Fukui and Ishikawa prefectures. Nor is it unusual to find shrines for the Sixteen Rakan and the deities of good fortune, Benzaiten and Daikokuten, who are sometimes included in the Shichifukujin pantheon (Seven Gods of Good Fortune: Ebisu, Daikokuten, Hotei, Benzaiten, Jurōjin, Fukurokuju, Bishamon). The gods are offered up in potpourri fashion, or as a buffet of offerings to lay believers.

The amalgamations between Sōtō Zen and folk religion are generally attributable to fourth-generation patriarch Keizan and the various lineages of his disciples. It seems that prior to this, many of the rural temples in the regions northeast and northwest of Kyoto, where Sōtō was spreading, were eclectic centers, formerly with a Tendai or Shingon affiliation. These sites were used for the performance of rituals often based or adapted to the needs of the local population or to reflect the values of itinerant and irregular priests who had learned the techniques of mountain ascetic practices.

Keizan maintained Dōgen's twin emphases on continuing a commitment to rigorous meditation as expressed in the *Zazenyōjinki*'s instructions on zazen and adhering to monastic regulations as explicated in the *Keizan shingi* code of rules. But he also rather extensively assimilated many elements of Tendai esotericism as well as folklore religiosity in his approach to Zen. Before joining the Sōtō sect, Keizan had been a follower of the remnants of the Daruma school, which was proscribed by the government in 1227 for antinomian tendencies in rejecting the Buddhist precepts and persecuted by the dominant Tendai church. Many of the school's followers then became affiliated with Dōgen's movement, perhaps inspiring his move from the capital in Kyoto to the remote provinces near Hajakuji temple, a last stronghold for Daruma school followers, and eventually formed the main component of the Sōtō sect. Through Keizan's efforts, Sōtō Zen spread primarily northward from Echizen to the Noto peninsula, where Sōjiji temple was originally established. Long a rival of Eiheiji for the designation of the school's head temple—Eiheiji enjoyed the prestige of the founder's legacy, but Keizan's temple could claim over nine times as many branch sites, in addition to imperial interest and support—Sōjiji was moved at the beginning of the twentieth century. The original remote location burned down in 1898 and was rebuilt and remains open, but the main activities of the temple were relocated to a new site in 1911 in the neighborhood of Tsurumi outside Yokohama in the Kanto region, which had become a major center of Sōtō school expansion during the Tokugawa era.

Apparently, Keizan's approach was to attract as many spiritual protectors as possible and to convert them all through supernatural encounters. He incorporated various esoteric rites syncretized with indigenous beliefs into Sōtō Zen, including geomancy, astrology, magic, visions, dreams, shamanism, and *yamabushi* techniques accompanied by the worship of Buddhist deities Bishamon and Rakan, native gods Inari and Hachiman, and numerous tutelary and local spirits. Yet, he never abandoned the practice of zazen, and his religious philosophy is a "fusion of vigorous Zen practice with an articulated faith in the efficacy of unseen Japanese spirits and Buddhist divinities."[30] As Heinrich Dumoulin reports, "Keizan's heart's desire was to affect [sic] a harmonious unity of Buddhist popular piety and its esoteric rituals with the serious practice of Zen meditation. This could not be accomplished, however, without compromise."[31] Whether or not such an evaluation, which implies a decline in the sect's integrity, is appropriate, it is clear that at least part of the fusion involved Inari. According to traditional hagiography, Keizan founded Yōkōji temple based on a prophetic dream of a white fox,[32] and his records in *Tōkokuki* note that he considered Inari to be the guardian spirit of Yōkōji and called the area of wild plants in the compound "Inari Peak."[33]

A key to the success of his lineage's growth was Keizan's evangelical disciple Gasan Jōseki, who was abbot of Sōjiji for forty years. Along with a troupe of energetic followers, such as Tsūgen Jakurei in the first generation and Ryōan Emmyō and Jochū Tengin in the next two generations, Gasan fostered the rapid spread of Sōtō Zen in the countryside. He did this by taking over many abandoned Tendai and Shingon temples and assimilating folklore divinities, which were called upon to protect the welfare of the sacred sites.[34] While greatly concerned with construction projects for bridges, dams, and irrigation canals to help win popular support, Gasan was also a scholastic monk who promulgated the dialectical doctrine of the "five ranks" (*go-i*), which is rooted in Chinese texts, especially in the teachings of founding patriarch Tung-shan.

Types of Sōtō Prayer Temples

One of the legacies of the popularization campaign is that some of the most prominent Sōtō temples are associated with shamanistic and esoteric practices. They are best known to their congregations of lay followers for espousing a syncretic approach to attaining worldly benefits, such as prosperity, fertility, or safety during travels, rather than for traditional Zen practices of meditation and monastic discipline. This section discusses a range of prayer temples selected for their affinity toward—or, conversely, for their divergence from—the standard seven-hall model in order to demonstrate the process and extent of the eclipse of the Buddha through local gods and other non-Zen objects of devotion. The temples range from those that are closest to the conventional model in creating a compromise by combining tradition with innovation, including Sōjiji temple near Yokohama and Saijōji temple outside of Odawara, to examples like Kōganji temple in the Sugamo neighborhood of Tokyo, which seems to bear no resemblance to what is generally understood to constitute a Zen temple compound. Following this is an in-depth case study of the two branch sites of Myōgonji temple, one in the town of Toyokawa in Aichi prefecture and the other in the neighborhood of Akasaka in Tokyo, both of which venerate the fox deity Inari, which eclipses the Buddha.

All of these prayer temples abandon to varying degrees the traditional layout in favor of syncretic forms of worship. Typical lay followers and participants who flood these sites for New Year's Day and other annual festivals may not even be aware of the Zen identity of the temple grounds, or that rituals and chants are being performed by monks trained in meditation at monasteries with the aim of overcoming worldly attachments. Furthermore, the two temples in Tokyo, Kōganji in Sugamo and Myōgonji in Akasaka, are noteworthy because their functions are largely indebted to a transectarian network of sacred sites and linkages with civic associations and community groups in their respective neighborhoods. The non-Zen shrines in these neighborhoods are based on similar kinds of worship, Jizō and Inari, respectively, regardless of label or sectarian identity, with crossover connections supporting joint festivals and outreach events throughout the yearly cycle of activities.[35]

Sōjiji: A Monastic Temple with Prayers

The first temple, Sōjiji, is anomalous and may not seem to fit in the group of sites mainly founded in late medieval or early modern times when popular religious movements were on the rise. It may even appear to represent the antithesis of the prayer temple in a way that gives credence to the TZN claims of asceticism. As indicated above, Sōjiji moved in 1911 to its current location in Tsurumi in the Kanto region from the Noto peninsula, where it was founded by Keizan in the fourteenth century. The layout closely resembles the seven-hall model by including a large temple gate at the entrance; a Samgha Hall, or *sōdō*, where trainees undertake the main activities of eating, sleeping, studying, and practicing zazen; and a Buddha Hall which contains statues of Sakyamuni, Tung-shan (the founder of the sect in China), Dōgen's Chinese master, Ju-ching, and the indigenous deity cum bodhisattva, Daigenshuri *bosatsu*. The Samgha Hall on appropriate occasions also serves as the Dharma Hall, or *hattō*; however, not having a Dharma Hall as a separate structure in which the abbot may address the assembly of clerics tends to detract from a sense of its adhering to the seven-hall model.

In addition to monastic training activities, Sōjiji is a focal point for lay worship, and many of the structures were designed to accommodate this function. The two largest and most significant buildings on the compound are the Founder's Hall (*daisodō*), for the veneration of Keizan (known as the sect's "great patriarch," or *daiso*, with Dōgen representing the "high patriarch," or *kōso*), and the Spirit Hall (*goreiden*), which honors the memory of Keizan's patron, Emperor Godaigo. Godaigo apparently helped the priest to construct nearly ninety buildings at the original facility in the Noto peninsula, which has been reconstructed to resemble the medieval style. In addition, there are several important popular religious elements at the south end of the Sōjiji compound. One is a shrine known as Baiyuan for abortion repentance rituals (*mizuko kuyō*), and there is also a small shrine for a manifestation of the divine fox, Anakuma Inari, complete with a small tunnel of vermilion *torii*. As shown in Figure 3.2, icon shops in the area sell statuary with folk religious themes.

Saijōji Temple: Combining Monasticism with Ritualism

The next temple on our list of Zen sites with an emphasis on prayer, Saijōji, is characterized by a similar but much more complex combination of monastic and folk religious elements weighted toward the veneration of deities and symbols through rites of obeisance and purification. The temple's self-explanation indicates that it prides itself on fostering a harmonious interplay of meditative and popular levels of religiosity. Saijōji, located near Odawara, an Edo period castle town in Kanagawa prefecture, is also called by two other designations. One is Daiyūzan in honor of the Chinese master Pai-chang. Pai-chang's temple was located near Ta-hsiung (J. Daiyū) peak in Kiangsi province south of the Yangtze River, where he was said to practice meditation in a small hermitage away from the main temple situated on a nearby hill.[36] Pai-chang, as we have seen, is also regarded as the founder of Ch'an/Zen monastic rules who lived by the communal work ethic of "a day without working is a day without eating." Therefore, the temple's moniker suggests that Saijōji is committed to strict Zen discipline. A large statue of Pai-chang sitting on the high seat while holding a

FIGURE 3.2. At a shop selling icons for graveyards and gardens outside of Sōjiji, the Laughing Buddha is for sale along with Inari in the background. Author's photograph.

fly whisk is held on the grounds, although it is usually kept out of view as a hidden icon (*hibutsu*) and is not part of what most pilgrims would be allowed to view. Sōtō monks carry out training activities in accord with Pai-chang's instructions, such as a week-long period of intensive meditation (*sesshin*) leading up to Rohatsu (Buddha's enlightenment day) on December 8.

The other, perhaps better known designation, is as the home for enshrining Dōryōzon, also known as Dōryō *daigongen* (or great avatar) or Dōryō *bosatsu* (or bodhisattva). Dōryō was a fifteenth-century priest who was said to have taken the form of a mountain goblin to become the guardian deity of the sacred site of his master and temple founder, Ryōan Emmyō, a second-generation follower of Keizan. Dōryō, at first a wayward, mischievous monk who overcame his faults through monastic training, eventually transformed into a winged Tengu riding atop a flying white fox (see Figure 3.3) to enhance his powers for protection of the temple grounds and was so spiritually powerful that he became recognized and venerated as a bodhisattva. Even so, Kannon is celebrated at the temple and its image is sometimes juxtaposed with or seems to eclipse the Tengu as a kind of reemergence of the buddhas (but not Buddha!), as shown in Figure 3.4.

FIGURES 3.3 and 3.4. At Saijōji, the Tengu appears on a flying white fox, yet from a side angle this image is eclipsed by a larger icon of Kannon. Author's photographs.

The temple is situated magnificently in the forested mountains heading west from Tokyo-Yokohama toward the Hakone hiking course, and in the Edo period this was a stop on the pilgrimage route heading from Tokyo to Ise shrine as the ultimate destination. The pathway to the compound is lined with tall cedars, and the layout features a rock garden, along with a variety of blossoms that convey the beauty of nature and rotation of the seasons. Throughout the area, there are streams and waterfalls, as well as steep stairways that lend a sense of elevation and mystery and create a path for walking meditation. The central section of the compound, as shown in Figure 3.5, features some of the structures of the traditional Zen temple layout, including a gate; a Monks Hall, where trainees meditate, sleep, and do their chores of cooking and cleaning; and the White Cloud Pavilion (*hakuunkaku*), where itinerant monks congregate and stay. The Dharma Hall (referred to as the Main Hall, or *hondō*) and the adjacent Scripture Hall (*shoin*) are the largest buildings and command the attention of all those who enter the compound.

However, lay congregants who visit the temple grounds for festivals and other events come with the primary motivation of finding a method for healing and attaining worldly benefits. Pilgrims converge from all over Japan

FIGURE 3.5 Overview of Saijōji compound, with the inner sanctuary housing the Dōryō icon at the top center. From *Daiyūzan: Daiyūzan Saijōji kaisō roppyakunen hōzan* (Kanagawa-ken, Japan: Daiyūzan Saijōji kaisō roppyakunen hōzan jimuchō, 1994), p. 10.

seeking to drink or wash from a sacred spring of water gushing forth on the compound, which has been said since the Tokugawa era to have miraculous healing or rejuvenating powers. Or, they view the enormous, oversized Japanese wooden shoes (*geta*) said to have been worn by Dōryō, which have a talismanic effect.[37]

The declared aim of Saijōji is not to foster a two-tiered institutional structure in which elite monks focus exclusively on meditation while uninformed believers take part in a uniform and segregated fashion in folk ritual practices. Rather, through a focus on Dōryō and rites related to his veneration, Saijōji creates a dynamic integration of complementary elements of traditional Zen monastic discipline and popular religiosity and festival life. It serves at once as the main training center and the most lucrative fundraising temple of the network affiliated with Sōjiji.[38] These interrelated dimensions converge in legends concerning two impressive rocks on the temple grounds. One is the "zazen stone" (*zazen seki*) shown in Figure 3.6, which is located down the path from the entrance and across a bridge over the Daiyū River. According to tradition, this was where Ryōan practiced meditation for weeks

FIGURE 3.6. Zazen stone at Saijōji. Author's photograph.

at a time until he wore down the surface of the mighty rock. The other is the "one-strike stone" (*ittekiseki*) located in front of the Founder's Hall, which marks where Ryōan was able to find the proper location for constructing the temple when a spirit told him to heave the large stone that was obstructing his path and to build where it landed.

The temple strives to create a seamless integration of monastic and popular, elite and devotional practices through seasonal festivals in which monks demonstrate the prowess of their training and discipline in a way that fully engages and inspires lay participants. The greatest and most solemn celebration is the Sacred Food Offering Festival, which is held on the twenty-seventh and twenty-eighth days of three different months (January, May, and September), in honor of the fact that Dōryō once served the temple as the chief cook (*tenzo*). During this rite, three priest/cooks wearing white attire and having prayed and purified themselves with austerities for seven days previous, cook steamed rice as an offering. At night, they rush up the imposing 350 steps from a bridge near the Repentance Hall (*gokudō*) to the Inner Sanctuary (*oku no in*) without pausing and offer the steamed rice to Dōryō *bosatsu*.[39] After the conclusion of the ceremony, the congregants are served a vegetarian feast in the Dharma Hall, whose function has been eclipsed by the hidden icon of Dōryō held in the sanctuary. As seen in Table 3.2, the festival year for the lay community culminates with a fire ceremony and purification rite held on November 27 performed by the abbot and other head monks. This is another occasion of vicarious fulfillment, in which lay believers are inspired

TABLE 3.2. Yearly Rites at Saijōji Temple.

January 1	New Year's bell ringing
January 26	Dōgen memorial
January 27–28	Sacred Food Offering Festival
February 3	Setsubun (Chinese New Year)
March 25–26	Founder's Memorial
April 8	Buddha's birthday
May 27–28	Sacred Food Offering Festival
July 1–12, 27	Visitor's feast
September 27–28	Sacred Food Offering Festival
October 5	Bodhidharma memorial
November 21	Keizan memorial
November 27	Sacred Fire Festival
December 1–8	Sesshin (intensive meditation)
December 8	Rohatsu (Buddha's enlightenment)
December 27	Preparing *mochi* (New Year's cakes)

by a performance that demonstrates the monks' prowess in monastic training and spiritual realization.

Kōganji: A Full-Fledged Prayer Temple

The next site on this list, Kōganji, located in the Sugamo neighborhood of Tokyo, is based entirely on devotion to Buddhist deities rather than either a Zen patriarch or local spirits. This approach to ritual practice is reflected in the temple layout, which is far removed from any resemblance to the traditional compound. Togenuki Jizō is another designation for this temple, which worships the image of Kannon through a bathing ceremony in honor of a manifestation of Jizō, who once saved a girl by pulling out (*nuki*) a splinter (*toge*) stuck in her throat. Since the temple, originally founded in the Ochanomizu neighborhood at the end of the sixteenth century and later moved to Ueno, was again relocated to the current site during the Meiji era, it has become a center for a popular healing cult that attracts the elderly from all over the city and the country.

Togenuki Jizō is particularly known for addressing ailments and health concerns of elderly women, and temple rites cater to this clientele. There is no Main Hall, and instead temple practice revolves almost entirely around believers performing a brief bathing ceremony of the statue known as "*arai* (washing) Kannon." Lay visitors line up for hours on festival days (the fourth, fourteenth, and twenty-fourth days of every month) for the opportunity to participate in the bathing rite, and even a typical dreary, rainy day off-cycle finds the temple frequented with a long line of devotees awaiting a chance to approach the icon. Accompanying this rite, Sōtō monks provide acupressure therapy or sell fortunes or talismans for healing at the gateway to the temple.

The surrounding neighborhood in the district of Sugamo is called *obaa-chan no Harajuku* ("granny's Harajuku," with Harajuku being a fashionable area for young people in an upscale part of the city near Shibuya and the Meiji shrine). In shops and stands throughout the area, various kinds of herbal remedies, Chinese medical supplies, and miracle cures (including a shop that specializes in red underwear, as shown in Figure 3.7, which supposedly creates a youthful effect for the elderly) are offered to the festival throngs.[40] Furthermore, this temple participates in a network of Jizō sites that populate the larger Sugamo area as indicated on the map in Figure 3.8, which greets visitors who get off at the rail station (with a Denny's restaurant in the background and a notice for the Sugamo graveyard at the bottom of the sign). Each of the sites on the tour has a special approach to veneration of its local deity and affiliation with one of the various Buddhist sects.

FIGURE 3.7. Red underwear for youthfulness for sale in a Sugamo area shop. Author's photograph.

FIGURE 3.8. Street sign promoting the Jizō pilgrimage network in Sugamo. Author's photograph.

Syncretism in the Myōgonji/Toyokawa Inari Network

The pattern of Sōtō Zen Buddhist–folk religious syncretism is perhaps most evident in the network of Myōgonji temples, which, although affiliated with the Eiheiji wing of the sect, has a head temple in Toyokawa city in Aichi prefecture, southeast of Nagoya, and several subsidiary temples. These include an important branch in the Akasaka neighborhood of Tokyo (with other branches in Osaka, Yokosuka, Fukuoka, and Sapporo). In addition to the branch temples, there are numerous locations referred to as "divided spirit sites" (*bunreisho*) in which the spiritual power has been transmitted from a parent to a daughter shrine through an icon, which is ritually animated and empowered.[41] At both the Aichi Toyokawa and Tokyo Akasaka sites, the main icons on the compound are not images of the Buddha but of the Shinto rice harvest and fertility god in the form of its chief messenger and avatar, the fox deity, Inari. The fox represents an indigenous manifestation (*gongen*) or guardian spirit (*chinju*) of the universal Buddha-nature enshrined as a main Buddhist object of worship (*honzon*), to which monks routinely pray for the protection and prosperity of their institution. Inari is also assimilated with an esoteric deity, Dakini-shinten, which became a spiritual force protecting the Buddhist teachings.[42]

Myōgonji temple, or Empukuzan Myōgonji, is a Sōtō Zen institution, yet to most people, including many of its patrons, casual visitors, and tourists, it is better known as Toyokawa Inari. This in large part reflects a deliberate strategy by the Sōtō sect to promote the site as a prayer temple rather than as a place for meditation. Toyokawa Inari is second only to the Fushimi Inari shrine in southeastern Kyoto in importance for the overall cult of Inari, which is spread throughout large sectors of both Shinto and Buddhism, and in some senses, especially but not limited to the impact on Zen, its significance as a ritual center surpasses the other shrine's. Even more connected with the worship of an indigenous god than is Saijōji temple, Myōgonji's use of the Inari designation as the primary moniker gives the site more cachet for promoting its worldly benefits orientation. The red votive banners that decorate the walkway in Figure 3.9 are typical of Inari shrines (that is, non-Buddhist sites).

Myōgonji temple in Tokyo plays a role as a link in a chain of sites in the Akasaka neighborhood that is similar to Kōganji temple's participation in the Jizō network in Sugamo. The Toyokawa Inari site in Akasaka is situated in an upscale modern business district that has historical importance as an area in close proximity to the imperial palace and capital buildings, which was its

FIGURE 3.9. Row of votive banners at Toyokawa Inari in Tokyo, Akasaka. Author's photograph.

prime location in the Tokugawa era. In addition to numerous Buddhist temples, Akasaka also features at least three other major shrines that venerate various forms of Inari, including one (Hie Sannō Jinja) affiliated with Fushimi and two (Akasaka Inari Jinja and Hikawa Jinja) that are part of networks in greater Tokyo. Part of the appeal is that the atmosphere of these shrines evokes a sense of nostalgia for the Edo period. While the Hie Sannō and Hikawa shrines actually date back to that era (Hie Sannō may be much older, originating in some of the earliest Edo settlements), Toyokawa Inari probably came to be located in its present site during the Meiji era, with the Tokugawa dating representing an "invention of tradition."

Assimilationist Trends

The Myōgonji temple foundation legend (*engi*) is only available through an unreliable historical source reported in the temple's publicity literature and pamphlets (some of the details of which apparently have been changed over the years).[43] Its (mythical) history is also cited in the modern dictionary of Zen compiled by Sōtō scholars, the *Zengaku daijiten*.[44] The legend refers to a narrative about the origin of Dakini-shinten, originally a Hindu deity, although its name seems to be based on a Tibetan Buddhist term. The deity came to be enshrined and worshiped in Japan, which indiscriminately absorbed many Indian gods whether of Hindu or Buddhist origin, and was assigned the role of the *honzon* and Inari as the *gongen*. Although Dakini-shinten is labeled Buddhist in Japan, the formation of its imagery and iconography actually has little precedent in Indian or Chinese models and seems to reflect a prior syncretism with the native god Inari. Sōtō clergy, many of whom are trained at Eiheiji, for which Myōgonji serves as a regional training temple, perform the rites, festivals, and chants for the worship of this deity. This occurs despite— or perhaps because—of the fact that medieval folklore records contain numerous tales in which Sōtō monks, other Buddhist practitioners, and non-Buddhist shamans and wizards are known for their ability to recognize and exorcise demonic trickster foxes.

According to the foundation legend, Kangan Giin Zenji (1217–1300), the third son of Emperor Jotoku and a Sōtō sect disciple of Dōgen, had a spiritual experience (*reiken*) while visiting China to show the deceased master's writings to his former colleagues at Mt. T'ien-t'ung temple near Ming-chou (present-day Ning-po). Giin envisioned the deity Dakini-shinten carrying a rice plant on its back and riding a white fox as a benevolent kami (*zenshin*) and a protector deity (*chinju*) of the Buddhist dharma. Based on his vision, Giin had a statue constructed of Dakini-shinten. In 1441, during the era of rapid provincial Sōtō expansion in the late medieval period, a sixth-generation follower of Giin's enshrined this icon along with a thousand-armed Kannon at Myōgonji (the current compound in Aichi prefecture dates from 1536 and gained a sizable *danka*, or parish, in the Edo period). The statue was later brought to the residence of Ōoka Echizen no kami (Akasaka Hitotsugi in Tokyo), once a disciple of an Aichi Myōgonji priest, where it remained until it was enshrined in 1887 in its present location at the Tokyo branch of Toyokawa Inari temple in Akasaka.

It is not clear how Dakini-shinten or Myōgonji temple became associated with Inari the rice god, but it is possible that the connection was made after Giin's statue was built simply because the fox iconography was common to both beliefs. It is plausible that Myōgonji was first an Inari shrine and subsequently converted to Buddhism or that both Inari and Dakini-shinten were enshrined there at the same time. The whole question of the relation between the white fox in its various manifestations and legends and the typical Fushimi Inari fox, which in some representations is also white although not necessarily so, is obscure. There is also no systematic theological discussion of gender symbolism regarding the connection of Dakini-shinten with either female portrayals of Inari or folklore conceptions of the vixen Kitsune as a trickster, who appears as a femme fatale who seduces and abandons men who are vulnerable to duplicity. In any case, according to the current beliefs, Dakini-shinten functions as the *honzon* and Inari as the *gongen*. Yet, it is important to point out, as indicated above, that Dakini-shinten cannot be considered a Buddhist deity that assimilates Inari for it is, no doubt, a result of intensive indigenization and syncretism probably influenced by preexisting Inari beliefs. Also, several Sōtō temples that enshrine the fox, although not necessarily those in the Myōgonji network, consider the indigenous deity Inari, rather than the imported god, to be the *honzon*. The view portrayed today may well be shaded by the legacy of *shinbutsu bunri* (the forced separation of kami and Buddhist gods), which was imposed as a national policy in the Meiji era.

In Japanese religion, the cult of Inari is surely one of the oldest and largest organized folk religious movements.[45] According to legend, the origin of Inari worship is traced back to 711 A.D., when a bird's flight auspiciously sited the first shrine on a mountaintop at Fushimi on the southern outskirts of Kyoto. The cult was also patronized in its early years by Kūkai (774–835), who declared Inari to be the protector deity of Tōji temple, which was built with wood from Fushimi Mountain. Fushimi Inari began receiving imperial patronage during the Heian period, when the first large shrine building was erected in 823 in gratitude for successful prayers for rain. A century later, three shrines were built on separate hills that established a connection between Inari, based initially on the local, seasonal, rice-growing gods of the paddy fields (*ta no kami*) who regularly return to the mountains (*yama no kami*) for winter hibernation, and the classical Shinto mythology of Kojiki/Nihongi fertility gods. Inari, which according to traditional etymology means "rice plant (*ine*) growth (*naru*)," was linked to Ukemochi, a female deity who, it is said, was disembodied by an angry father and gave rise to vegetation which sprang from her interred body parts.[46] Although the legends of pre-Heian Inari activities are unreliable, it is plausible that some of the rituals for rice planting, transplanting, and harvest that were incorporated into the cult actually stemmed from local fertility rites and field dances originating from much earlier, pre-Buddhist times.

The fox deity may well have existed before Kūkai, but one Inari tradition maintains that on his deathbed he named the original Buddhist ground (*honji*) Mandarajin, made up of Benzaiten, Shōten, and Dakini-shinten, with Inari/fox as the local expression (*suijaku*).[47] Yet, as indicated, there are many reversals of this pattern, in which Inari takes precedence over the Buddhist gods, including Kannon or Sakyamuni, or in which Dakini-shinten alone is elevated to the most venerated status or stands alone as the *gongen*.

Despite its size, endurance, and pervasive cultural resonances, Inari/fox worship is generally classified as an example of *shinkō*, a cult based on folk beliefs and practices, as opposed to a *shūkyō*, a sect officially affiliated and registered with one of the major traditions, Shinto or Buddhism. Whereas a *shūkyō* has one main temple or shrine that oversees numerous branch institutions, while often allowing for tremendous regional diversity and flexibility of interpretation or application of doctrine, a *shinkō* refers to a loose-knit, diffused network of associations and amalgamations without a clear, official center of authority. Although it played such a key role early on, the Fushimi shrine has probably never functioned as a central authority, and most other Inari shrines have remained at least quasi-independent. Since the period of Heian imperial patronage, the prominence of Fushimi has declined, and it was not recognized as part of "sect Shinto" in the Meiji era.

However, it is necessary to qualify the above distinction between *shinkō* and *shūkyō* for several reasons. First, the complete history of Fushimi Inari is difficult to determine because a fire during the Ōnin War in 1468 destroyed all of the existing records. Also, the government-sponsored Meiji era campaign for the separation of Buddhism and Shinto caused the elimination, rewriting, or distortion of many of the records and remainders of Inari worship and its connections with Buddhism, including the Shingon temple, Aizenji, once at the foot of Fushimi. Furthermore, Inari worship is different from some other kinds of *shinkō*, which are localized and limited to a particular region, such as a sacred mountain or shrine, or to a specific deity. There are over 30,000 Inari shrines, from large, sprawling compounds to some as small as a single *torii* gate, incorporated into hundreds of non-Buddhist sites and Buddhist temples throughout the country, such as Sōjiji. But the main qualification regarding Myōgonji involves the intimate, syncretistic relation between the Inari cult and the Sōtō Zen sect almost to the point of indistinguishability between the folk religion and Buddhism, which contributed to the premodern *shinbutsu shūgō* (unity of kami and buddhas) tradition that prevailed until it was challenged by the Meiji era policy of dividing the religions.[48]

A major study in a volume edited by folklorist Gorai Shigeru of the relation between Buddhism and Inari *shinkō* in over five dozen temples examines a variety of categories. These include temples founded as Zen institutions and others converted in the medieval or early modern periods, along with temples that primarily venerate either Fushimi Inari or Toyokawa Inari as a *honzon* in addition to temples whose fox images have roots in different folklore beliefs.[49] Many of the temples that favor Toyokawa Inari or Dakini-shinten also enshrine Fushimi Inari as either their *gongen* or *chinju*, sometimes based on the founder's having received a dream oracle (*mu-koku*) or on local village or clan ancestor rites.

The Myōgonji compound in Aichi has two central buildings, a Dharma Hall where Dakini-shinten is enshrined and a Shrine Hall for Toyokawa

Inari—these are separate structures although, as we have seen, at Saijōji the terms are used interchangeably. Dakini-shinten is assigned the role of the original source of Toyokawa Inari, although both are portrayed riding white foxes. The adjacent halls are separated only by a *torii* gate. Also, Inari fox statues often decorated with red bibs stand protectively outside the Dharma Hall. In the Tokyo Akasaka branch temple, there is only one center referred to as a Shrine Hall, generally a term for non-Buddhist sites, where Dakini-shinten is enshrined with foxes standing guard outside the hall. In other words, the two Myōgonji temples primarily service Inari rites to gain worldly benefits rather than support zazen, although its practice does take place in Aichi.

Both Myōgonji temples have festivals based on the cycle of the seasons and Buddhist repentance days (*uposatha*) that occur fortnightly. For example, the observance of the *hatsu-uma sai* rite is celebrated shortly after the lunar new year in February when, as a holdover from agrarian times, the local mountain god is supposed to return to the paddy field (*ta no kami*). Toyokawa Inari in Aichi is particularly known for *mikoshi*-carrying festivals with adults and children wearing costumes or traditional garb and some believers donning oversized fox masks. The temples offer worship for protection in the secular realm. For instance, Tokyo Akasaka has regular festivals to pray for traffic or travel safety (*kōtsū anzen*), with the main celebration held every twenty-second day of June.

Both sites have a grove (*reikozuka*) with at least several dozen small fox-spirit statues, rather than stupas, which are offered as memorials in honor of the deceased. The Myōgonji temples also offer a potpourri of other forms of worship. The temple in Aichi enshrines a thousand-armed Kannon and the Sixteen Rakan, and has numerous statues and portraits (*chinsō*) of Giin. Tokyo Akasaka, which is dedicated to Yakushi and Sakyamuni and is adorned with red lanterns lit up every night, evoking an Edo period atmosphere against the background of downtown Tokyo, enshrines Kannon, Jizō, and Benzaiten. It also has a Sanshinen (Hall of Three Gods: Tarō Inari, Tokushichirō Inari, and Ugajin), and in the inner area of this shrine the Shichifukujin pantheon is enshrined.

Coexisting Exorcistic Trends

The picture that emerges from an examination of Toyokawa Inari and related forms of worship involves multiple images of fox iconography that are at once intertwined and conflicting, or overlapping and competing. These include Buddhist and indigenous orientations, icons that are enshrined in a Dharma Hall or Shrine Hall and are either more or less valued than traditional buddhas, and images positive and negative of the fox as protective and inspiring worship or demonic and requiring exorcism. At the same time that Zen Buddhism identifies the fox-as-Inari with sacredness, influenced by another dimension of folk religions it also seeks to eliminate the fox when it is understood as a conniving trickster or Kitsune. Kitsune is generally understood in East Asian society as a demon or a cultural indicator of mischievous, dispersed, and chaotic forces that are in need of being tamed and controlled.[50] The dual elements of fox veneration and exorcism, which seem to be in conflict, coexist within Zen discourse and ritual practice. It appears that part of the background for Japanese views of Kitsune is the portrayal of the fox only as a malevolent trickster in Chinese folktales in texts such as the tenth-century *T'ai-p'ing kuang-chi* (J. *Taiheikōki*). Here, there is little suggestion of the positive, self-sacrificing image of foxes found in subsequent Japanese folktales that serves as a model for veneration and worship in the Inari cult, which was widespread in Japan since the eighth century and penetrated into the Sōtō sect by the 1400s.

A prime example of the exorcism of the demonic side of the fox by Japanese Buddhist ritualists is found in the morality tale in the text *Konjaku monogatari* 16.17. This tells the story of a husband and father named Yoshifuji, who is led astray by a beautiful vixen and who goes off with his illusory bride and thinks he sires a child. In the midst of his enchantment, Yoshifuji feels that he has not a care in the world, but his worried brothers recite the *nembutsu* and chant sutras, calling on Kannon to help them find him. Suddenly, a man with a stick, a messenger of the Buddhist deity, arrives at his new, imaginary house and scares everyone in the household away. According to the tale, Yoshifuji crawls out from the storehouse under his real home, and the truth is revealed. He starts to show off his new son to his older boy, declaring the youngster to be his true heir, but there is in reality no one with him, and meanwhile a servant finds lots of foxes scurrying under the storehouse.

It turns out that Yoshifuji had been tricked into marrying a vixen. A yin-yang diviner—with spiritual power of equal value to Buddhist ritualism—is called upon to perform an exorcism, and eventually Yoshifuji comes to his senses. He realizes, "The thirteen days he had spent under the storehouse had seemed to him like thirteen years, and the few inches of clearance between the ground and the floor of the building had looked to him like a stately home. The foxes had done all this."[51] In this case, a moral lesson is learned by a wayward soul betrayed by a seductive apparition of a fox about the need for loyalty and commitment by overcoming temptation and rising above self-deception.

The connections between Sōtō Zen and ritual purification include the fact that the most famous of all legends of fox exorcism performed by Buddhists

FIGURE 3.10. Exorcism of the killing stone as depicted in Noh theater. From Janet Goff, "Foxes in Japanese Culture," *Japan Quarterly* 44/2 (April–June 1997): 71.

involves Gennō Shinshō, a disciple of Gasan Jōseki, the main descendant of Keizan and abbot of Sōjiji temple, whose followers are credited with the tremendous regional expansion of the medieval sect by subduing and converting local spirits. According to legends recorded in Sōtō texts and popular literature, in 1389 Gennō exorcised one of the most demonic of vulpine forms, the infamous, malevolent nine-tailed fox (*kyūbi kitsune*) that took possession of a killing stone (*sesshō seki*) from which it was murdering people and other living things. A famous floating world print (*ukiyo-e*) by Kuniyoshi, known for his compelling fox paintings, depicts a *musha-e* (picture representing a fight or struggle) of the wicked nine-tailed fox fleeing from the palace of King Pan-Tsu of India. According to this cycle, which appears in other East Asian cultures, including Vietnam, the nine-tailed fox stayed with the Indian king for years as his mistress before revealing its true nature and then fleeing to China and finally to Japan and elsewhere in the twelfth century, where it continued to work its evil magic.[52]

According to one version of the origin of this anti-shrine, the fox spirit dwelling in the stone located in a moor near Mt. Nasu north of Nikko was originally expelled from India and took the guise of a woman, who married an emperor in Japan. When the emperor recognized her vulpine status, the fox spirit turned itself into this noxious stone.[53] The stone is actually volcanic rock emitting poisonous gases. Bashō, traveling in this area on the way to see

Saigyō's weeping willow at Ashino, as recorded in *Oku no hosomichi*, reported that the "stone's poisonous vapors were as yet unspent, and bees and moths lay dead all around in such heaps that one could not see the color of the sand beneath."[54] Legends record that yin-yang master Abe no Yasunari, featured in numerous *setsuwa* tales and a Noh drama (Figure 3.10), had already expelled the demon from the capital and into the provinces. There it was subdued by Gennō's use of a purification stick and his chant based on one of the best-known phrases of Dōgen (1200–1253), "*genjōkōan* [everyday realization] is the great matter."[55] This legend highlights the twofold approach-avoidance, embracing-rejecting relation between Zen and folk beliefs.

On Eclipsing the Buddha

Table 3.3 sums up some of the main differences among the various temples examined in this chapter concerning their main structures, deities, functions, and the issue of the relation of Zen to folk religious elements of practice.

The various examples of Sōtō–folk religion syncretism highlight the apparently sharp contrast between the exclusive emphasis on the attainment of worldly benefits and healing in Inari, Tengu, and Jizō worship and the focus on zazen only as espoused by TZN. To appreciate the diversity of rites and the atmosphere they create, let us consider that a visit to the non-Buddhist Fushimi Inari shrine on a festival day finds believers climbing the mountain through a tunnel of *torii* gates among throngs who are making offerings, watching *kagura* dances, or listening to the chanting of priests. The pilgrims may see the construction of new shrines or icons in the compound while stopping at a café or vending machine for refreshments. The aim is to appeal to, stimulate, enhance, and celebrate the world of sensation while finding spiritual release through an integration and elevation of everyday affairs. By

TABLE 3.3. The Range of Beliefs at some Sōtō Prayer Temples.

	Sōjiji	Saijōji (Daiyūzan)	Myōgonji (Toyokawa Inari)		Kōganji (Togenuki Jizō)
Location	Tsurumi	Odawara	Toyokawa, Aichi	Tokyo, Akasaka	Tokyo, Sugamo
Main structure	Daisōdō	Hondō (Hattō)	Honden/Hattō	Honden	Icon/Honden
Main deity	Sakyamuni	Doryōzon	Dakini-shinten	Inari	Arai Kannon
Main function	training plus benefits	healing and benefits	benefits plus meditation	benefits	healing
Zen or folk?	Zen (folk)	synthesis	folk (Zen)	folk	folk

contrast, at the opposite end of the spectrum, a Zen monastic-training temple, whether the Sōtō sect's Eiheiji temple or Daitokuji or Myōshinji temples in the Rinzai sect, creates a contemplative sense of calm amid nature and detachment from worldly striving or activity. Its simple layout and minimalist construction, with its emphasis on varying shades of gray, tries to compel a visitor to appreciate a transcendental spirit. The atmosphere at Saijōji and Myōgonji temples, which both attempt in their own way to achieve a fruitful admixture of worldly and transcendental dimensions, has become a prime example of what Allan Grapard calls the "combinative" character of Japanese religion, which goes a step further in involving Buddhism in syncretism than was the case in China. In that sense, "the words Shinto, Buddhism, sect, and religion are inadequate because they compartmentalize a reality that is not cut up in the manner implied by those words."[56]

While there are historical and ideological roots in Chinese folklore and Ch'an sources, the kinds of syncretism embodied in these examples seem distinctive to the context of medieval Japan, when Zen monasteries assumed the need to make peace with, rather than to try to eradicate, the local deities, in order to receive their protection for the sites of the institution. Japan, like China, is one of the few countries where its two main religions have mingled and blended along with local indigenous rites. Despite repeated governmental attempts to separate them, Buddhism and Shinto have remained intertwined. Even more than in the case of China, this has resulted in an elevation of mischievous spirits such as Kitsune or Tengu to the status of the primary objects of reverence. Although Toyokawa Inari is one of the main examples, dozens of other Buddhist temples, including those in Rinzai Zen and the Nichiren and Pure Land schools, contain a fox shrine in addition to shrines with icons of some other local animistic deities.

The situation in which a native spirit becomes more highly venerated than Buddhist gods by a Sōtō temple supposedly dedicated to the practice of zazen, and yet still is recognized as having a malevolent potential requiring exorcism, becomes a focal point for rethinking the function of syncretism in Zen. It also calls for a reevaluation of the two-tiered, "trickle-down," assimilative model of *honji suijaku* theology of Buddhist gods serving as the original ground for indigenous spirits as their local expression. A central question concerns the extent to which these cases of syncretism reflect, as Heinrich Dumoulin has suggested in the comment about Keizan's evangelism cited above, a "compromise" of Buddhist values for the sake of accommodation with autochthonic beliefs. The debate among HCC critics has to do with whether the elevation of local gods should be evaluated either as a natural outgrowth of the open-endedness of Zen thought, which is admirable (in Duncan Williams), or as representative of a fundamental, fatal weakness, or a "fault line" in Zen ideology (in Bernard Faure), which is reprehensible (as Dumoulin's comment suggests).[57]

Rhetoric of Antisupernaturalism, Practice of Supernaturalism

One approach to wrestling with these concerns is to consider, without trying to eliminate artificially a sense of conflict or contradiction, that there are several levels of discourse coexisting in Zen's view of syncretism that help to justify various aspects of both the TZN and HCC perspectives. A primary level of discourse in classic (Sung Chinese and Kamakura Japanese) Zen literature is the rhetoric of antisupernaturalism, in which kōan records disavow and mock the claims of supernatural beliefs from a transcendental perspective. The various roles of fox spirits as they appear in Sung Chinese records, for example, all derive from a basic image of the "wild fox" as a symbol of counterfeit enlightenment or of a rogue element in practitioners who deceive themselves and others into believing they have genuine realization. The main example is *Wu-men kuan* (J. *Mumonkan*) case 2 (also *Tsung-jung lu* case 8), in which an old monk reveals that he has suffered 500 incarnations as a wild fox for having misunderstood—long ago, in a lifetime prior to the era of Sakyamuni—the meaning of karmic causality. The monk/fox is released by the "turning word" of master Pai-chang expressing the inviolability of karma.[58] Other texts that use the term "wild fox" in the same fashion include the *Pi-yen lu* (J. *Hekiganroku*) cases 1, 73, and 93 and several passages in the records of Lin-chi. That is, the Sung records transmute the folklore elements based on supernatural images of bewitching, seductive vixens into a demythologized rhetorical device indicating false enlightenment.

However, even though the Zen scholastic tradition of recorded sayings and kōan commentaries often refutes and makes a mockery of supernaturalism, these texts are frequently ambivalent and open-ended rather than one-sidedly critical. They use tongue-in-cheek rhetoric to remain noncommittal about avowing or disavowing folk religiosity, thereby leaving the door open to forging various kinds syncretism. For example, Dōgen's *Shōbōgenzō* "Raihai-tokuzui" fascicle seems to endorse fox worship, in asserting that "we revere the Dharma, whether manifested in a round pillar, a garden lantern, a buddha, a fox, a demon or deity, a man or a woman,"[59] although it is not clear that this refers specifically to Inari *shinkō*.

This discursive level expresses an ironic, self-reflective sidestepping of the issue of supernaturalism versus antisupernaturalism, as in a kōan case cited in the "Raihaitokuzui" fascicle, which asserts the equality of male and female practitioners. According to the case record, the monk Chieh-hsien is sent by his teacher, Lin-chi, to study with a female master, Mo-shan. On their first meeting, the nun asks the seeker where he comes from, a typical encounter-dialogue query about the student's background designed to test whether it can elicit a spiritual, and not merely factual, response convincingly demonstrating a student's identity. He gives an answer which literally means the "mouth-of-the-road" village, and Mo-shan retorts, "Then why didn't you close [your mouth] when you came here?"

On being outsmarted by the philosophical pun of the woman cleric, another example of an elderly, seemingly unsophisticated woman with great wisdom, reminiscent of similar kōan episodes involving Te-shan and Chao-chou,[60] the monk prostrates and becomes her disciple. Later, he asks, "What is the summit of the mountain?" (the literal meaning of the name Mo-shan), and she replies, "The summit of the mountain cannot be seen." "Then who is the person in the mountain?" he continues, demanding to know her essential spiritual identity. "I am neither male nor female form," she responds, recalling a debate found in the *Vimalakirti Sutra* and the *Lotus Sutra* about whether enlightenment must be realized in a male body (requiring a reincarnation for females) or can be considered to transcend gender differences. "Then why not transfigure into some other form?" he asks, and she concludes the dialogue with an ironic reference to supernaturalism. "Since I am not a fox spirit, I cannot transfigure." Once again, the monk bows, decides to serve as supervisor of Mo-shan's temple garden for three years, and proclaims her teaching to be the equal of Lin-chi's.

The interesting aspect of this passage is that it acknowledges the reality of a fox metamorphosis precisely through denying its relevance for the Zen doctrine of the nonduality of male and female, human and animal, natural and supernatural realms. It creates the possibility, while also implicitly dismissing the need, for the multitiered, multidirectional Buddhist–folk religious syncretism, which coexists with its own level of ironic, skeptical discourse.[61] While irony and ambiguity about offering criticism or praise, or some combination, infuses Zen rhetoric, which helps to reinforce the TZN perspective, it is clear that in the realm of practice, amalgamations with supernaturalism, which integrate indigenous gods into the mainstream ritual structure, are commonplace and widespread. In support of syncretism, there develops a theology of deference toward—or empowerment and elevation of—native animistic spirits, which are not only accepted but also fully absorbed and promoted.

This level of discourse, which supports and sustains supernaturalism, is crucial for the process of eclipsing Buddha through the absorption of folk religions. The process of completing and fulfilling the dynamic process can be analyzed in four stages, as reflected in the panels of Figure 3.11. The starting point of the process, as illustrated in panel 1, is the "twofold nature" of indigenous spirits. The Japanese refused to separate their older Shinto gods from the new Buddhist religion, and still fearing the power of kami and local spirits, they did not want to upset or abandon them but rather tried to tame and rehabilitate them.

Figure 3.12 outlines how the twofold quality of the fox makes it at once a mischievous trickster (Kitsune) that causes conflict and turmoil and a benevolent god (Inari) that offers benefits and freedom. In the context of Buddhist–folk religion amalgamations, the bivalency is never fully cast off or abandoned; instead, the creative tension is used as the basis of inspirational morality tales as well as temple festivals and rites.

Like the relation between Kitsune as negative and malevolent and Inari as the positive and benevolent side of the fox image, the Tengu is twofold in

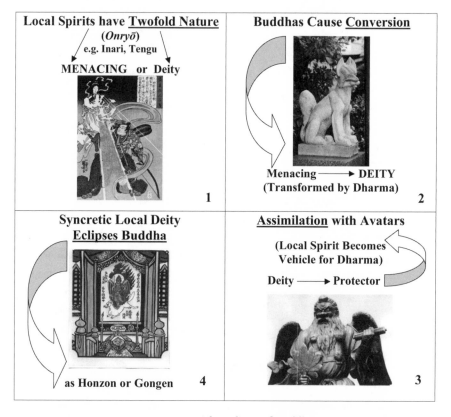

FIGURE 3.11. The eclipse of Buddha.

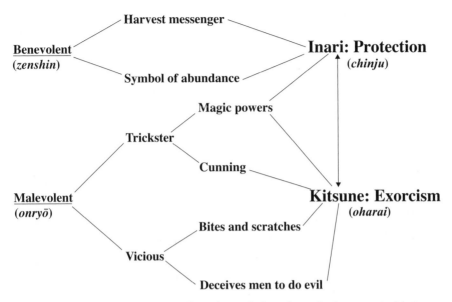

FIGURE 3.12. The two-sidedness of the shape-shifting fox and other marginal beings.

nature. It is associated with or can be considered a kind of outcast and is part of the broader category of nonhuman beings (*hinin*), which includes gods and demons which can be menacing and conflictive (*onryō*). As such, the Tengu, assumed to exist on the outskirts of mainstream society or to be confined to the river banks and other marginal areas that are part of the geography of liminality and exclusion, are defiled (*kegare*) and in need of purification or exorcism (*oharai* or *tsuina*). But categories of marginal beings are twofold in nature. Status on the fringes can also mean or evoke the transcending of relations (*muen*), which covers the category of an ascetic priest or recluse who has the spiritual power to perform exorcisms. This power is accentuated by its association with impurity, in that its strength has been tested and proven.

Part 2 of the process depicted in Figure 3.11 is the exorcism and "conversion" of the *onryō* spirits. Charismatic Zen monks turn Shinto or native gods into—or even make them superior to—buddhas. Sacred images are seen as having a demonic, malevolent potential, which, when improperly unleashed, requires an exorcism that transforms the power into a Buddhist framework. This is done through ritual that is either homeopathic (using one image of the fox to defeat another fox image) or nonhomeopathic (using symbols antithetical to indigenous fox worship, such as traditional Buddhist divinities or chants). Thus, the empowerment and elevation of the indigenous gods are not only accompanied, but are actually enabled by a legacy of criticism and purgation as a crucial step in the process. By treating menacing spirits like people who have moral intentions and a longing to change their ways, Zen Buddhism provides a persuasive narrative of how the suffering spirits are liberated by the power of the dharma.

The tradition, however, contains no clear, systematic explanation of the purpose of exorcism, which is disclosed through legends and rites rather than written discourse. One way to interpret this process is to highlight the verb *bakasu* (also pronounced *ke* or *ka*), which can mean "seduce or bewitch" but also can imply any change or metamorphosis, including the compassionate manifestation of a buddha or bodhisattva (*keshin*). This term functions as a neutral category encompassing possessions which are invited, as in the case of oracles (*kamigakari*) sought by shamans, diviners, and healers through dreams and visions, and those which are uninvited, as when someone's spirit is invaded by a demonic force (*tsukimono*) that requires purification. The category of *bakasu* includes top-down and bottom-up, as well as beneficial/protective and demonic/intrusive theological perspectives. It helps to explain the twofold, bivalent function of *bakemono* such as the serpent, which has been characterized as the "snake of salvation" (manifested as a deity who offers Buddhist redemption) interacting at every turn with the "salvation of the snake" (which appears as a demon in need of being redeemed by a Buddhist saint or divinity).[62]

Part 3 of the process of eclipsing the Buddha, as shown in Figure 3.11, covers the embracing and "assimilation" of the transformed mischievous spirits. Despite having a menacing nature, local gods were more familiar and accessible than were the buddhas and were sought out as protectors who eventually gained the benefit of representing Buddhism and its official pantheon of gods once the purgation and purification were completed. The paradigm of exorcism enabled the spirits to receive and to be transformed by, and then to serve as disseminators of, the merits of the precepts.

In panel 4, the completion of the "eclipse" of the Buddha, we find that the former native gods have become such powerful images in Buddhism that they surpass the prominence of the Buddha and buddhas, as well as the contemporaneous temple abbot. Their innate spiritual powers, now shorn of mischief and used for compassionate, beneficent purposes, make them a compelling force that is equal or even superior to the foreign elements. This leaves the imported religious image somewhat distant and remote, while indigenous spiritual beings remain an important part of everyday Japanese mythology, receiving the participants at the temple gate and helping to guide them through their visit.

Nevertheless, there remains a hierarchy of forces based on the extent and magnitude of power. These range from the *chinju*, or tutelary god, who oversees a particular location, and the *garanjin*, or monastery god, whose power can be transported to a branch site, to the *gohōjin*, or protector of dharma, who has a more widespread appeal. The progression of spiritual power advances to the level of *gongen*, or avatars, who have universal power and can manifest at any time and place, and finally to the *honzon*, or main icon, which is considered to rule supreme as the source. As has been shown, whereas in the case of China, the local gods are generally subsidiary to the Buddha, in some prominent instances of Japanese Zen, the *honzon* is selected from among the native gods, so that the tables are fully turned in that buddhas are seen as their manifestations or emissaries.

Zen: Bending or Breaking?

Zen discourse ranges from rejection to veneration with exorcistic trends never disappearing, and the haughty disdain for supernaturalism in some records coexists with full-scale syncretism that includes purification rites. This range in the levels of discourse of Japanese amalgamations offers many striking contrasts with the nonassimilative, intolerant interactions between Christianity and medieval European paganism. Like Buddhism, Christianity in its spread during medieval times encountered a variety of healers, diviners, soothsayers, and prophets whose teachings were based on visions, spells, remedies, and magic that derived from a premodern animistic belief in the power of nature spirits, including trees, animals, waters, crossroads, etc.

Therefore, the reversals of theological hierarchy coupled with a legacy of exorcism in Buddhist–folk religious amalgamations suggest that syncretism in Zen is considerably more complex than the usual treatment of the notion of *honji suijaku* as a two-tiered, trickle-down, assimilative model. One of the limitations in the two-tiered view is the assumption that popular religion is a lesser version of the elite intellectual tradition. According to Whalen Lai, the roots of this assumption are based on developments in Western intellectual history:

> There is a tendency to regard philosophy as elite reflection while
> relegating magic to the base level of folk superstitions, conveniently
> dividing thereby the intellectual few from the vulgar many. How-
> ever, this two-tiered model of society first employed by David Hume
> in his essay *Natural History of Religion* and followed by many mod-
> ern scholars of religion, more often distorts reality than clarifies it. It

is not uncommon that we find both aspects together in one text, revered by social elites and common folk alike.[63]

Lai's critique of Humean thought needs to be balanced by the fact that the two-tired model preceded Hume with early medieval Christian refutations of "vulgar" or "rustic" (i.e., pagan) religiosity.

More significantly, the two-tiered view is not merely a Western invention imposed on China and Japan, as it has deep roots in East Asian thought, for example, in Hsün-tzu's critique of the supernaturalism embraced by the common folk: "Hence the gentleman regards ceremonies as ornaments [*bunsoku* in Japanese], but the common people regard them as supernatural [*jinsoku*]. He who considers them ornaments is fortunate; he who considers them supernatural is unfortunate."[64] Buddhism similarly distinguishes between the pursuit of the true dharma (*shōbō*) and superstition (*meishin*), and between the legitimate use of supernormal powers and miscellaneous, irregular, wild fox practices (*zatsu shinkō*), as seen in the passage from *Tsung-jung lu* case 10 cited above and related texts.

A prime example is the cult of the dog saint, or the "holy greyhound," St. Guinefort, which was popular in country chapels throughout medieval France. According to legend, St. Guinefort was martyred while saving a child from being eaten by a snake. The official church policy as expressed by Stephen of Bourbon, who learned of the existence of the cult while taking confession from women, was to dismiss and destroy it as the work of the devil:

> Offensive to god [*sic*] are those [superstitions] which honour demons
> or other creatures as if they were divine; it is what idolatry does, and
> it is what the wretched women who cast lots do, who seek salvation
> by worshipping elder trees or making offerings to them; scorning
> churches and holy relics, they take their children to these elder trees,
> or to anthills, or other things in order that a cure may be effected.[65]

From the standpoint of the church, "With superstition, then, God, is the victim and the devil the beneficiary ... its only purpose being to seduce [*seductio*] and to mislead [*ludificatio*]."[66] Yet the situation is more complex than this, because while the dog cult and other examples of paganism were attacked as superstition and eliminated through exorcism on one level, some of the elements of folk religiosity, including sacred symbols and sites, were at the same time preserved through conversion into Christian rites.

Therefore, "pre-Christian magical practices did not vanish. However, they existed now in an entirely new mental context. Their practitioners and participants had to become aware of the limits of magic and had to develop a critical attitude towards it."[67] To some extent, then, both Christianity and Buddhism have refuted and exorcised yet preserved and converted indigenous spirits. A main difference is that, whereas Christianity one-sidedly rejected the power of the native gods and did not allow them to stand as such, the strategy of Japanese Buddhism was to transform and elevate even the most demonic of spirits. Once converted, they became protectors of the dharma: "Thus evil and pollution are not only defeated by ritual, but are 'saved' in a Buddhist sense...[which] involves the conversion of pollution, not merely its defeat or neutralization."[68]

Joined by some sympathizers among HCC analysts, TZN argues, whether or not lay followers are conscious of this, that at the root of seeking worldly benefits there lies an awareness of the realm of emptiness or the ultimate truth of nonsubstantiality that purifies and justifies all expressions in the realm of conventional truth. That is, the doxa, or doctrine, of nonduality makes sense of any praxis, or practice, that operates in the realm of dualism. According to Saijōji temple literature, for example, "Whether performing Zen meditation or praying to the gods and buddhas for help, one is 'throwing away' one's self, affirming one's faith, and achieving rewards for behaving well."[69] The conceptual divide is not a problem at Daiyūzan, which makes a deliberate attempt to synthesize the realms of supernatural belief in the power of the Tengu and the antisupernaturalism of the Eiheiji-based monks who perform the rites.

While a "soft" HCC outlook acknowledges and admires syncretism in accord with TZN, a "hard" HCC approach skeptically raises the question of whether and to what extent folk amalgamations are an expression of skillful means or a matter of duplicity and corruption. As suggested by Heinrich Dumoulin, the pursuit of worldly benefits could be considered an ignoble use of Buddhist discipline, long rejected in early texts such as the *Digha Nikāya*, as that pursuit is based on the desire for personal gain rather than for genuine self-overcoming and self-mastery. HCC critics ask whether approaches sympathetic to folk magic expressed by TZN advocates are successful in dealing with the dilemma of reconciling transcendence and practicality, or in resolving "the serious tensions that keep orthodoxy and superstition apart."[70] Or, do the explanations and rationalizations end in affirming the separation and only declaring "an uneasy truce to prevent open conflict"?[71]

The eclipse of the Buddha by local gods, while seemingly inevitable for cultural reasons and apparently advocated for evangelical purposes, can have a problematic aspect. When left unacknowledged or not accepted for what it is by the elite level, it functions beneath the surface of official institutional policy. As indicated, many participants in Toyokawa Inari festivals for travel safety or Kannon bathing rites to gain healing at Togenuki Jizō are not even aware that these are Zen temples. Can monks, even if they are free of desire, cultivate rituals designed to cater to laypersons' attachments and longings and still remain immune to corruption? Or, should questions raised about compromise in the name of a standard of incorruptible purity be set aside as the unrealistic expectations of an idealism that is not appropriate to observing Buddhism on the ground?

For HCC, contradictions infecting the matter of rites open the door to a much more forceful critique asserted by both Japanese and Western scholars on issues regarding Zen rights in relation to modern society.[72] The next chapter considers the TZN view that Zen is optimally suited to address contemporary social ills in the postmodern era in light of the HCC criticism of Zen's moral deficiencies.

4

Zen Rights

A Series of (Un)fortunate Social Events

Whom Do We Meet at Zen Temples?

Whom should we expect to meet at a Zen temple? Like-minded monks ranked by seniority and function who practice meditation with diligence and intensity in a group spirit and hold regular public meetings and occasional private sessions with the abbot, in addition to performing a daily routine of cooperative tasks and chores? Would not Zen monks known for their strict discipline and moral fortitude, as well as an irreverent, iconoclastic, tables-turning attitude, be assumed to have a strong commitment to social equity and a willingness to challenge authority when they find injustices being perpetrated? What would be the implications if it were shown that much of the organization of temple life from the time of the origins of the sect was greatly affected by revenue derived from the patronage of government officials and the stewardship of land holdings that included servants and/or slaves? What would be the impact of learning that the Zen sect and other Buddhist schools in modern Japan have continued to endorse the segregation of the outcast community (*burakumin*) and women[1] and have participated in pre–World War II era militarist/nationalist ideology? The pervasiveness of practices infected with social discrimination (*sabetsu mondai*), particularly in the funerary rite of bestowing posthumous initiation names (*kaimyō*), in addition to widespread participation in the rhetoric of "Imperial Way Zen" (*kōdō Zen*), seems to indicate a fundamental breach with the basic Zen philosophical notion of nonduality, which advocates the equality and inseparability of all beings, transcending conventional divisions.

A classic expression about nondual philosophy is sixth patriarch Hui-neng's query recorded in the *Platform Sutra* and contained in case 23 of the *Wu-men kuan* collection: Chased into the mountains by a rival for monastery leadership, Hui-neng throws down the robe awarded to him by the fifth patriarch, which proves immovable. He then asks rhetorically, "Thinking beyond good and evil, just at this moment, what is your original face before your father and mother were born?" This emphasis on realizing the "original face" suggests that if one purifies one's own mind and beholds one's own true nature in a spontaneous experience of realization, there remains no lingering duality of good and evil. The main traditional Zen narrative (TZN) argument is that it is precisely because in a liberating experiential moment Zen overturns and abandons the polarity of good versus evil, and therefore an attachment to one-sided judgments, that the practitioner is able to function constructively and decisively by making appropriate distinctions within the realm of good versus evil. The paradox prevails such that a transcendence of ethics creates the possibility for dynamic, immanent applications within the ethical realm.

But for historical and cultural criticism (HCC), the claim of ethical paradox is a red herring that distracts from awareness that Zen's failure to resist and renounce intolerance and militarism is ironically derivative of traditional principles when misunderstood or when applied, sometimes purposefully, in an inappropriate way. For example, the modern Sōtō master Harada Sōgaku, who in the years leading up to World War II referred to the Japanese as "a chosen people whose mission is to control the world," also said of the "unity of Zen and war," "[If ordered to] march: tramp, tramp, or shoot: bang, bang. This is the manifestation of the highest Wisdom [of enlightenment]."[2] Here, Harada appears to distort deliberately for nationalist purposes the meaning of Zen sayings such as, "When hungry I eat, and when tired I sleep," or "When cold, be thoroughly cold; when hot, be hot through and through," thus turning notions of mental clarity and equilibrium into vehicles for enforcing an oppressive social order. The Tokugawa era sword master Takuan Sōhō perhaps paved the way for such a misappropriation when he stated in *The Unfettered Mind*:

> The accomplished man uses his sword.... When it is necessary to
> kill, he kills. When it is necessary to give life, he gives life. When
> killing, he kills in complete concentration; when giving life, he gives

in complete concentration. Without looking at right and wrong, he
is able to see right and wrong; without attempting to discriminate, he
is able to discriminate well.[3]

These associations, which link premodern works with ethically deficient
standpoints in the modern world, may cause us to cast aside commonplace
and somewhat naive assumptions about Zen's promoting harmony (wagō)
and cooperation, and instead see it as a primary reason rather than as a
remedy for many of the ills of Japanese society.

Of the three main topics discussed in this book, including language
(writes) and ceremonies (rites), the issue of social ethics (rights—or, for HCC,
"wrongs") is by far the area of the greatest contention and harshest mutual
criticism between the TZN and HCC standpoints. On the matter of writes,
although some critics associated with the dissolution thesis find Zen discourse nonsensical, the analysis by the HCC realization thesis of the re-
markably rich variety of literary styles produced by classical masters tends to
enhance TZN claims for Zen's distinctive creativity. In terms of rites, the
HCC focus on the role of prayer temples seems to expose a commercialization
of religion. This dimension is nevertheless somewhat complementary to the
TZN view that ritualism functions on a lesser but necessary level of the
Mahayana Buddhist notion of two levels of truth, the ultimate/absolute and
the conventional/mundane.

In contrast to discussions of the matters of writes and rites, which lead to
a sense of compatibility or, at least, lack of conflict, between TZN and HCC,
the issue of Zen rights (and wrongs) creates a fundamental discord that may
leave observers with a sense of disconnect or dysfunction in coming to terms
with the real Zen Buddhism. TZN asserts that Zen's approach is meritorious
and invaluable. Kyoto school thought influenced by Western phenomenology
and existentialism along with other kinds of ideological affinities with philosophy and ecological consciousness demonstrate that Zen is ideally suited to
the complex modern era. Modernity—or, according to some, postmodernity—
has come to reflect the relativist, nonlogocentric, and conservationist outlook
that Zen monastic life fosters. HCC, on the other hand, condemns Zen for
contributing to a long list of social ills, and in particular bashes the Kyoto
school for its involvement in imperialism. Therefore, the strong suit cited by
TZN as desperately needed for the recovery of a world plagued by the threat of
environmental disaster and nuclear holocaust is precisely the weakest link,
according to HCC, which lies at the root of many of today's social problems.

Since the mid-1990s, several prominent HCC-oriented books have dissected the problematic state of modern Zen Buddhism with regard to social

ethics. For example, *Rude Awakenings*, a collection of essays originally presented at a conference held in the early 1990s, is dedicated to "questioning"
(to cite the book's section headings) the sociopolitical leanings of Zen and its
two major modern proponents, D. T. Suzuki and Nishida Kitarō, associated
with the Kyoto school.[4] Here and elsewhere, Zen thinkers are criticized for
presenting a nativist orientation that helped to feed the Japanese war machine, much as European intellectuals, including Martin Heidegger, Paul de
Man, and Mircea Eliade, have been questioned and challenged for their
shortcomings in apparently succumbing to and supporting Nazi hegemony.
For example, Robert Sharf rebuffs the "polemical intent behind the modern
Zen nativists' rendering of East Asian Buddhist history," according to which
"Zen survived in its 'pure' form only in Japan." Of claims made by advocates
like Suzuki and Herrigel that only Asians can really understand Zen, Sharf
wonders, "Why, we might ask, would anyone in the West take this view of Zen
seriously?"[5] Furthermore, he suggests that such reverse Orientalism has been
a ploy to avoid the need for confronting the issue of social reform: "The
purveyors of Zen insight would like to expurgate this gap between the world
of human affairs and the world of Zen through rhetorical fiat" (that is, with
words only, but not through taking action).[6]

For HCC, the marrow of Zen is its duplicity and complicity in unseemly
social agendas, while the skin is its commitment to monastic discipline, which
only helps to cloak a lack of genuine concern for society. To put the matter in a
broader context, the relation of mysticism to morality is often controversial
because of an implicit gap between the ideal realm of spiritual attainment
(enlightenment) and the real or practical realm of ethical decision making. This
gap frequently leads to charges of escapism, amorality, or antinomianism—all
forms of a basic moral blindness—which haunt many spiritual traditions, including Zen. The blindness ranges from a passivity in overlooking or ignoring
social problems and moral dilemmas to a more aggressive side, which actively
participates in or causes examples of intolerance and militarist excess, including
atrocities committed during the World War II era in Nanking or with regard to
the plight of the "comfort women" (Asians forced into prostitution by the
Japanese military).

William James argued at the beginning of the twentieth century that there
is an unavoidable link between mystical thought and moral (or amoral or immoral) practices. James asserted that mysticism should not be considered an
abstract realm of pure consciousness unaffected by the vicissitudes of daily life
but part of everyday, lived experience, encompassing ethical implications and
moral accountability. Mystical traditions, whether they like it or not, are not able
to remain indifferent and ostrich-like; rather, they must take responsibility,

for better or worse, for the impact that their teachings and practices exert on the social world. From this standpoint, Zen's theoretical emphasis on the role of actualizing enlightenment in the concrete world, which is expressed in sayings such as "everyday mind is the Buddha," may ring hollow in light of the actual historical record. Zen remains ensconced in a cloak of purity without a full consideration of the moral implications of contemplation for the realm of impurity. Because Zen overturns good versus evil on the ideal level, it loses sight of the significance of problems involving good versus evil in the real realm, which are not adequately addressed due to a shirking of responsibility and lack of remorse for transgressions.

At the other end of the spectrum, defender of the faith Kirita Kiyohide replies to charges of exclusivism and nativism attributed to the philosophy of Suzuki, who he feels strove for a genuinely universal interpretation of Zen, by arguing, "Nothing could be further from the truth in Suzuki's case, and only a complete disregard for context can yield such conclusions."[7] In regard to their role during the prewar period, TZN advocates portray Zen intellectuals as heroic figures tragically condemned to a miserable political situation that they tried valiantly to resist without offending authorities in a counterproductive way. Any shortcomings that might be pointed out are probably based on misunderstandings after the fact and turf battles extraneous to actual circumstances. In noting the vagaries of political discourse surrounding religious traditions, which get placed in a lose-lose, "darned if you do, darned if you don't" situation, Nishitani Keiji remarked that the Kyoto school has been criticized by both sides of the political fence. "During the war," Nishitani said, "we were struck on the cheek from the right; after the war we were struck on the cheek from the left."[8]

When acknowledged, problems regarding Zen rights are seen by TZN as skin, flesh, and bones relative to a record of outstanding accomplishment in addressing the greater needs of humankind and the potential that Zen has at its core, or marrow, to achieve much more in the social realm than other less philosophically consistent spiritual outlooks or less disciplined forms of religious training. To put it crudely, according to TZN, Zen and only Zen, which functions seamlessly in both the ideal and real realms, is capable of embarking on a worldwide mission to save modern civilization from its own undoing. But according to HCC, the Zen approach, in which there festers an irresolvable gap between realms, has already shown its failure to address some basic matters of inequity within the narrow context of Japanese society and should not be let off the hook.

Does either side benefit from this kind of (non)dialogue?[9] Or does each approach only tend to get ever more hardened—perhaps rightfully so, from their own perspectives—in the conviction that their adversaries are hopelessly misguided and so cannot help but misunderstand and misrepresent their critique? What is the interested or, for that matter, disinterested onlooker to this discussion of the real Zen to make of the lack of constructive interaction? If Zen is two-faced, is it the double visage of Janus or the schizophrenia of Jekyll and Hyde? Is there a way to break through this impasse? In other words, will the real Zen Buddhism please stand up?

Functions of the Samgha Hall

An assessment of the conflict between the TZN and HCC standpoints on the issue of rights requires an understanding of the structure and function of Zen's interior institutional organization and its standing in connection to the outside world of commerce and culture. One of the main claims of distinctiveness suggested by Zen's traditional self-definition compared with other Buddhist schools involves the construction of the Samgha Hall or Monks Hall, which is considered "the most important place in the monastery in the life of a monk."[10] An indication of the significant role of this hall is that after Dōgen returned to Japan in 1227 from China, where he learned the authentic Ch'an style of monastic life, it took him nearly six years until he opened his first temple, Kōshōji, in 1233 in Fukakusa, just outside of Kyoto. The temple featured what was considered the first Japanese Samgha Hall, and this gave Dōgen an advantage over other temples in recruiting monks.[11] A decade later, Enni Ben'en, who also had completed a pilgrimage to China, opened Tōfukuji temple up the road from Kōshōji and enjoyed support from the imperial court. For this and other reasons, Dōgen left the Kyoto area to establish Eiheiji temple in the remote mountains of Echizen province.

In earlier forms of Buddhist monasticism from India to China and Japan, monks were housed in cells built in blocks around the central lecture and worship halls. According to the TZN reading of history, this approach emphasized individuality at the expense of the group spirit, but in Zen, supposedly for the first time in the history of Buddhism, there was a single open hall in the monastery. In a relatively lengthy passage that is part of a very short text, the *Ch'an-men kuei-shih* (CMK) describes the Samgha Hall's functions:

> Regardless of whether their numbers are great or small, or whether they are of high or low social status, those who have joined the community as monks reside together in the Samgha Hall, with seniority based strictly on the number of summers since the time of their ordination. Platforms [for resting] are to be built along the side

of the hall and should include a stand for each monk's robes and other belongings. The proper position is to lie on the right side—the position of the Buddha's final repose [at the time of entering *parinirvana*]—with the headrest set at the edge of the platform and the hands used to support the head. The period of rest should be short even if it comes after a lengthy session of meditation. This is not considered a time for sleeping but for "reclining meditation." It is part of the practice of the four observances [of *gyōjū zaga*, or walking, standing, sitting, and lying down as forms of meditation].

The Samgha Hall is where all monks are required to reside together and meditate in common quarters, with seniority based on the length of stay, as in the Vinaya. Having this home base for all ordained monks—which might have included several hundred or even up to a couple of thousand clerics in the larger monasteries of the Five Mountains system, such as Mt. T'ien-t'ung, visited by both Eisai and Dōgen during their stays in China—enabled Zen to develop its own special pattern of monastic life. In the seven-hall monastic compound, the primary learning and meditation activities took place in the two most essential temple buildings, the Samgha Hall and the Dharma Hall. The Samgha Hall remained the center of Zen life up to the fifteenth century, when its role was overtaken by a variety of factors. These included an increasing emphasis in Japanese monasteries on the role of the Abbot's Quarters (not one of the original seven structures), the proliferation of subtemples especially for prayer rites and related ceremonial functions, and the soldier's torch, as many Zen institutions were burned down or destroyed during periods of ongoing civil warfare and sectarian conflicts.[12]

According to the *Ch'an-yüan ch'ing-kuei* and as indicated in Figure 4.1, the Samgha Hall was a large building divided into an inner and an outer hall surrounded by enclosed corridors that connected it with various nearby ancillary facilities. The outer hall was linked by a passageway to the inner hall, and between them were two light wells. The inner hall was reserved for monks formally enrolled, who were given a spot on the platform just deep enough to allow them to stretch out and sleep for the few hours of rest allowed. On their single mats, monks spent long hours in silent meditation and eating in silence two vegetarian meals, which were completed by midday, as required by the Vinaya.

The monks' primary possessions, their clerical robes, rested on the lip of the platform during meditation and were also used as headrests at night. Their bowls hung above their seats, and other personal effects and training implements were stored in boxes to the rear of the platform area. The outer

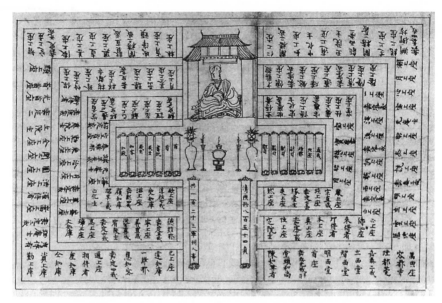

FIGURE 4.1. The ranking and seating arrangement in a traditional Samgha (Monks or Meditation) Hall (sōdō or zendō), after *Shina zensatsu zushiki*. Anonymous thirteenth-century depiction of Tōfukuji temple in Kyoto appears in Helmut Brinker and Hiroshi Kanazawa, *Zen: Masters of Meditation and Writings* (Zurich: Artibus Asiae, 1996), fig. 32, p. 61.

hall was known as the Cloud Hall (undō) as itinerant monks came from all directions "like clouds and vapors" to visit and temporarily train at the important temples. New arrivals were formally registered as guests, and there was also a place for lay visitors to sleep alongside the monks' common quarters. The corridor by the outer hall was used for walking meditation exercises (kinhin).

A part of the hall was considered the chamber of the "holy monk," Manjusri, who represented not a magical form as in other images of the manifestations of the bodhisattvas but an ideal of monkhood to which all trainees could aspire.[13] In addition to meditation and meals, the Samgha Hall was used for other kinds of religious practices designed to focus the mind, for example, as a ceremonial site for the recitation of nien-fo (J. nembutsu), which helped monks to remain mindful of impermanence and the need to strive earnestly for salvation. The Samgha Hall was also the location, according to the *Ch'an-yüan ch'ing-kuei*, for conducting the tea ceremony and for the reading, chanting, or writing of sutras, although it was recognized that these activities, if not mastered and managed carefully, could interfere with an attitude of introspective concentration. Furthermore, monks performed prayers for longevity and the success of the imperial reign, the flourishing of Buddhism and spread of the dharma, and for protection of the monastery community by tutelary deities, in addition to the prosperity of patrons.

Crimes and Punishments

In creating a cohesive and collaborative community, the Samgha Hall represented principles of democracy in terms of the horizontal unity of all monks practicing under a single roof, but at the same time a strict vertical hierarchy in acknowledging and honoring rank and seniority. A democratic outlook is expressed in the injunction for communal labor, mentioned briefly in the CMK, which requires universal, compulsory labor among members of the samgha:

> All members of the community must participate equally in carrying out the practice of communal labor (C. *p'u-ch'ing*, J. *fusei*).[14] Ten tasks for the regulation of the community are assigned to specific officers, each officer taking responsibility for the supervision and fulfillment of the duties assigned to his role. (For example, the monk who supervises vegetables is referred to as the Vegetable Steward.)

This dovetails with several anecdotes from Pai-chang's recorded sayings, especially his saying "A day without work is a day without eating." This injunction was tested when he was elderly and his disciples took away his tools one day to see his reaction, and Pai-chang refused to eat. This anecdote inspired monks to work and to sacrifice personal needs for the good of the group, which is said to have been self-sufficient and autonomous, although there is little historical or economic evidence to suggest what the texts depict, so that the independence of Zen temples based on an agrarian lifestyle is little more than a rhetorical device.

Hierarchy was reflected in that the meditation chair of the abbot, who lived and gave instructions in separate buildings (either the Dharma Hall or Abbot's Quarters), was placed just inside the northern portal of the entrance to the inner hall of the Samgha Hall. He sat facing the holy monk Manjusri, the patron and true spiritual leader of the hall. Senior officers and other assistants and attendees sat to the right of the abbot, and their comings and goings were carefully prescribed in rules texts. Of the ten main officers, the rector, or supervisor, along with the monitor of the Samgha Hall had special responsibility for overseeing and managing the behavior of resident and itinerant monks and of meting out punishments appropriate for wrongdoers or troublemakers.

As a relatively new and growing religious movement in the competitive environment that was T'ang/Sung China and Kamakura Japan, where all Buddhist sects had to deal with Confucian, Taoist, or Shinto rivals as well as government supervision and oversight, the Zen approach to the self-definition and self-regulation of its monastic community presented an image at once thoroughly mainstream and distinctively innovative. According to the CMK, Zen represents a middle way, or third way, between the extremes of the precepts of Hinayana, which emphasize discipline and self-control, and of Mahayana precepts, which emphasize freedom and release from constraints:

> We must seek a middle ground that at once synthesizes the spirit of these approaches and lies beyond them in establishing regulations that are most appropriate to our style [of practice]. In that way [Pai-chang] conceived the idea of instituting the first genuinely indepen-dent monasteries of the Zen sect.

The Zen regulations claim to represent an admixture and transcendence of Hinayana and Mahayana precepts, although in actuality both sets of behav-ioral codes were required in Zen in China and for the most part in Japan as well.[15]

It is important to clarify the way that Zen saw the need for and sought to carve out its middle way position. What the CMK and other texts seem to suggest is that the Hinayana list of 250 precepts as articulated in the *Prati-moksha*, which prescribed specific, detailed codes of conduct, was considered essential for monk making but too narrow and legalistic if followed without some modification or moderating factor. At the same time, the Mahayana list of 48 bodhisattva precepts was overly abstract and idealistic without incor-porating concrete guidelines for carrying out virtuous behavior. What type of compromise did Zen bring about? The Zen middle way approach was not a matter of taking some ideas from one side and some from the other and mixing them together to get a new concoction. Rather, Zen tried to show that it was just as or even stricter than the Hinayana approach, yet not attached to external guidelines as an end in itself, and put just as much or more emphasis on subjective realization as the Mahayana approach without sacrificing the need for behavioral guidelines.

Perfecting the attitude of being stricter than the strictest and more mystical than the mystics required a delicate balancing act, and in the end mysticism won the day. The detailed rules of deportment and etiquette in the *Ch'an-yüan ch'ing-kuei*, which covers nearly every aspect of behavior including the equipment needed by monks and the correct way to pack and carry them, were among the injunctions used in commanding and reprimanding Zen practitioners. According to the text, all forms of inappropriate behavior—congregating, shuffling feet, releasing a curtain noisily, making other kinds of noises, blowing one's nose, spitting, making medicine pills, leaning on railings of shrines, being publicly naked—are forbidden. For example:

> When traveling on the road, [the monk] should not let his arms hang down or swing his body from side to side. He should not have a springy gait, and when resting he should not sit in a squatting position or stand with arms akimbo. His demeanor should not be arrogant or wild, and he should not speak with the use of his hands. When walking, he should step heel first. His gaze should be solemn and respectable, and his eyes should be fixed no more than eight feet ahead of him.[16]

Furthermore, monks are encouraged to exchange words of gratitude with each other and with their guests, donors, or other lay members of the samgha.

To confirm and enforce these guidelines, Zen established a firm, nononsense, zero-tolerance policy that contained harsh punishments for transgressors, including excommunication. According to the CMK:

> Anyone who makes a false claim of membership or is insincere or deceitful in his practice and abuses his office, or anyone who breaks the rules or otherwise stirs up trouble among the dedicated members of the monastic community, will be punished by the rector [C. *wei-na,* J. *ina,* Skt. *karmadana*], who is to remove the imposter's possessions from the Samgha Hall and to expel and excommunicate him from the compound. This severe discipline serves as a warning to the other monks of the humiliation and disgrace that will ensue should a similar offense be committed.

The rector had the authority to punish and expel anyone committing an offense, but while he might have set any punishment process in motion, it was the abbot who had the responsibility to administer corporal punishment to the miscreants with his staff, burn their belongings, and banish them from the temple grounds. According to the CMK, "An offending monk will be flogged with the abbot's staff [C. *chu-chang,* J. *shujō*] and, after finding that his robes, bowl and other belongings have been burned in front of the entire assembly, he will be unceremoniously dispatched through the side gate." Doing this means "that word of the incident will not spread outside the monastic compound in a way that would call into question the integrity of the sect."

No doubt, what was meant by a serious offense harked back to the early Vinaya rules concerning the four *parajikas* (killing, stealing, sexual indiscretion, or misusing supernormal powers gained through meditation). However, the Zen recommendations seem to be much stronger than those in the traditional Vinaya, which allows for various methods of confession, penance, and repentance for those who admit their transgressions and are reembraced by the community. Rather than merely receiving reprimands, serious offenders were shunned in order to preserve the faith of worthy monks, save the reputation of the samgha, avoid litigation, and prevent word of monastic misbehavior from spreading to the community at large. The last three reasons suggest a preoccupation with sidestepping any embarrassment that might invite harsh criticism from Confucian and other rivals. As Zen sought to succeed and thrive in a competitive religious setting and a cultural environment largely influenced by Confucian mores, which emphasize ethics grounded in filial piety, it was necessary for monastic leaders to be sure that any wrongdoers or troublemakers did not create a bad impression in the general society.

While much of the Zen approach to monastic rules may sound legalistic and mechanical in providing instructions, restrictions, and punitive measures, key passages make it clear that the attitude or state of mind that underlies behavior is also of utmost importance. The *Ch'an-yüan ch'ing-kuei* states, for instance, "When the rector recites a prayer or strikes with the mallet, he must be careful to do so clearly so as to generate good thoughts in the minds."[17] In his famed instructions for the chief monastery cook, the *Tenzokyōkun*, Dōgen asserts that the most important thing in preparing a meal is not the ingredients or cooking skill. Rather, it is the outlook of the monk who pours his heart and soul, so to speak, into the process. "In the art of cooking," he writes, "the essential consideration is to have a deeply sincere and respectful mind regardless of the fineness or coarseness of the materials. Isn't it so, that by offering to the Tathagata a bowl of water with which she had washed rice, a woman obtained inconceivable merit throughout her various lives?"[18] That is, the right attitude accompanying the proper ritual could eradicate impurity and redeem personal karma. According to the CMK, not only cooking but also eating is to be considered essentially a state of mind: "The monks eat two simple vegetarian meals daily according to the routine schedule. These are prepared and served with utmost frugality to demonstrate that the activity of eating is an opportunity for realization of the Dharma."

A key example of the internalization process to foster subjectivity and avoid a mechanical approach to ritualism involves the Zen view of periods of confession and repentance that are followed by all members of the samgha based on Vinaya codes. The traditional emphasis on monks repenting for transgressions has two main components. The first of these is the fortnightly confession, or *Uposatha* (Buddhist Sabbath), when the entire assembly of fully ordained monks comes together before the abbot to recite the 250 *Pratimoksha* vows one at a time, and those who have violated any of the precepts are required to confess while those who have not remain silent.[19] The other component is the three-month rainy season retreat extending from the full moon of the fourth month to the full moon of the seventh month. At this time, the precepts are recited for the opening (*pravarana*, lit. invitation) and closing (*kathina*, lit. distribution of new robes) ceremonies, and ample time is provided to reflect on their applicability for behavior and the extent to which they have been followed.

Both of these confessionals have generally been followed in temple life, although the timing of the *pravarana* cycle may vary based on cultural modifications from the schedule delineated in the early canon. Yet, Zen also rejected and to some extent abandoned a Hinayana-like emphasis on routine, mechanical repentance ceremonies in favor of a new emphasis on the doctrine of "formless repentance." This doctrine suggests that a realization of the fundamental emptiness (*sunyata*) of all phenomena, or the realm of the formless, makes one aware that the realm of form is basically irrelevant, so that it is not necessary to confess particular, or form-based, transgressions. The classic justification for this is the *Platform Sutra*'s focus on the nonproduction of evil:

> What is repentance [made up of two kanji, C. *ch'an*, J. *zan*, and C. *hui*, J. *ge*]? Confession (*ch'an/zan*) is the non-production [of evil] throughout your life. Regret (*hui/ge*) is to realize your previous evil karma and never let this slip from your mind. There is no reason to make a verbal confession before buddhas. In my teachings, forever to engage in non-production is the meaning of repentance.[20]

Furthermore, there tends to be a general lack of evidence in traditional monastic codes or recorded sayings for Zen's involvement in repentance. Yet there is also no attempt in Sung Zen texts to offer a sustained refutation or explanation for a deemphasis of a practice that was so prevalent in many other kinds of medieval East Asian Buddhism, particularly Ch'an's main rival as a school based on meditative discipline, the T'ien-t'ai school, in a way that would be comparable to Luther's criticism of the sacrament of penitence.

The justification for the deemphasis on repentance seems to be based on Zen's self-power ideology and skeptical view of the efficacy of formal, external ritualism without inner realization, as in the sayings "kill the Buddha" and "burn the sutras." Further in this regard, despite an apparent emphasis on uniformity and ceremonialism on many levels of religious practice, several of the most prominent masters of the medieval period were known for a rugged individuality and eccentricity in their commitment to a life of poverty and reclusion, as well as the creative expression of self-awareness. This is shown through dramatic examples of irreverent, iconoclastic behavior that deliberately rebuffs and flaunts conventions.

For TZN, the radical irreverence of figures like Ikkyū and others, which is based on subjectivity and includes a deemphasis on repentance rather than following objective, external standards for behavior, demonstrates the genuine ingenuity and innovation of Zen at once transcending and contributing to social ethics. The question posed by HCC is whether such antistructural behavioral may at times go too far in the direction of antinomianism and lose an appropriate sense of the balance of external reinforcements and subjective realization that ends up ignoring problems in the everyday world and thereby reinforcing and embracing rather than reforming the status quo. HCC asks, for example, whether too much power and leeway rests in the abbot as a figure of authority without any supervisor or management body to which he must have to answer. Does the undercutting of ritual confessionals by the notion of formless repentance render these rites insufficient vehicles for enacting a sense of genuine repentance and the reversal of unfortunate deeds, resulting in a failure to enact an ongoing commitment to ethical concerns and social reform?

Zen Rights

For TZN advocates, the strength of the Zen approach, which constructively links mystical realization and moral applications, derives from several historical and ideological factors inspired by, yet not limited to, activities performed in the Samgha Hall and related temple chambers. Historically, Zen was a tradition of strict discipline and training for monks, who despite an aloofness born of transcendence from worldly attachments, were involved in developing a powerful legacy of commitment to social advocacy. This approach, which began in medieval Japan, is considered to be applicable to overcoming many of the deficiencies of the modern world, which is characterized by moral relativism and threatened by the deleterious effects of science and environmental concerns.

Historical and Ideological Background

TZN acknowledges that during its peak institutional period, Zen had close affiliations and received significant support from the elite classes in both China (among scholar/officials and literati during the Sung dynasty) and Japan (among samurai and those affiliated with the newly dominant Hōjō and Ashikaga warrior clans during the Kamakura and Muromachi eras, respectively). Even Dōgen, known for his integrity and commitment to reclusion, could not have established Eiheiji temple without the benefaction of his chief patron, the one-eyed samurai retainer Hatano Yoshishige. The positive side of maintaining these connections is that Zen learned a mastery of organizational structure and techniques for community relations and outreach. Furthermore, the historical development of Zen in medieval Japanese society was somewhat different than in China, as Zen monks also formed strong affinities with outcasts and the downtrodden. As Matsuo Kenji points out, the founders of Japanese Zen during the thirteenth century, Eisai and Dōgen, traveled to China to learn the monastic system and literary tradition, but in returning and creating a new religious school in their native country they also became a central part of the trends of the so-called new Kamakura era Buddhism (*shin Kamakura Bukkyō*).

This period saw a dramatic shift from official monks (*kansō*), who first were initiated into the Tendai and Shingon sects that dominated the Heian era, to the patriarchs of new Buddhism, a group of reclusive and fiercely independent monks (*tonseisō*) which also included Hōnen, Shinran, Nichiren, Myōe, and Eizon. According to Matsuo's theory, a key element that entered into the Zen approach and allowed it along with some of the other new movements to succeed where the Heian schools were failing was the reclusive "monks' view of themselves as free to associate with ritually impure people." "In particular," he writes, "they could pray for the salvation of women and lepers, conduct funerals, and collect contributions, all of which had previously been regarded as involving impurities."[21]

While Eisai's Rinzai sect became known as "shogun Zen" because it gained support from the militaristic Hōjō government that established power in the thirteenth century, Dōgen's Sōtō Zen sect, sometimes referred to as "farmer's Zen," used a broad range of evangelical and public works projects to spread into the countryside, especially in the northern provinces. These included mass precept ceremonies and summer retreats for laypersons, as well as large-scale bridge building and irrigation installations. Through these methods, Sōtō Zen was especially successful in trying "to reach the social classes that had been unable to participate in the formal Buddhist funerals and memorial services of the older sects—Shingon, Tendai, and the Gozan Zen schools."[22] Therefore, in many ways, Zen in medieval Japan exercised a commitment to social reform through the overcoming of discrimination and injustice and by increasing the base of those who benefited from the spread of the dharma.

In terms of ideology, TZN responds to criticism regarding amoral tendencies infecting Zen by pointing out that Zen philosophy epitomizes the nondogmatic, open-ended outlook of the Buddhist middle way, which does not speculate on unedifying metaphysical questions but addresses pragmatically the concrete matter of how to conquer suffering in all of its manifestations. Furthermore, Zen prides itself on maintaining an unwavering focus on the Mahayana Buddhist goal of universal salvation. Flexible and adaptable to any particular situational setting without ever becoming doctrinaire or stiffened in its approach, Zen thought transcends all forms of attachment, including the pernicious clinging to nonattachment. Zen represents a therapeutic outlook that offers provisional teachings to keep a baby from crying, according to Ma-tsu, or to cure an illness, according to Lin-chi. In a number of examples of kōan literature, Zen's overcoming of attachment is symbolized by the saying that, whether answers are right or wrong, they deserve "thirty blows of the stick," or by the disingenuous blasphemy of insulting and castigating the patriarchs, including Sakyamuni and Bodhidharma. Casting aside any subtle residue of clinging is also the meaning of *Wu-men-kuan* case 38, "Wu-tsu's Buffalo Passes through the Window," in which the head, horns, and four legs of the buffalo pass through, so why, it is asked, does not its tail? This shows that the smallest element can represent a major obstacle if not overcome.

According to TZN, the Zen approach, while ensuring purity and integrity in the monastic setting through rigorous discipline and adherence to rules, and despite an emphasis on mountain asceticism and a lifestyle of reclusion, does not represent a withdrawal into the cocoon of mystical contemplation cut off and detached from the need to address problems in the concrete world. Rather, Zen transmutes the lofty indifference of the contemplative life into an eminently active approach that is open-ended, fair-minded, and well suited to dealing creatively with the ethical and environmental predicaments of modern society. This view is summed up by *Not Turning Away*, the title of a recent sourcebook highlighting a network of Buddhist practitioners who advocate nonviolent, spiritually based activism in the social, political, and economic affairs of the day.[23]

Reinforcing this point, Kyoto school thinker Masao Abe, who took part in a dialogue on comparative ethics with Christian scholar/mystic Paul Knitter, thinks through his partner's summary of religious differences in characterizing the Buddhist view as "You cannot change the world unless you sit," versus the Christian view, "You cannot sit unless you change the world." Knitter, though sympathetic to Zen in many ways, uses the distinction he draws out regarding the respective religious outlooks to highlight the superiority of Christian activism, which refuses to sit by idly while social problems fester and relaxes only after community reforms have been accomplished, over Buddhist passivity. According to this analysis, Buddhism is content to focus on individual enlightenment or an attainment of an ideal spiritual realm through sitting meditation at the expense of ignoring concrete problems in the everyday world.

Abe inverts the assessment, however, by pointing out that Knitter conflates two different meanings of the word "sit," one that suggests passivity and irresponsibility and the other that suggests sustained effort through meditation. Knitter creates an additional misimpression in using "before" in a literal, chronological rather than an ontological sense. Knitter mistakenly indicates that Buddhists sit quietly in the midst of turmoil prior to reacting to the tide of events, instead of seeing that they engage in an ongoing investigation and awakening of true selfhood while, and as the metaphysical ground of, being eminently active beyond the conventional duality of action-reaction. Abe argues, "Zen sitting in meditation does not exclude activities but provides the basis for our vital activities.... this activity includes the investigation and formation of the world and history."[24] Thus, the sitting occurs "before" in the distinctive sense of transpiring as an earlier mental process that accompanies and occurs simultaneously with bringing about change in the world.

Kyoto School Teachings

The Kyoto school has been a primary vehicle for expressing the relevance of traditional Zen doctrines for the contemporary world (and also the main object of criticism for HCC). In addition to interfaith dialogues with Knitter and a host of other Western religious thinkers,[25] Kyoto school approaches include the establishment of the F.A.S. Society for promoting world peace by charismatic Zen priest Hisamatsu Shin'ichi and Nishitani Keiji's critical examination of modern science from a Zen perspective, especially in *Religion and Nothingness* (Japanese title: *Shūkyō to wa nanika* [What Is Religion?]).[26] There are also a number of analyses and comparisons of Zen ethical thought with Western philosophical pragmatism, postmodernism, environmentalism, and deep ecology.

The F.A.S. Society, established in 1958 and based at the Rinzai sect's Myōshinji temple in Kyoto, has been an instrument for promoting the mutual understanding of worldwide religious and philosophical viewpoints and an advocate for harmony. The acronym stands for three main factors:[27] F represents an experience of awakening to the *formless* self, or the investigation of true selfhood infused with all-encompassing compassion; A designates the method of viewing the world from the standpoint of *all* humankind, which overcomes any racial, national, and class barriers; and S indicates a *suprahistorical* understanding, which seeks the real meaning of history in origins and purposes beyond current circumstances. Taken together, according to Hisamatsu, F.A.S. suggests that Zen is a timeless view committed to activating and liberating the universality of humankind through the realization of authentic self-discovery here and now.

A more sustained theoretical discussion is offered by Nishitani, who applies his teacher Nishida Kitarō's distinction between two levels of nothingness: relative (in the world of form) and absolute (formlessness). In several of Nishitani's works, including *Religion and Nothingness*, Zen is understood as a self-surpassing standpoint that attains a realization of absolute nothingness yet functions as a tool to assess critically and provide a solution for deficient tendencies that plague modern society. The key factor in Nishitani's analysis is science, which lies at the root of the problems of modernization and creates the catastrophic threat of nuclear conflagration and environmental disaster.[28] The early twentieth-century optimism concerning science, which at first challenged and threatened to replace traditional religion as an explanation of the origin and meaning of the world, has proven false or misguided since the advent of the nuclear age. Religion, which initially responded by condemning or ignoring science and then reluctantly accepting it as an alternative viewpoint as in the case of the (still prevalent) debate regarding evolution, has begun to face an even deeper challenge: overcoming the inadequacies and potential devastation that science and its by-product, technology, cause.

The issue of religion and science has an immediacy and urgency for Nishitani, recalling the works of Nietzsche and the later Heidegger's examination of *techne*. This is motivated by the need for a universal spiritual recovery in an era when nihilism reigns and the constant yet frightful specter of indifferent or even exploitative applications of so-called technological advances destroying creation itself is irrevocably felt. Now, science functions in some ways as the enemy rather than as the usurper of the role of religion in terms of morality. Yet traditional religion, once attacked at its core for being irrational or illogical, cannot easily reclaim and assert its position of moral superiority without undergoing a thoroughly penetrating and transformative self-analysis of its own foundations and relation to science. This process, according to Nishitani, is facilitated with reference to Nishida's philosophy of

Zen based on absolute nothingness, which refers to the ultimate state of existence, which is characterized by contradictory self-identity that is prior to any human conceptualization and therefore overcomes all attachments. Absolute nothingness, expressed in Hui-neng's notion of original face, can best be realized through the existential experience of great doubt, a state of profound questioning and anxiety that leads in turn to the great death, or a transformation from being bound to conventional structures to absolute or unbounded awareness.

In contrast to Zen's emphasis on absolute nothingness or the relativity and fundamental unity of all phenomena beyond the dichotomies of subjectivity and objectivity or universality and particularity, science sees the world from the standpoint of mechanistic causality in which reality consists of lifeless material objects devoid of spirit or underlying aim and direction. Unfortunately, the Christian approach to *telos* and teleology, which highlights and affirms the role of future possibility through the attainment of eternal salvation, overlooks here-and-now existence. Nietzsche, influenced by Buddhist thought, was the main Western philosopher who accentuated the transience or incessant change that characterizes the flow of time when he spoke of "the 'moment' as the twinkling of an eye [*Augenblick*]," Nishitani maintains. "But it is a moment standing against a background of Eternal Recurrence and hence does not possess the bottomlessness of the true moment. Hence, it cannot signify the point where something new can truly take place."[29] For Nishitani, it is medieval Christian mystic Meister Eckhart's organic conception of the "eternal now" that comes closest to the Zen view of absolute nothingness. Eckhart, considered a heretic by the church, according to Nishitani's analysis viewed the godhead (*Gottheit*) from the standpoint of the ultimate identity of affirmation and negation, eternity and the present, life and death, in the concrete moment of fully realized subjectivity which embraces clear objectivity.

The Zen perspective can thus lead to a demythologization of Christian teleology because it involves a radical reversal whereby the self finds its *telos* not in the anticipation of heaven but in the self itself and at the same time finds it in all other beings. In this light, Christian piety can be interpreted not as a dedication to the memory of the events of God's creation or Christ's resurrection but as the bottomless and holistic moment "when the self experiences *metanoia* [repentant conversion] to faith that represents the solemn moment when the solemnity of those other moments is truly realized."[30] The here-and-now moment of faith experience thereby encompasses all previous and forthcoming sacred events.

In a compelling essay, "Science and Zen," Nishitani applies the Zen perspective on time and nothingness to an overcoming of the ideological limitations in the scientific world view. He examines several noted Zen kōan cases concerning the mythical eschatology of the "kalpa fire," which is symbolically analogous to the imminent possibility of the cosmic conflagration that science and technology have wrought. In the first case, a monk asks the master, "When the kalpa fire flares up and the great cosmos is destroyed, I wonder, will 'it' perish or will it not perish?" The master replies, "It will perish." According to Nishitani, the "it" refers to the inner dimension of self-realization, thereby giving an existential interpretation to the myth, or a demythologization whereby the scientific and/or apocalyptic possibility is understood as the existential actuality of a here-and-now encounter with the transformative experience of the great doubt/death, that is, profound anxiety leading to genuine self-discovery following the demise of the ordinary ego.

In a similar case, a Zen master is asked, "How is it at the time of the all-consuming kalpa fire?" and he responds, "An unspeakably awesome cold." The paradoxical response, expressing the bottomless depths of absolute nothingness, suggests a level of religious experience unknown to science, which forces a reorientation and reevaluation of the presuppositions of the scientific world view. "*In the religiosity of Zen Buddhism,*" Nishitani maintains, "*demythologization of the mythical and existentialization of the scientific belong to one and the same process.* Religious existence in the Great Death makes possible at once the demythologizing of the myth of eschatology and the existentializing of the scientific actuality of the cosmos."[31]

Nishitani's central contribution to the Buddhist philosophy of the Kyoto school lies in his reclamation and revitalization of Zen in the arena of contemporary international social ethics. Nishida and Suzuki demonstrate that Zen is not an anachronistic mystical standpoint that retreats to nature and rejects civilization but an essential and meaningful contributor to modern philosophy and religious thought that ponders and helps to remedy the future of human society. Nishitani extends their approach in a bold new direction by declaring that Zen will inevitably occupy the forefront of postmodern ethical developments. The Zen experience of the great death is the paradigm of transformation not only for world religions but for all current and possible ideologies. It constitutes the primordial realization from which other standpoints in their partiality arise and the standard that can revise and redeem them.

Thus, Nishitani has recast and reversed the question that modernity seems to pose—can the seemingly archaic naturalistic outlook of Zen survive in an industrialized world?—by asking: Will technological culture itself endure without the metanoesis, or profound conversion or transformation, uniquely expressed in Zen's view of absolute nothingness? In so doing, however,

Nishitani's ontological clarification of Zen, Christianity, and science implies that Zen has a corresponding ethics that will be effective and purifying in the crises faced by contemporary society. But this seems to beg the question of whether Zen has traditionally ever been strong in the formation of ethical theory. Zen offers a phenomenological analysis of the "is-ness" (*arinomama*) of reality, yet does not necessarily explain "ought-ness" on a collective and historical basis beyond the requirements for individual meditation and the monastic order. The limitations in Zen's approach to moral practice have been exposed by Mishima Yukio's *Temple of the Golden Pavilion*. Although Nishitani highlights the flexibility and open-ended quality of Zen as the basis for philosophical dialogue, he does not account for the historical weaknesses of Buddhism in Japan and other Asian countries, which is crucial to interpreting its concrete role in future cultural developments. Nishitani's suggestion that the synthesis of Christian morality and Buddhist metaphysics will only result from a metanoesis of the ontological shortcomings of Christianity may be valid, but he probably also needs to develop an argument from the other side about the transformation of Zen ethics.

Zen and Western Pragmatism and Environmentalism

There have been other fruitful inquiries into Zen rights in a comparative context with Western philosophical and environmental perspectives. In *The Social Self in Zen and American Pragmatism*, Steve Odin effectively constructs and critiques Japanese philosophers from the standpoint of raising basic ethical questions about the role of Zen Buddhist thought in the modern world that have been brought to light by the association of traditional ideals with twentieth-century nationalist/imperialist agendas. For Odin, the key to Zen is not meditation in a manner that remains detached and isolated from society but a realization articulated by modern philosophers that is firmly rooted in a sense of "betweenness" (*aidagara* or *ma*, in Watsuji Tetsurō) or the "place" or topos (*basho*, in Nishida Kitarō) of intersubjectivity. According to Odin's analysis of the traditional series of the Ten Oxherding Pictures attributed to twelfth-century Rinzai master Kuo-an Shih-yuan, "the Zen process of becoming a person culminates with the realization of the true self as a compassionate Bodhisattva located in the *between* of I and Thou as the standpoint of Nothingness." The sequence of drawings "thereby makes fully explicit that the goal of Zen is not simply an inner state of tranquility but the social reconstruction of the self."[32]

For the book cover, Odin uses the final image in the series by Sung master Kakuan (illustrated by the modern artist Tokuriki Tomikichiro), which shows the boy who, having tamed the ox and returned from a realm of primordial nothingness, is now entering into the marketplace, thereby unifying ultimate and mundane reality, or nirvana and samsara. This entrance, or reentrance, into concrete experience after having apparently fully transcended it exemplifies Odin's focus on the social side of Zen. His choice of the last picture for his book's cover implies not a sense of completeness or finality but an ever-continuing process of becoming within the social realm.

Odin primarily deals with Watsuji, Nishida, and psychologist Doi Takeo in his comparison with American pragmatism and demonstrates how George Herbert Mead, often an overlooked figure, was the fulfillment of a movement that included such luminaries as Peirce, James, Royce, Cooley, Dewey, and Whitehead (and, more recently, Buchler and Hartshorne). Despite his sympathetic understanding of Japanese thought, Odin is wary of facile or biased arguments for social selfhood in Japanese philosophy, which tend to lead to an overemphasis on the value of loyalty to the group as an end in itself or to a suffocating communitarianism such that the "odd nail gets hammered into place" (deru kugi wa utareru). He reverses the outlook of many comparativists who favor the East in his conclusion that "only the Whiteheadean process framework of G. H. Mead clarifies the asymmetrical nature of these relations so as to allow for individuality and sociality, creativity and contextuality, indeterminacy and determinacy."[33]

For Odin, Mead surpasses the Kyoto school because he has stripped away the kind of thinking that is vulnerable to charges of nefarious political associations:

> Like Mead in American pragmatism, Nishida Kitarō develops an explicit theory of the social self based on an I-Other dialectic which overcomes Cartesian subjectivism while preserving the "I" of creative human agency and the acting self. Similar to the I-Me dialectic of Mead, the I-Thou dialectic of Nishida underscores the irreducible self-creativity and radical discontinuity of the individual I as over against the social determinism of the "Thou." However, at the political levels of analysis, it has been seen that whereas the social self and I-Thou dialectic of Nishida is used to support the emperor system, the social self and I-Me dialectic of Mead instead functions as the basis for a liberal democratic society.[34]

Odin cites criticisms of the Kyoto school and of abuses of Buddhism leading either to antinomian or fascist associations that have come from non-Buddhists in the postwar period, such as Maruyama Masao, and Western skeptics, such as Peter Dale who has sought to expose the "myth of Japanese uniqueness."[35]

However, he remains in the TZN camp in that he does not follow through with this line of criticism to the extent seen in a collection of articles originally presented at a symposium on modern Japanese intellectual history and the prewar-postwar period, *Rude Awakenings*.

Another TZN approach considers traditional and modern Zen sources in relation to contemporary environmental ethics.[36] While not inherently "green" in the current sense of ecology, Zen evidences quite a number of core qualities and values that can be considered ecofriendly and help it serve as a model for new theories that address problems of conservation and pollution control.[37] Traditional Japanese society is characterized by an approach based on healthy, efficient, and convenient living derived from a mental outlook that makes the most of minimal natural resources.[38] Zen particularly endorses the values of simplicity, in that monks enter the Samgha Hall only with robes, bowls, and a few other meager possessions; thrift, by making a commitment to waste nothing; and communal manual labor, such that through a rotation of chores everyone contributes to the upkeep of the temple. The image of dedicated monks sweeping the wood floors of the hallways by rushing along on their hands in a semi-prostrate position is inspiring. Furthermore, the monastic system's use of human and material resources, including natural space, is limited and spare in terms of temple layout, the handling of administrative duties and chores, and the use of stock items. The sparse, spartan, vegetarian Zen cook, who prepares just enough rice gruel for his fellow monks but not a grain too much or too little, demonstrates an inherent—if not necessarily deliberate—conservationist approach. The minimalist aesthetic of rock gardens highlights the less-is-more Zen outlook that influenced the "Buddhist economics" evoked by E. F. Schumacher in *Small Is Beautiful*.[39]

For Zen, unsullied natural beauty serves as a symbol of purity. However, the approach is different from the utopian Taoist poem by Tao Yuan-ming, "Peach Blossom Spring," in which a fisherman wandering in the remote mountains stumbles on an idyllic village where people have no conflicts and achieve a remarkable longevity, but then he is unable to relocate the lost land on a second journey. Instead, Zen is eminently practical in seeing nature as a model for human behavior to learn and practice the way of the dharma. For example, the pine trees weathering the harsh winter storms teach a lesson in the value of dedication and determination in pursing the path to enlightenment; bamboo branches that sway but are not broken by the breeze teach flexibility and the need to overcome stubborn one-sided or partial views; and evaporating dew, which accepts its brevity and inevitable demise, shows the significance of adjusting and abandoning resistance to the impermanence of reality. These natural images, which are used extensively in the Chinese and

Japanese poetic traditions, frequently enter into various styles of Zen verse and prose, not just as rhetorical flourishes but as indicators of inner spiritual transformation.

In addition to serving as a behavioral role model, the Zen view of nature also becomes the basis for a holistic standpoint that defeats anthropocentric tendencies in Western approaches by highlighting the intrinsic value and sacredness of sentient beings—and, especially in Japan, of all phenomena whether animate or inanimate—which are said to participate in the universality of Buddha-nature. The following Dōgen passage from *Tenzokyōkun* depicts a celebration of mountains, trees, and waters as embodying the sutras that compel the reader to recognize and appreciate all aspects of reality from an ecological or cosmocentric, rather than human-centered, perspective with equilibrium and nondiscrimination (or an "equal eye"):

> "Great mind" is a mind like a great mountain or a great ocean.
> It does not have any partiality or exclusivity. You should not re-
> gard a pound as light or a ton as heavy. Do not be attracted by the
> sounds of spring or take pleasure in seeing a spring garden. When
> you see autumn colors, do not be partial to them. You should al-
> low the four seasons to advance in one viewing, and see an ounce and
> a pound with an equal eye.[40]

Another important element for understanding Zen's relation to contemporary environmental issues in this and related passages is that practitioners are motivated to follow a realization-based, or a unity of means and end—rather than an instrumental, or means leading to an end—attitude and approach to their training. Moreover, pantheistic implications that suggest that the whole world is contained in a speck of dust provide the basis for an imperative that, if one person practices zazen for a single instant, the effects continue to reverberate and to help redeem karma throughout the entire universe.[41] The combined impact of these doctrines is to inspire those working for ecological reform not to be overwhelmed and demoralized by the extent of the problems faced. Instead, they dedicate their efforts to accomplishing seemingly small or insignificant tasks here and now while having the determination to prevail and the faith that these activities will eventually have a greater, transformative impact on the whole society. Reformers can learn from monks, who spend countless hours cooking or cleaning the grounds or raking the garden, and can view each and every task, no matter how menial or seemingly trivial, not simply as a means to an end, which is frustrating if the final goal seems remote or unattainable. Rather, the tasks are seen as ends in themselves to be celebrated as eminently worthwhile, which paradoxically enhances their possible benefit for the future.

Zen Wrongs

HCC reverses many of the TZN evaluations in its view that from the time of its inception Zen was a compromised institution. The HCC critique begins by pointing out that the historical conditions in the formative period in China and Japan were somewhat tainted and corrupted through concessions and compromises of Zen ideals made with ruling powers, and this corruption eventually became the basis of the ethical deficiencies evident today. Following its period of hegemony in medieval Japan, when it had nearly full government support and subsidy, the role of Zen over a period of several centuries beginning around 1600 was subjugated to other religious traditions, including Confucianism in the Tokugawa era and Shinto beginning in the Meiji era.

By the Taisho-Showa eras (1912–1989), when state Shinto was first established and then rebuffed after World War II, Zen had become an institution preoccupied with preserving its status quo. This was its reaction to a society that enforced government regulation of clerical life and was rocked by upheavals during the pre- and postwar periods, which created tremendous political pressures for conformity to which Buddhism almost invariably succumbed.[42] Along with these factors, the primary role of Zen and other Buddhist sects in Japanese society was not based on a striving for the attainment of enlightenment. Rather, it was preoccupied with the performance of a series of ancestor rituals and funeral rites for the lay community collectively known as "funerary Buddhism" (sōshiki Bukkyō), ranging from the O-Bon or Ghost Festival to funerals and memorial services.[43] As a consequence of the conflux of circumstances, a tendency born of anxiety and defensiveness became ingrained in Zen and Japanese Buddhism more generally to turn a deaf ear— and, at worst, to lend comfort and support—to examples of extreme nationalism and intolerance for the downtrodden in Japan. It is in this light that comments by TZN apologists, including Suzuki and Herrigel, to the effect that "only Japanese can really understand Zen" seem to ring hollow in evoking the excesses of reverse Orientalism.

Therefore, HCC critics undertake a forceful and sometimes scathing attack on Zen's role in relation to contemporary social issues. The two main targets for criticism are participation by Kyoto school members and other Zen spokespersons in the rhetoric of imperialism/militarism leading up to World

War II and discrimination against the outcast community, which is evident in the manner of awarding posthumous initiation names (*kaimyō*) during funeral ceremonies. The basic ethical flaw that links the seemingly disparate issues of militarism and discrimination seems to be located somewhere between amorality, or a failure to address moral concerns because of historical circumstances, and the more virulent flaunting of convention that characterizes antinomianism. It is a deeply entrenched problem reinforced by centuries of misguided behavior, which though now acknowledged and identified, is by no means easily overcome.

There have been several sources of HCC criticism regarding the problem of Zen involvement in social wrongs encompassing both insiders and outsiders to the tradition. Following the war, Japanese social commentators ranging from left-leaning public intellectual Maruyama Masao to novelist Mishima Yukio on the right wing exposed the inability of the traditional Zen monastic system to overcome corruption and capitulation to authority. Also, non-Zen Buddhists like Pure Land school thinkers and historians, including Tanabe Hajime and Ienaga Saburō, who expressed in varying ways regret for Japan's handling of the war, stood in contrast to Kyoto school thinkers who seemed to offer no regrets or apologies for their support of imperialism.[44] Another source of criticism from within Japan has included organizations representing antidiscrimination positions, such as the Hisabetsu Burakumin Kaihō Dōmei (Burakumin Liberation League) and advocates for women's rights, who have charged that Zen and other Buddhist sects hinder their cause of protesting intolerance and the mistreatment of minorities.[45] While the Zen organization may have at first tried to ignore these criticisms, over time it has come to realize the value of constructive interaction and dialogue.

Interestingly, much of the harshest criticism has come from Zen insiders, including several scholar/clerics. Ichikawa Hakugen, a leader of Hanazono University in Kyoto during the Vietnam War era, chided Zen for contributing to, yet failing to acknowledge, Japan's wartime responsibility. Hakamaya Noriaki along with Matsumoto Shirō of Komazawa University developed the critical Buddhism approach in the 1980s when injustices connected with the practice of *kaimyō* were becoming a heated topic in Buddhist circles. In addition, Brian Victoria, an American researcher who became an ordained Sōtō cleric during his long stay in Japan in the 1960s and 1970s, has published two provocative books, *Zen at War* and *Zen War Stories*, about Zen's involvement in prewar nationalism, both of which have received notice in the Japanese press and have stimulated international debate.

Kyoto school thinker Ueda Shizuteru has been a staunch defender of Nishida against criticism of the founder of his intellectual lineage's apparent sympathy for and reification of the imperial household, which may have influenced his disciple Nishitani's participation in the suspect symposium "Overcoming Modernity", which was held at the peak of the war effort in the early 1940s. Yet even Ueda seems to support the weight of HCC criticism when he scoffs at any ambivalence on the part of wartime intellectuals regarding Japan's role in imperialism, which has been justified as a struggle to liberate East Asia from Western colonialism. Ueda maintains, "The war in question *was* a war of aggression against the countries of East Asia. For us Japanese to equivocate on this point is morally unacceptable."[46]

Historical and Ideological Roots

The HCC analysis draws a direct connection between the initial formation and organization of the samgha and current deficiencies in Zen's relation to society. From the outset, Zen has harbored a degree of corruption in making compromises and accommodations with state and local authorities and donors, which has led to many of the social problems evident in modern Japan. As stipulated in the *Ch'an-yüan ch'ing-kuei*, for example, it became customary for abbots in China and Japan who were delivering public sermons (*jōdō*) in the Dharma Hall to include, as part of the cycle, memorials for the emperor and other powerful figures. Matsuo notes the tendency to acquiesce to powerful officials that was part of the success of new forms of Kamakura Buddhism, "The regular task of reclusive monks was to pray in response to the individual needs of believers, but the monks also sometimes prayed for the welfare of the emperor and the nation."[47]

Christopher Ives comments on the significance of self-interest and self-preservation in maintaining institutional longevity (rather than integrity) as a driving force shaping Zen's close relationships with the ruling powers. "The symbiosis and embeddedness," he writes, "reached its apogee during WWII in the form of Imperial Way Zen (*kōdō Zen*), a modern instance of 'Buddhism for the protection of the country' (*gokoku Bukkyō*)."[48] Similarly, in an article titled "Japanese Corporate Zen," a precursor to his books mentioned above, Victoria shows how techniques used by corporations today to instill loyalty and subservience in company recruits are an extension of Zen's long-standing role from the Kamakura era in supporting samurai training for the sake of promoting the state. According to Victoria, "This relationship [between Zen and corporate training]...is based on more than 700 years of Zen cooperation with, and support for, the power structure of the day. Its reform will be no easy task."[49]

Therefore, for HCC, an examination of the origins of the Zen community cannot be limited to the supposed purity of the Samgha Hall as defined by an arcane set of monastic rules, but must take into account a much broader sociopolitical context. HCC asks how the role of patronage and government support was crucial for the growth and spread of Zen. For example, what parties paid for building and maintaining the hall, and why? The same set of questions applies to the transmission of the lamp records, the main Ch'an/Zen literature of the classical period, which were generally commissioned by leaders of the Sung state. These texts often reflected sectarian agendas in that a master's life was selected for inclusion or was highlighted to suit the ideological bent of the funding sources. As Albert Welter points out, "In contrast to Chan myth that characterizes the master as aloof from political and secular concerns, the history of Chan is in fact predicated on the relations between clerics and officials."[50] Furthermore:

> The interplay between political and religious authority is inevita-
> ble whenever the implicit influence of religious functionaries and the
> explicit power of secular officials is recognized. In spite of the image
> of Chan masters enshrined in legend as "pure" recipients of declined
> favors, the reality is one of Chan masters accepting official honors.[51]

Because of this level of intrigue, it seems that transmitting the dharma was jeopardized in many cases in that the transmission meant nothing more than assuming the abbotship at a temple. It was no guarantee of spiritual quality but merely offered the legitimating of authority that may have been the result of a political payoff. A related issue regarding the economic background and organization of the Zen community is the way private retreats were often set up by monks who retired and used juniors as servants, and they probably helped to finance this by managing large estates that generated a significant amount of revenue.

Several scholars have pointed out that in most ways the Zen approach to institutional expansion was not much different than the organization and management of the main schools that preceded the rise of Zen, the Lü (or Vinaya) and T'ien-t'ai schools in China, and the Tendai and Shingon sects in Japan.[52] The basic operation of Buddhist temples in East Asia cut across sectarian lines as all schools were competing for external resources and support. This argument, if valid, in some ways lets Zen off the hook, so to speak, in that other forms of Buddhism were more or less guilty of some of the same excesses and lacunae. But at the same time, this argument under-mines TZN claims for the uniqueness and purity of the Zen agenda vis-à-vis other Buddhist schools.

Zen's historical development as an institution from the formative period to modern times was largely based on capitulation and acquiescence to authority.

ZEN RIGHTS 143

An attitude of complacency is evident in two basic theoretical factors that are seemingly opposite but converge, according to the HCC analysis, in reinforcing the social deficiencies of Zen ideology, which reifies the status quo and lacks a mechanism for reform. On the one hand, Zen stresses an affirmation of everyday reality through such expressions as "ordinary mind is Buddha," "every day is a good day," and "sitting quietly, doing nothing, the seasons turn and spring comes of its own accord." This emphasis on the quality referred to as "is-ness" is intended to evoke the primordial incorruptibility of nature prior to human intervention. It can imply an overcoming of petty human strife and conflict, but unfortunately, all too often it has led to the passive acceptance of "things as they are" (another typical Buddhist phrase) without advocating change or demanding that those in authority be held accountable for their actions. Despite the rhetoric of antistructuralism and antinomianism, there is precious little in Zen, save for a few exceptions that seem to prove the rule, that reflects resistance or rebellion regarding what the monastic system or individual monks are told to do, and this translates into a larger-scale lack of commitment to creating change in society as a whole.

At the other end of the ideological spectrum, Zen, as we have seen, is also well known for its emphasis on irreverent and often outrageous and blasphemous masters, as portrayed in the classic narratives, who slapped or tormented each other and found a variety of ways to express a boldly creative wildness through no-holds-barred, unchecked antistructural behavior. While seeming to demonstrate a radical creativity that is anything but passive, the result of this approach, ironically, is to give license to the leaders of the school to act without being bound by any system of checks and balances. Idiosyncratic and erratic, or domineering and overbearing, forms of behavior—or misbehavior—on the part of leaders could not be questioned or challenged. The appointment of abbots was regulated by the government system, which politicized the process and helped to create a sense that once in a position of authority masters were often considered beyond reproach by their disciples, who had no recourse if there was an abuse of power.

One of Ikkyū's noted calligraphies contains the saying "Entering the realm of Buddha is easy, entering the realm of the demon [ma] is difficult." An implication of the saying is that asserting the priority of purity while occupying a state of transcendence is a relatively simple task that is not as demanding as maintaining a genuinely enlightened state of mind while being tempted and tested in the midst of impurity. An underlying theme is that Buddha and demon are not distinct, but symbolize interior forces of wisdom and delusion that are inextricably and dialectically linked as complementary opposites embraced by a deeper level of nondual awareness.

However, this expression, along with Ikkyū's controversial lifestyle, which included the celebration of visits to brothels and the "red thread" of passion, could also be interpreted as deliberately defying conventional ethics and endorsing the kind of antinomianism that was praised in some of the biographies but consistently rejected by Zen monastic rules texts. Like Shinran's True Pure Land statement, "If good people can be saved, how much more so evil people," in the sense that these are the ones who most need the benefits of Amida's grace, Ikkyū's saying perhaps opens the door to distortion and licentious behavior. While relevant and meaningful to the select few who are inspired and who do not take advantage of the ethical loopholes, unfortunately the Zen approach is so open-ended, vague, and elusive that it can be interpreted in any way and even used as a rationale for making accommodations with the powers that be, whether the Hōjō shogunate in the medieval period or the Hirohito imperial family in the twentieth century.

"Warmongering" Zen

Nishitani's comment about getting slapped by the right before the war and by the left after the war suggests that the Kyoto school took an essentially moderate approach that was criticized by extremists on both sides. While it is no doubt the case that prewar Kyoto school writings were attacked by nationalists for not being sufficiently right-wing, HCC would not want to be considered the flip side, or another excessively negative attack. Rather, it questions whether Nishitani's defense is credible or is a ploy to skirt the issue of taking responsibility for his own failings. Responsibility is a key term highlighted in a breakthrough work by Ichikawa Hakugen, *Bukkyōsha no sensō-sekinin* (Wartime Responsibility of Buddhists), which remains timely and relevant nearly four decades after its publication.[53] Ichikawa has called for Buddhist intellectuals to share accountability for Japanese atrocities committed during the war, as these were ultimately founded on the false sense of harmony and compliance with the totalitarian regime that was supported by religious movements, including—or, given its history of militarist endeavors, especially—Zen.

Ichikawa rejects the notion that there was a sense of ambiguity in the views of Kyoto school and Zen thinkers that can be used to defend what they wrote before and during the war. Any vagueness about a commitment to nationalist agendas embedded in their wartime writings was actually a pretext to avoid scrutiny and to hedge bets rather than an expression of a genuine sense of searching for, or an uncertainty about, the truth.

According to Bernard Faure, Kyoto school thinkers must be "held accountable" for the implications of equating universal harmony and nondiscrimination with the state in statements asserting that both individuals and the whole society "mutually negate themselves for the emperor." According to Faure's critique of Nishitani's thought influenced by Nishida's reconciliation of the paradoxical ideal of absolute contradiction with the state, "This [process] seems to have as its center this contradictory self-identity that is the Imperial Household."[54] A prominent example of nationalist rhetoric that has been dissected extensively since the 1990s by scholars on both sides of the Pacific is "Nishida's assertion of *kokutai* ('national polity') ideology, according to which there is an essential identity between the divine realm of the *kami*, the divine Emperor, and Japan, the 'divine land' (*shinkoku*)."[55] This appears to be a grotesque distortion of Zen principles for the sake of a political accommodation foreshadowed by medieval institutional origins and culminating in a reprehensible political discourse centuries later.

Although not explicitly expressed this way, one implication of Nishida's view, as indicated in Figures 4.2 and 4.3, is to identify the imperial palace grounds in central Tokyo with the empty circle (*ensō*) featured in the Ten Oxherding Pictures and in numerous examples of calligraphy. Both represent an image, to allude to Nishida's main philosophical phrasing, of the logic of the "place" or "locus" (*basho*) of absolute nothingness, which is supposed to suggest the Zen state of mind that has eliminated all distractions. From an aerial view, the palace, which appears amid the swirling, labyrinthine streets of Tokyo and looks like the eye of a storm, seems to manifest such a symbol.[56]

The criticisms proffered by Ichikawa are not limited to the war itself, but are wide ranging as he explores multiple ways in which Zen ideology easily gets corrupted and exploited by nationalism and corporatism.[57] He has in particular criticized easy converts and confessors who, after the war, renounced their ties to imperialism only when it was convenient and fashionable to do so, and without expressing any real conviction about remorse for transgressions.[58] Ichikawa suggests that the confessors never would have engaged in reform-minded social consciousness without the external pressures created in the shifting political climate of the Occupation and emerging cold war periods pushing them in this direction. It has also been pointed out that some, like Nishitani, never even made such a confession/conversion.

However, there are certainly defenders of the Kyoto school who claim that the real distortion is on the part of overeager, even vehement detractors who generate more heat than light through unfounded attacks. According to this analysis, as part of the trendy deconstructionism pervading some approaches to Japanese intellectual history, which debunks any and all arguments for the distinctiveness of Japanese culture, HCC criticism is based on "irresponsible . . . accusations of fascism or ultranationalism" backed up by "vague generalization

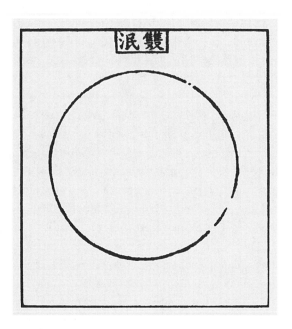

FIGURES 4.2 and 4.3. Image of the empty circle from the Ten Oxherding Pictures (by Sung master Kakuan, illustrated by Tokuriki Tomikichiro) juxtaposed with the Imperial Palace in the center of Tokyo.

and innuendo," and otherwise "flimsy grounds."⁵⁹ According to the defense, critics tend to overlook the historical context whereby Japanese intellectuals in the 1930s were reacting to a century of Western colonialism in East Asia. This left China encroached by European powers to the west and Japan itself threatened by American presence in the Philippines to the east and by conflicts with Russia over contested islands to the north. It can be forgiven that Zen thinkers were caught up in these global trends.

Greatly influenced by the wing of HCC that does not find exceptions or concede forgiveness except in isolated cases, Brian Victoria mounts a blistering attack on the embracing of wartime ideology by leading Zen masters and practitioners in Japan.⁶⁰ Following Ichikawa's lead, Victoria shows that the attitude characteristic of numerous eminent Zen monks and scholars was not a matter of only benignly resisting, or even passively accepting, the rhetoric of Imperial Way Buddhism by clergy who were pressured and powerless to stand up to authorities. Nor was it an example of innocently recognizing historical and ideological affinities between Zen monastic discipline and military training.

On the contrary, the Zen masters enthusiastically endorsed some of the most excessive aspects of imperial ideology in the name of a corrupted vision of spiritual realization as a tool to spread the Greater East Asia Co-Prosperity Sphere, itself a grand ploy to disguise colonialism as a force for liberating the rest of Asia from the West. They also used Zen wedded to hypernationalism and imperialism as a tool to misread the historical records of their own tradition and to help transport Japanese supremacy to China and Korea, while refusing to acknowledge or repent for their actions after the defeat of Japan. This outlook infected numerous politicians and military figures who turned to Buddhism as a way of explaining away or masking their problematic political roles leading up to, during, and after World War II.

In *Zen War Stories*, Victoria documents several masters who have become icons in the West for their apparent adherence to Zen tradition linked with their ability to address contemporary culture. After showing that Ōmori Sōgen, praised for his prowess in swordsmanship and other arts, had a fascistic, "Mr. Hyde" side as manifested in the founding in 1932 of the Kinnō Ishin Dōmei (League for Loyalty to the Emperor and the Restoration), Victoria turns to the case of Yasutani Haku'un. In "Zen Master Dōgen Goes to War," he shows that Yasutani, known as the teacher of Philip Kapleau and inspiration for *The Three Pillars of Zen*, wanted to smash all universities for harboring traitors. Yasutani was a fanatical militarist who "transformed the life and thought of Zen Master Dōgen (1200–1253), the thirteenth-century founder of the Sōtō Zen sect in Japan, into a propaganda tool for Japanese militarism."⁶¹

In particular, Yasutani tried to argue that Dōgen's famed pilgrimage to Sung China in 1223 was triggered not by a simple but intense longing for attaining the Buddhist dharma, as traditional sources explain it, but by a sense of disgust with the new shogunate and infatuation with preserving the imperial household at the beginning of the Kamakura era. According to Victoria, Yasutani's corrupted spirituality did not end with support for militarism. He was also even more "ethnic chauvinist, sexist, and anti-Semitic" than his teacher Harada Sōgaku, cited at the beginning of this chapter for celebrating tramping and shooting at the enemy as the epitome of enlightenment.

In "Zen 'Selflessness' in Japanese Militarism," Victoria discusses how Zen's historical relation to the samurai was deliberately misinterpreted by D. T. Suzuki and other prominent representatives of Zen, including former Eiheiji temple abbot Kumazawa Taizen, to support imperial ideology about the acceptance of death. He then considers examples of the involvement with Buddhist thought by military and political leaders. While this discussion is less devastating as a critique of Zen than of Japanese Buddhism and society in general, Victoria explains in "Buddhism: The Last Refuge of War Criminals" how easily the moral basis of religion can be distorted and subverted. For example, as recollected by Buddhist studies scholar Hanayama Shinshō, seven Class A war criminals who were condemned to death continued to cling to Buddhism while on death row in order to find a feeling of solace and justification for their immoral behavior. Hirota Kōki, for example, never abandoned his sense of Zen's identification with the warrior class, and used meditation to stiffen his resolve to "die naturally...returning to nothingness."[62]

"Discriminatory" Zen

Critical Buddhism has argued that there is a fundamental connection between Zen's support for the war and its involvement in discriminatory practices based on deficiencies in ideology that have left East Asian Buddhist schools drifting and without a moral compass. Hakamaya and Matsumoto are part of a widespread response to a sense of frustration and disappointment in Zen Buddhism, which has appeared to be an anachronistic, authoritarian, dogmatic, and socially rigid institution instead of a genuinely contemporary, progressive, and flexible advocate for justice and reform. As with the case of its apparent warmongering, there is a long history of Zen's participation in discriminatory practices connected with mortuary rites. This has been especially true since the Tokugawa era, when the government introduced policies of intolerance, and both Rinzai and Sōtō along with other Buddhist sects created a tradition of suppressing the rights of outcasts through the way funeral rites were conducted, including the granting of *kaimyō* to the deceased based on social rank and the donations made to the temple.

A fascination with honoring and at the same time conquering death was characteristic of Chinese Ch'an, which developed elaborate mortuary rites for deceased monks and also worshiped the mummies, relics, and portraits (*chinsō*) of deceased patriarchs. These objects were often installed on the high seat of the Dharma Hall or in the Samgha Hall to preserve the sacred presence of abbots and other venerated leaders after their demise, even though this seems to contradict the traditional Buddhist emphasis on accepting impermanent reality.[63] Memorial services were performed for honored secular figures, such as members of the imperial family and local patrons. While the elite members of Buddhist and non-Buddhist society were elevated and eulogized in funerary practices, at the other end of the social spectrum there was a practice of mistreating the dispossessed classes in China through their exclusion from the temple grounds or by their serving in the role of slaves. Nevertheless, these sectors of the population were served during the annual Ghost Festival held at the time of the full moon of the seventh month of the lunar calendar. Buddhist rituals played an important purification function by placating spirits of the dead who were visiting the living.

Buddhism in Japan complemented the indigenous religion (Shinto), which did not provide rituals of burial or memorial for other than the elite but did offer rites of veneration for deceased ancestors. In addition to inheriting some of the legacy of Chinese Buddhism, ranging from memorials for patriarchs to the Ghost Festival, a distinctive practice to Japanese Buddhism soon developed: bestowing a *kaimyō* to ensure that the deceased attains nirvana (*nehan*) in the afterlife. In the *kaimyō* rite, laypersons are treated once they have died as if they were monks through applying Buddhist symbols, such as shaved heads, robes, ablutions, etc. Although the *kaimyō* rite does not identify social status directly, it has a built-in hierarchical approach in that different kinds of names are given to advanced and junior monks, clerics and laypersons, males and females, and a variety of ranks and roles in society, from nobility to poverty.[64] Acquiring a name invariably requires a family's donation to the temple, and in most cases, more prestigious *kaimyō* can be purchased or obtained through political influence. A basic problem with the system is that the deceased's behavior in their lifetime seems to be of less importance than financial considerations or social connections harnessed at the time of their death.

It has been noted that in medieval times special techniques were developed to keep outcasts "off the registry," while handwritten inscriptions (*kirigami*, lit. paper strips) were composed for protection from the spirits of the discriminated, who would be seeking to wreak revenge (*tatari*) on the per-petrators.[65] The damning names still given to *burakumin* in modern times further reinforces the hierarchical process by deliberately identifying their untouchable status in a disguised way during a ceremony that purports to guarantee their salvation in democratic fashion.[66] Figure 4.4, a photo of the gravestone label of an outcast, dramatically demonstrates this point.

Among several important accounts of the historical and ideological roots of discrimination, in *Sei to sen* (Sacred and Profane), Noma Hiroshi, a renowned modern novelist and follower of Shinran who befriended and supported

Kanji for "Beast"

FIGURE 4.4. The third character from the top on the gravestone literally means "beast," but for purposes of decoying or concealing the use of slander, it can also be read as two separate characters, which would render a meaning of "dark field" as a way of coding an outcast's status. From Shimada Hiromi, *Kaimyō: Naze shigo ni namae o kaeru no ka* [Posthumous Initiation Names: Why Are Names Changed Posthumously?] (Kyoto: Hōzōkan, 1991), p. 73.

several prominent *burakumin* writers, stresses two main points.[67] One is the influence of Shinto views on ritual contamination or impurity (*kegare*, the kanji for which is also pronounced *e* as in the derogatory term *eta*, which is traditionally used for *burakumin*) accompanied by an abhorrence of death. The other is the impact of the caste system and practices of untouchability in India and other countries on Japanese Buddhist conceptions of karmic defilement and social stratification. The term *sendara* (Skt. *candala*) for untouchables in the Indian caste system was appropriated in Buddhist texts as a designation for those whose evil karma prohibits them from being receptive to the Buddha's teachings.[68] The term may have been initially intended as a way of evaluating the evil karma of murderers and mercenaries. In Japan, it became a tool to discriminate against those who performed legitimate social functions in killing or handling dead animals because these activities were not sanctioned by the samgha.

The community that came to be known as outcasts by the Tokugawa era apparently played a much more ambiguous role in medieval society, when they were given comfort in Eizon's reform-minded Ritsu sect, or even favored status by some forms of Buddhism since their lives of itinerancy resembled those of wandering monks. Institutionalized and rigidified discrimination commenced in the Edo period when Buddhism became a vehicle for promoting rather than a possible source of release from the oppression of outcasts through the role of the parish (*danka*) system in the shogunate society, which kept tabs on all citizens who were required to be affiliated with a temple.[69] Many untouchables were further "tainted" by being forced by the Tokugawa shogunate into the role of torturers, executioners, or disposers of corpses.

An interesting example of how traditional terminology has been used on behalf of intolerance is a kōan cited in the *Eihei kōroku* (9.67) in which a butcher, asked for the best slice of meat, responds that all slices are equally valuable. The conventional interpretation highlights the notion of nonduality and the innate equality of each portion of the whole object. Yet in Japan, the kōan has been extracted out of its original philosophical context and used— even though the term may not have carried the same stigma in the original Chinese setting—in an insidious fashion to label *burakumin* as "butchers."[70]

Critical Buddhist thinkers Hakamaya and Matsumoto in following the lead of Ichikawa have focused their criticism on how the notion of original enlightenment thought (*hongaku shisō*) in traditional Mahayana and Zen texts can ironically foster social discrimination in the name of pointing to the attainment of liberation through epistemological nondiscrimination. Matsumoto shows how the rhetoric of universality is undercut by the category of *sendara*, which is similar to the term *icchantika*, or exceptions to the rule who are said to be incapable of spiritual attainment. The real aim of original enlightenment thought is to assimilate local animistic/naturalistic cults for commercial purposes, as discussed in chapter 3. In justifying this ideology, the doctrine also denies causality on the basis of nonduality or absolute contradiction, and thus tends to foster a false sense of equality that mitigates the need for social responsibility to right the wrongs of injustice and intolerance.

According to Critical Buddhism, original enlightenment and related doctrines, such as *tathagatagarbha* and Buddha-nature, espouse an uncritical syncretism that fosters such problematic viewpoints as the demand for societal harmony over individuality and a tacit compliance with militarism. These attitudes are in turn supported politically by totalitarian and nationalist ideologies and intellectually by *nihonjinron* (Nihonism or Japanism) rhetoric that ends up abetting ethnic discrimination. The basic weakness of Mahayana thought is that ontologically it does not allow for the existence of an "other" since all things are considered to arise from the single, undifferentiated primordial *dhatu*, or locus, and epistemologically and ethically it is rendered incapable of dealing with the complex manifestations of otherness that force concrete choices. Therefore, Hakamaya maintains that the original enlightenment and Buddha-nature doctrines lack a basis for developing situationally specific, ethically evaluative judgments, and the result is an unreflective and reprehensible endorsement of injustices:

> Although some interpret the doctrine of original enlightenment as a theory of equality since it claims to recognize the fundamental universal enlightenment of all people, this is actually a gross misunderstanding. In fact, the doctrine of original enlightenment, which in a facile way requires seeking out the fundamental unified ground of enlightenment, must be considered the primary source of [social] discrimination.[71]

Sallie King further suggests in a discussion of the doctrine of Buddha-nature:

> [T]he texts prized in East Asian Buddhist traditions have tended to emphasize such things as nondiscrimination [in the epistemological rather than social sense] and non-conceptual wisdom, which are difficult to reconcile with the complexities of resolving competing claims, for example, or balancing needs against resources, which require that one be very precise in the distinguishing of particulars, that one make informed judgments, and that one regard such activities as important and valuable.[72]

In Japan, this means accepting or even supporting the myth of Japanese uniqueness and the related nationalist/nativist/Nihonist rhetoric that pervaded post-Tokugawa and especially prewar intellectual life. Zen, in particular, has often hidden its support for the status quo behind what is, in effect, an elitist aestheticism based on the notion that everything reflects Buddha dharma.

Thus, the Buddhist view of personal liberation, lofty in an ideal sense, has been subverted and reduced in the real world to an approach based on *jigo jitoku*, an idiomatic expression that literally means "the karma created by self is received by self," or "the self gets back the karma it causes." This turns into a "you get what you deserve," blame the victim, "what goes around comes around," "you made your bed, now lie in it" type of justification for social oppression, providing a pseudohistorical mythology that rationalizes the devaluation of "vile occupations." (According to the writings of B. R. Ambedkar, untouchables in India were long reluctant to convert to Buddhism because of this tendency.) Since people deserve their karma, there is no need to take responsibility to bring about social change along with tacit support for the status quo and complacency.

For Critical Buddhism, in the cases of both discrimination and nationalism/imperialism, Zen has had an unfortunate tendency to comply tacitly and at times overtly, or at least to fail to resist and protest the manipulation and exploitation of minority and stigmatized groups imposed by a hierarchical authoritarian order.[73] This "don't rock the boat" mentality unfortunately gets associated with the Zen sense of naturalism (as-it-is-ness) and a capitulation to imperialism by a subdued, obedient, nonconflictive, detached, aloof institution that unquestioningly accepts holy war. This is the reason that through much of the twentieth century Zen has cloaked itself in the ideology of being a part of the "great (imperial) family" (*dai-kazoku*).[74]

On the issue of rights and wrongs, TZN and HCC have grown so far apart that they appear separated by a canyon of differences and discrepancies. The epilogue explores ways of trying to reconcile the TZN and HCC approaches to the issue of rights. It evokes the notion of repentance, originally included in the Vinaya code and abused or neglected throughout the centuries, as a means of presenting a constructive compromise that puts forward the strengths of Zen without trying to conceal its weaknesses.

Epilogue: The Real Zen Buddhism

Engaged, Enraged, or Disengaged?

Whither Zen: Repentance or Nonrepentance

This concluding chapter marks a departure and transition from the approach and content that characterized the first four chapters, which were descriptive and nonjudgmental with regard both to the diverse phenomena manifesting Zen Buddhist theory and practice and to various ways this material has been interpreted by the traditional Zen narrative (TZN) and historical and cultural criticism (HCC) viewpoints. Here, in pursuit of Zen's skin vis-à-vis its marrow, I move cautiously and in preliminary fashion toward a normative approach. This involves making some recommendations about how the conflict between TZN and HCC can be overcome, such that the merits of Zen Buddhism proffered by TZN are recognized and restored in light of the need for self-criticism and reform engendered by the outlook of HCC.

The key to this bridge, I maintain, is to highlight the importance of repentance, long a basic Buddhist ritual tool for moral purification and spiritual renewal, as the basis for undertaking the reformation of Zen. In this context, I suggest making a basic distinction between mechanical or liturgical repentance, referred to in some texts as *zange metsuzai* (terminating transgressions through repentance), and the more self-reflective and open-ended attitude of *Zangedō* (creative pathway of repentance). The latter notion is a term borrowed from Kyoto school thinker Tanabe Hajime, Nishida Kitarō's foremost disciple known for his Pure Land background and emphasis on the act of repentance, or metanoesis (as influenced by early Christian theology), in a prominent book published at the conclusion of World War II. Tanabe's *Zangedō toshite no tetsugaku* (Philosophy as Repentance), which appeared near the close of 1945, was the thinker's opportunity to express regret and remorse and to recommend methods of repentance for reversing deficient Buddhist attitudes and achieving reform. Nishida died that year and was not able to respond to the end of the war, so one can only speculate how he would have reacted. There are indications that he might have gone in the direction of expressing an awareness of wrongdoing and regret like Tanabe, as there are historical reconstructions suggesting that Nishida's approach was, especially behind the scenes, not nearly as problematic as has been charged. Or perhaps he would have ended up dismissing and refusing to address the matter like another of his disciples, Nishitani Keiji.

In any case, *zange metsuzai* is taken here to represent the skin. It is a superficial, facile approach that implies that an externally based ritual can rid a person or institution of impurity and eradicate any sense of sin and guilt. *Zangedō*, on the other hand, represents the marrow because it conveys a thoroughgoing, internal introspection and investigation of the roots of wrong-doing and the means of overcoming this tendency and undertaking the good. However, it is necessary to keep in mind that, as we have seen in previous discussions, skin and marrow can easily end up being reversed from different perspectives or due to various applications of the respective approaches. Nothing is quite what it seems to be when examined for its full implications and repercussions.

Janus or Jekyll and Hyde?

In considering the issues of Zen writes and rites, we have found a basic sense of compatibility and at times complementarity, despite some lingering conflict and controversy, between TZN and HCC regarding the questions of meaning and sense (or nonsense) in Zen literature and of whether a decline due to commercialism is evident in Zen popular religiosity. On the matter of writes, the HCC dissolution thesis is critical of the elusive, hard-to-decipher quality of traditional Zen literature. But the realization thesis shows that the extensive literary production of the Sung Chinese and Kamakura Japanese eras demonstrates the ingenuity and creativity of classical Zen thinkers, as well as their ability to absorb influences from a variety of non-Buddhist intellectual and aesthetic movements that pervaded East Asian culture. On the matter of rites, the HCC emphasis on the range of ritual practices in prayer temples further supports the TZN view of Zen's flexibility and adaptability in assimilating native gods and rituals that strengthen the overall appeal and dissemination of the sect. However, the issue of incorporating indigenous rites does open up an area in which conflict emerges. While TZN apologists tend to slough off references to folk religiosity as a concession to local styles that does not detract from Zen ideology, some, though by no means all, HCC critics accuse Zen of rather shamelessly compromising its ideals of worldly detachment and renunciation for the sake of self-promotion.

In considering the issue of rights, there emerges a rather fierce sense of hostility and betrayal.[1] TZN advocates find in Zen a socially vibrant tradition that holds the secret to spiritual healing for an ailing world, whereas HCC critics see Zen as a morally complacent institution in need of drastic changes before it can claim to contribute to modern society. Divisiveness over these views has resulted in a Leonard Cohen–esque "war" about the war. In this battle, TZN maintains that Zen rhetoric, with its paradox and wordplay conveying nonduality and freedom from mental constraints as preserved in recorded sayings and kōan commentaries, is a supremely inventive form of literature that Western culture has only achieved in the past century, in part due to Eastern influences, including Zen-oriented literary forms such as kōans and haiku. HCC, on the other hand, tends to view Zen writes as deliberate ambiguity and obfuscation for the sake of concealing its true intention to support unworthy social causes. This purposeful hocus-pocus, as Arthur Koestler has charged, resembles Orwellian double-think, which "means the power of holding two contradictory beliefs in one's mind simultaneously, and accepting both of them."[2] In the case of Zen, the ideal of harmony (which devolved into cooperation with and capitulation to political authority) and the reality of conflict and discord (regarding support for imperialism) seem to coexist, but with a sense of disconnect that is deliberately suppressed and hidden from view or simply forgotten.

If Zen is indeed two-sided, or two-faced, is it the double visage of Janus, as Williams's TZN-oriented "other side" image indicates, or the schizophrenia of Jekyll and Hyde, as HCC advocate Victoria has suggested of a prominent modern Zen master's darker side? Janus, the Roman god of gates and entranceways, represents the unity of beginnings and endings, and hence is portrayed with a double-faced head, each looking in opposite directions. Worshiped at crucial junctures, such as planting season and the beginning of the harvest, birth and marriage, and other periods of origins and/or fruitions that are important events in a person's or community's life, Janus also symbolizes the transition between primitive society and civilization, and between the countryside and the city, peace and war, and life and death.[3]

Whereas Janus, much in the style of Asian nondual theology, bridges gaps and unifies opposites in a constructive way, Robert Louis Stevenson's *Dr. Jekyll and Mr. Hyde* tells the story of Jekyll's ultimately flawed and failed struggle with his own hidden evil self lurking within, which captures the inescapable duality of human personality and behavior that inevitably comes to haunt even those who on the surface seem to have an unblemished character. According to one essay:

> Without much scientific detail or verisimilitude, through the inges-
> tion of a concoction of powders, tincture, and salt, Jekyll releases the
> character who resides in him—the thoroughly wicked Mr. Hyde.
> Jekyll may then, via Mr. Hyde, enact all the diabolical desires he
> otherwise suppresses. G. K. Chesterton wrote[,] "The real stab of the
> story is not the discovery that one man is two men, but in the dis-
> covery that two men are one man."[4]

This type of oneness underlying the apparent separation of the Jekyll and Hyde personas makes a mockery of the ideals embraced by the TZN perspective.

Is there a way out of the impasse regarding the Janus versus Jekyll/Hyde images? How can the Jekyll-like positive elements of Zen practice favored by TZN, such as naturalism, environmentalism, thriftiness, and commitment to human rights and social work, be salvaged in light of acknowledging the sometimes devastating criticism of HCC that the Hyde-like quality of Zen has endorsed discrimination and nationalism? It is essential not to sacrifice or diminish one side, and not to overlook or bypass the other side. We could try to apply the simple metaphor of a swinging pendulum to understand the situation of discourses by and about Zen. According to this model, for a time, the pendulum was pointing in the direction of traditionalism, and then it swung in the opposition direction, pointing to criticism, so perhaps it could now swing back toward the middle and find a happy compromise. However, the problem in evoking this image is that there does not appear to be a single pendulum that tends to one extreme or the other and then naturally seeks out a point of moderation. Rather, there now appear to be two separate pendulums, each stuck at the extreme angle and hardly swinging at all.[5]

In another work, Stevenson shows a different possible outcome of grappling with inner moral turmoil. Whereas the Jekyll and Hyde story ends in tragedy and hopelessness about the human condition such that base instincts and a lack of values and integrity cannot be overcome, in a story about criminal behavior, "Markheim," Stevenson explores not only misdeeds, but also the themes of "censure, conscience, redemption, moral uplift."[6] Here, he shows that the way to bridge the gap between polarized elements of one's personality and to heal the wounds is through an authentic internal process of undertaking repentance to gain redemption.

In pursuit of redemptive experience, we find that Nishitani demands confession of other faiths, including Christianity, but not necessarily of Zen, which is said to transcend the matter. However, Critical Buddhism has demanded that Zen undergo repentance in order to lay a theoretical ground for social reform. Critical Buddhism has both reflected and influenced the fact that most sects of Buddhism in Japan, known disparagingly as "funerary Buddhism," are involved in examining and seeking ways to rehabilitate themselves from the hypocrisy embedded in the kaimyō system.[7] Following a period of uproar and ongoing protests regarding burakumin rights in the 1980s, Sōtō Zen began to realize that it had been performing this ritual function for the lower classes in a reprehensible fashion, and critical Buddhism became one of the vehicles for change.

A report on the impact of discriminatory tendencies, which was commissioned by Eiheiji temple in the early 1990s, began with a specific focus on abuses in religious practices and investigated whether the roots of injustice are to be found in basic Buddhist doctrines and attitudes, and if so, how they can be overcome. This sectarian study went on to speak of the need to undertake a profound repentance for the mistreatment of the outcast community by recognizing that Zen needed to exercise confession and self-criticism in examining and correcting the abuse of its ideals.[8]

The Eiheiji document has been part of a wide-ranging admission of guilt offered by Sōtō Zen related to missionary work in Korea[9] and to support for World War II. This has also included the new recognition of Uchiyama Gudō as an honored figure in the history of the sect. Uchiyama formerly was a pariah because of the controversy he generated in the early twentieth century by protesting the imperial government, which eventually led to his execution. As stated by scholar and sectarian leader Nara Yasuaki, former president of Komazawa University:

> In 1992 the Sōtō Headquarters published an official acknowledgement of guilt for its role in supporting military conquest and an apology for the activities of Sōtō missionaries in occupied territories, especially Korea. Sōtō temples now perform annual memorial rites on behalf of the victims of Sōtō religious discrimination and Japanese military aggression.[10]

Yet the continued existence of so-called eta-dera (outcast temples) and eta-za (outcast seats) in some areas, well over a century since the burakumin were legally "liberated" in 1871, testifies to the great difficulties involved in weeding out centuries of ingrained behavior. Does this indicate that proclamations of contrition and culpability, along with the implementation of supposedly reform-minded rites, cannot help but be disingenuous? Do they represent little more than the artificial posturing of political correctness, and empty words or lip service used to save the hides of individuals and institutions put on the defensive by external pressures from forces of protest and criticism? Modern world history has consistently shown that legal methods can neither support discrimination when there is resistance nor wipe it away when there is a reluctance or unwillingness to change.

History of Form and Formless Repentance

What is the path to awaken and activate a genuine sense of repentance? Expressing regret and remorse for deep-seated amoral and antinomian behavioral trends requires a wholehearted and open-ended examination of the roots of discrimination and a willingness to challenge and change, rather than merely reluctantly concede, the problematic side of Buddhist teachings and institutional organizations. The questions of what constitutes genuine repentance, or lack of it, and of whether Zen is capable of enacting a constructive approach, given its historical and theoretical predilections, have become an important focal point in debates between the TZN and HCC standpoints.

The traditional Zen outlook claims to offer a middle way between mechanical repentance, associated with traditional Vinaya rituals of confession, and antistructural iconoclasm, associated with the doctrine of formless repentance as developed in the *Platform Sutra*. However, it seems clear that claims of a middle path have not always borne the desired results. What has gone astray, and how can it be corrected? Who or what principle is to serve as the guiding light for Zen to acknowledge and reform its deficient attitudes by accepting responsibility for the past while constructively offering alternative solutions suited to problems plaguing contemporary society?

A consideration of this issue calls for a brief yet broad-based critical appraisal of the role of repentance in the history of Zen thought. Table E.1 outlines how the polarity between form repentance and formless repentance has evolved historically, through an overview of the development of different thinkers, works, schools, and movements, as will be explained more fully below. This helps to explain the reasons for an apparent deemphasis on form repentance because of proclamations of irreverence and iconoclasm supporting formless repentance functions in a tradition that otherwise proclaims itself

TABLE E.I. Historical Overview of Trends in Repentance, with Possibilities for Middle-Way Perspective versus a More Problematic Compromise.

Form Repentance	Time Period	Formless Repentance
Vinaya	early Ch'an	*Platform Sutra*
Tsung-mi	T'ang China	Hung-chou school
punishment	CMK era (Sung)	emphasis on abbacy
precepts	medieval Japan	iconoclastic approach
mechanical ritual	modern Japan	*Shushōgi*
HCC ◄	recent scholarship	► TZN
	► *zange metsuzai* (problematic ◄	
	compromise) versus	
	Zangedō (constructive middle way)	

to be based on strict discipline and harsh punishment for offenses. It also shows how the question of deemphasis is related to an understanding of the current debate between the TZN and HCC views.

Like all schools of Chinese Buddhism, Ch'an monastic life inherited the Vinaya rituals of fortnightly confession and summer retreat from early forms of Buddhism, and these practices are still maintained in Zen training monasteries in Japan today. As with some of the T'ang dynasty schools, especially T'ien-t'ai, Chinese Ch'an also questioned the validity of traditional styles of repentance in favor of the notion of the nonproduction of karma. T'ien-t'ai teachings integrated repentance involving ritual ablutions in sacred chambers into the practice of the four samadhi meditations. This was based on Chih-i's fundamental distinction in the *Fa-hua san-mei ch'an-i* (*Taishō* 46:949a–955c) between form repentance, or repenting for misdeeds committed in the realm of phenomena, and formless repentance, or recognizing the principle of the absolute nature of reality. Formless repentance means that since all things, including sins and karmic transgressions, are empty of own-being (Skt. *svabhava*) in the realm of principle or the absolute beyond concrete phenomena, the need to repent for actual misdeeds is vitiated.[11]

Perhaps influenced by this approach, the *Platform Sutra* implements the transmission rite by enjoining the assembly of monks to "receive with your own bodies the formless precepts"[12] and to undertake formless repentance, which obliterates negative karma built up from unwholesome activities. The text's view of the nonproduction of evil, which stresses that one's apparent karmic burden must be seen as originally empty and thus part of the purity of self-nature, is in accord with basic Mahayana Buddhist doctrines and seems to coincide with the T'ien-t'ai view of defining formless repentance. The main difference, however, is that whereas the T'ien-t'ai school acknowledges the enduring role of form repentance as a necessary check and balance for monastic behavior while also advocating its transcendence, the *Platform Sutra* denies this function altogether as part of the world of delusion that must be rejected because it prohibits a realization of transcendence.

Once the basic opposition between form and formless repentance was incorporated into the Zen outlook, the Hung-chou lineage led by Ma-tsu became the mainstream approach in the Chinese Ch'an school in emphasizing the priority of formlessness by virtue of the fact that the dharma does not require seeking. It further supported the lack of any need for repentance (despite the fact that Ma-tsu's follower Pai-chang is said to have created the discipline-oriented CMK text). It did not take long for this outlook to be severely criticized and condemned in the ninth century by Tsung-mi, who surveyed the various Ch'an views and found this one particularly wanting. According to Tsung-mi:

> Now, the Hongzhou school says that greed, hatred, precepts [*sila*], and concentration [*samadhi*] are of the same kind, which is the function of Buddha-nature. They fail to distinguish between ignorance and enlightenment, the inverted and the upright . . . since water can both carry a boat or sink it, its merits and faults are remarkably different.[13]

Therefore, for Tsung-mi, the Hung-chou lineage threatens to sink the boat of Buddhism because it wavers in making a commitment to ethical responsibility.

By the Sung dynasty, the Ch'an school, having survived the suppression of Buddhism and other foreign religions in the 840s and emerged the stronger for it, was the dominant religious institution of the period. Ch'an seemed to recognize that it was necessary to seek a middle way that would encompass yet remain unbound by the alternatives of form and formless repentance. The aim of the *Ch'an-men kuei-shih* (CMK), which is attributed to Pai-chang but was no doubt crafted in the late tenth century and which served as the paradigm for later monastic rules texts, especially the *Ch'an-yüan ch'ing-kuei*, was to find a compromise not so much by locating a middle ground as by straddling the extremes. The CMK approach was stricter than the strictest discipline through enacting a system of potentially severe punishments culminating in banishment, so that even form repentance would not compensate for a major offense. It was also freer than the freest approach in resting authority entirely in the hands of the abbot, who as a living buddha venerated in the Dharma Hall had no need to offer repentance.

The CMK emphasis on the incontestable freedom of the abbacy was also supported by other literature from the period, especially the hagiographical narratives in the transmission of the lamp records about the exploits of individual masters, which reinforced Zen's highly individualistic and iconoclastic attitude. This approach gives free rein to the all-powerful master, thus giving rise to antinomianism that can stand in violation of conventional norms and social ethics, while also creating a contradictory, legalistic subjugation of rank-and-file monks whose behavior is subordinated to the rule of the abbot.

The CMK's attempt to straddle the extremes of harsh punishment for monks and supreme freedom for the abbot had the impact, whether intentional or not, of enhancing the deemphasis on repentance instigated by the *Platform Sutra* and sustained by the Hung-chou school. The ritual was seen as either not a strong enough vehicle for reform or an unnecessary, obsolete rite. In either case, its role was significantly downplayed. Nevertheless, the practice of the recitation of the vows during fortnightly and summer retreat rituals was perpetuated in what can be termed a mechanical fashion, since it may not have led to a thoroughgoing investigation of wrongdoing and the way to create a sense of spiritual renewal. Rather, confessional vows were primarily performed as a means of maintaining continuity with age-old Buddhist monastic traditions. Meanwhile, the rationale for the freedom of the abbot continued in the Sung dynasty, although this period was not known for eccentric, iconoclastic behavior to the extent of the T'ang Chinese or medieval Japanese masters.

As Zen entered Japan at the beginning of the thirteenth century, the double tendency of continuing the ritual of repentance on the level of monastic guidelines for behavior while debunking its merit as a tool for spiritual awakening was maintained. Eisai and Dōgen, to a lesser extent, stressed the importance of the precepts. For Eisai's Rinzai approach, the 250 *Pratimoksha* precepts were introduced and required along with the bodhisattva vows because this is what he had experienced in China. For Dōgen's Sōtō approach, a new, streamlined system of 16 precepts was initiated, which Dōgen claimed he inherited from his Chinese mentor Ju-ching.[14] Both Eisai and Dōgen vigorously condemned the Daruma school, which was proscribed by the government as early as the 1190s, although its followers lingered for several decades, because it dispensed with the precepts altogether in a radical reading of the notion of formless repentance. These criticisms of the Daruma school echoed Tsung-mi's condemnation of the Hung-chou school, demonstrating a pattern of internal criticism that has surfaced in recent years with the works of

Ichikawa Hakugen and Critical Buddhism. At the same time, as part of the discourse and debate about the priorities for religious practice leading to enlightenment, it became clear that Eisai and to a larger extent Dōgen had a preference for zazen perhaps taking priority over discipline. According to a frequently cited passage in the *Shōbōgenzō zuimonki*, Dōgen rhetorically asks, "When doing zazen, what precepts are not upheld, and what merits are not produced?"[15]

Medieval and early modern Zen practice was also greatly influenced by various elements in Japanese religiosity, including aestheticism and *bushidō* culture, which helped give rise to such luminaries as Ikkyū and Takuan, who in different ways disregarded and flaunted the traditional precepts. The greatness of Zen in these periods while the sect was spreading through the assimilation of esoteric Buddhist and popular syncretic (Buddhist/Shinto amalgamations) religiosity was due in large part to creative geniuses who broke the mold of conventional forms of behavior. These figures, who were inspiring in their literary and martial accomplishments, gained prominence by reconnecting with tendencies imported from China, which gave poetic license to the authority of masters whose activities frequently departed from or flaunted societal norms.

Among the exceptions in Ch'an/Zen writings to the absence or deemphasis on repentance have been Northern school texts such as the *Ta-sheng wu-sheng fang-p'ien men* and *Leng-ch'ieh shih-tzü chi*; two *Shōbōgenzō* fascicles, the "Keisei-sanshoku" and "Sanjigo"; Ming dynasty monastic revival texts by Chu-hung; and anecdotal, *monogatari*-like writings that refer to social leaders, such as samurai in Tokugawa Japan, who saw the error of their ways and repented before converting to Buddhism. An example of the last category is the case of Kume Heinai, enshrined at a subtemple of Sensōji temple in Asakusa, Tokyo, who repented for his life of killing people by converting to Zen and practicing meditation. At his death, he donated his zazen image made by a sculptor for burial at the temple so that people could tread upon it before it was properly set up. Eventually, Heinai became a folk deity to whom people pray in search of a future spouse by writing down their wish; this process is based on a pun as both "treading upon" and "writing upon" are pronounced *fumi-tsukeru*.[16] Nevertheless, Zen generally stands in contrast with several other Chinese or Japanese Buddhist contemplative traditions that did strongly emphasize repentance, such as the T'ien-t'ai/Tendai school. Also included in this category are miscellaneous practices based on a variety of mythological sutras dedicated to the supernatural powers of bodhisattvas, who have the capacity to grant mercy according to devotional and esoteric Buddhism. Another example is transectarian popular Buddhist *setsuwa* (morality) tales of drifters and philanderers who attained religious awakening through encountering and repenting their own sins.

In the modern period, Zen and other Buddhist sects were dramatically affected by a number of factors involving new restrictions regarding the traditional monastic institution and its practices. First, the Meiji era campaign of *haibutsu kishaku*, which denigrated Buddhist icons, as well as the program of *shinbutsu bunri*, which separated Buddhist temples from Shinto shrines, had the combined effect of delimiting the role of Buddhism in society and relegating it to secondary status compared to Shinto, which was supported by the state. Furthermore, a set of government instructions known as *nikujiki saitai*, which required monks to eat meat and to marry, forced clerics into a more lay lifestyle, while at the same time competition with Christian evangelism had the inverse yet complementary effect of encouraging Zen to improve its outreach to the nonclerical, lay community. All of these trends, which encouraged new styles of practice, led to a significant decline in the number of monks adhering to traditional monastic training and discipline.

A key text in the modern period reflecting the trend toward a new emphasis on lay Zen and the consequent rise in importance of the prayer temple is the Sōtō school's *Shushōgi*. This was created in the 1890s era by lay and ecclesial leaders who culled and edited Dōgen's sayings, mainly from the *Shōbōgenzō*, and it is still studied and recited during ceremonies by nearly all members of the sect.[17] However, the result was quite different from the source text, which puts a strong emphasis on zazen taking precedence over the precepts or other kinds of ritual activity, including repentance. Instead, the *Shushōgi*, targeting a general audience in an era of rivalry with other forms of lay Buddhism in light of Christian influences, does not mention meditation even a single time, apparently in the assumption that its primary readers had little time for or interest in this practice.[18] Rather, it emphasizes the role of *zange metsuzai*, a term featured in numerous scriptures, which implies the purification and eradication of evil karma via repentance obtained through the power of forgiveness of compassionate buddhas, bodhisattvas, and patriarchs.

Vinaya rituals of confession tend to operate within a closed ritual circle in the sense that they refer to repentance for transgressions committed against the Buddhist samgha and its precepts. Both the *Platform Sutra* and *Shushōgi* as examples of prominent classical and modern Zen texts seek to move beyond the ritual circle by highlighting the transformative capacity of self-nature (C. *chien-hsing*, J. *kenshō*) or Buddha-nature in providing redemption. These two texts may seem worlds apart since the former is by and for monks and justifies their abandonment of form repentance, while the latter is primarily geared toward the lay community who are instructed in the benefits of a mechanical approach to repentance. But both can be seen as expressions of formless repentance in stressing that an underlying metaphysical principle beyond karma is more relevant and effective in releasing one from a sense of sin than the act of confessing transgressions in the realm of form.

The strength of the approaches in the *Platform Sutra* and *Shushōgi* lies in their clarification of the soteriological significance of formless repentance, which focuses on a realization of emptiness surpassing and purifying actual deeds. But the weakness is due to their neglect of the ethical implications of deemphasizing form repentance, or of being aware and overcoming actual misdeeds. In that sense, these texts are not successful in breaking through the ritual cycle to a more expansive view of repentance, but rather tend to have the deleterious effect of continuing to rationalize and support constraints on its role. Therefore, the two texts, which are among the few Zen works that deal extensively with the topic of repentance, actually provide a reason to turn away from the need for recognizing the power of confession for transgressions in the traditional Buddhist sense, since the nonbeing of unwholesomeness is emphasized. Again, the case of the *Shushōgi* is complicated because its widespread use in popular religious functions also seems to encourage lay believers to accept *zange metsuzai* as a panacea for moral offenses, and this could be interpreted as calling for a belief in the value of a mechanical ritualistic approach, which the *Platform Sutra* opposes altogether.

Relating Repentance to TZN and HCC Views

With this overview of the legacy in mind, we can now situate the TZN standpoint as a kind of contemporary reflection of the notion of formless repentance. This was the mainstream approach expressed in the primary scriptures from different eras, including the *Platform Sutra* from the T'ang, the CMK, the transmission of the lamp records, other literature from Sung China and Kamakura Japan, and some examples from the early modern and modern eras. TZN has defended Zen against the charge of amorality that can be associated with the approach of formless repentance, which arises from denying ethics as an obstacle to enlightenment that must be transcended, by endorsing what has been called a "virtue ethic." According to Christopher Ives's explanation, "The pivotal question is what one should *be*, not what one should *do*. Zen goes a step beyond ethics in the ordinary sense in that it calls into question the moral agent rather than simply dwelling on a critique of the agent's actions."[19]

This contemporary notion based on realizing an interior quality emphasizes what sort of person one wants to be rather than being governed by an external set of rules and regulations, and seems to echo the way some traditional writings have advocated going beyond monastic codes that cover mainly the etiquette rather than the essence of temple life. Instead of focusing on moral principles, virtue ethics highlights the behavioral attitudes of the individual that are not necessarily bound by objectivity.[20] Virtue ethics is really an example of metaethics, which constructs appropriate ethical solutions and environmental reforms not by addressing them directly based on standardized, across-the-board criteria, but by adjusting individual attitudes to particular situational contexts. It claims to be based on a higher level of subjective realization that is superior to conventional ethics, which are derived from objective standards of assessment. A recent advocate of this approach said that the "living dharma" is not divisible into categories, and furthermore, "The Zen Buddhist does not ask what is right and wrong but rather, 'What am I to do at this point?' She has no opinion to put forth. She has learned not to acquire answers and to hold her questions open wherever she goes."[21]

The standpoint of HCC, on the other hand, reflects form repentance, which is at times unforgiving of the misdeeds of others and yet has its own ax to grind in advocating a harshly critical approach to some aspects of Zen. For example, Brian Victoria's work is admirable in uncovering the deficiencies of Zen masters leading up to World War II. Anyone reading *Zen at War* and *Zen War Stories* who is interested or intrigued by Japanese religion and culture as a model for behavior that is impartial and free from attachment will probably be disturbed by the words and deeds cited extensively in these works. The deficient ideas and actions on the part of Zen masters during the war are portrayed not as exceptions to the rule or unusual cases but as the widespread ethos of at least a "lost" generation or two of monks subverting spirituality for political partisanship.

However, Victoria in his two books does not take the opportunity to point beyond the regrettable shortcomings and glaring warts toward a compromise view of Zen and its complex connections with society, in a way that works constructively with the strengths as well as the weaknesses of the tradition. He endorses a Marxist and pacifist agenda that sees no hope for any ideology that falls short of the ideals he recommends. For those who care deeply about Zen and its place in Japan and the world, the challenge is to help define Zen's role creatively lest the tradition get buried under the avalanche of criticism or, contrariwise, lest the research behind these books gets relegated to the realm of sensationalism.

The Critical Buddhist project with its sometimes excessive rhetoric and hyperbole has been attacked for creating an inflated sense of purity and authenticity regarding Dōgen's later thought, after he rejected an offer from the shogun to lead a temple in the new capital of Kamakura and decided to return and remain ensconced in the mountains. Critical Buddhism claims this period of Dōgen's thought is free from the infection that plagues the notion of original enlightenment in other forms of East Asian Buddhism. Simultaneously, it denigrates much of the Sōtō sect's history after Dōgen, along with a host of prominent modern scholars of Buddhism, for making compromises with assimilative trends and amoral ideologies. For this reason, Critical Buddhism may appear exclusivist or even combative toward most of the already polarized and fragmented Chinese and Japanese Buddhist schools. Many feel that critical Buddhism is simply trying to "save" Dōgen from a host of challenges (although Hakamaya has claimed a higher regard for Hōnen as an advocate and model for social reform). The Critical Buddhist approach appears all too ready to abandon Sōtō and other syncretistic forms of East Asian Buddhism— as if any figure, Sakyamuni and Dōgen included, is immune from charges of absorbing influences from his surroundings. Although Critical Buddhism does not intend to foster a purely sectarian agenda, it is perhaps inevitable that its tone of being *engagé* and even *enragé* creates an impression of us versus them.

From *Jigo Jitoku* to *Jiko Hihan*

Both the TZN and HCC approaches seem trapped in the well-established pattern of polarization by either advocating too much freedom based on subjectivity or enforcing too great an expectation for discipline imposed from external regulations, without coming to a genuinely constructive middle way.[22] Unfortunately, the main parties among TZN apologists and HCC critics seem unable to get past an impasse in which they are not willing to give ground based on trying to uphold common principles, even though this renders them unable to look for constructive solutions or find a middle path resonant with the strengths and weakness of Zen theory and practice. How is it possible to remove this obstacle in order to challenge and overcome the polarity that separates form and formless repentance embedded in the respective TZN and HCC perspectives? A key to resolving this matter is to recognize that, despite their apparent conflict, both approaches—formless repentance based on neglect of ritual confession due to the priority of spiritual transcendence and form repentance based on ceremonial efficacy in which *repentance is ritually made toward Buddhism* as in the case of correcting oneself and accepting punishment after violating precepts—result in an indifference to overcoming moral concerns. An important consequence is the tendency to overlook the value of repentance as an ever-renewing vehicle for self-reproach, self-criticism, and self-correction.

However, it is not always the case that repentance functions in such a positive way. Indeed, the statement about the problems that derive from not having a sufficient degree of repentance is not meant to imply the converse, that is, an emphasis on repentance necessarily and without equivocation leads to ethical responsibility and reform. For example, the Jōdo Shinshū sect probably has shown more interest and follow-through than has Zen in rectifying the discrimination problem beginning with the *Suiheisha* (equality) movements in the 1920s. But this may reflect the fact that in the Tokugawa era *danka* (parish) system, an overwhelming number of untouchables were assigned to this sect, especially the Nishi Honganji branch. The legacy of the Edo sociopolitical situation fostered a heightened concern with managing a sector of the population, but this did not necessarily reflect an authentic commitment to repenting for the practice of discrimination.

In any case, the implications of repentance or reform for other schools of Buddhism must be examined on a case-by-case basis. The main point for our purposes is that a systematic deemphasis on repentance in Zen beginning with the *Platform Sutra* has perhaps helped to reflect and promote either antinomian trends or a general lack of regard for the importance of morality. While this may be conducive to the attainment of spiritual freedom on an individual basis, if unchecked on an institutional level it can end in counterproductive or even reprehensible forms of behavior. The tendency to turn away from direct dealings with ethical responsibility and decision making reinforces the status quo and supports the complacent outlook of *jigo jitoku*, defined as "you get what you deserve." This attitude implies that since each and every person in the end gets exactly what they deserve by virtue of the mechanics of karmic causality, there is no need to go out of one's way to change or reform the social order as it now stands. To some extent, Zen has cultivated this attitude deliberately, at least on a rhetorical level, in the name of a virtue-ethical perspective that claims to transcend conventional standards of good and evil in a quasi-Nietzschean sense, but this rationale has a hollow ring in light of Zen's acknowledged participation in discrimination, nationalism, imperialism, and corporatism. At the same time, the overreaction and overcompensation of having such severe penalties and punishments to enforce the system does not create balance nor promote moderation.

Instead of trying to compromise by embracing extremes of subjective freedom and objective discipline, it is necessary to try to find a true middle way by asking, what is the fundamentally strong suit of Zen, and how can it be brought to fruition in spite of Zen's weaknesses? Recent reflections by concerned Buddhists on the issue of discrimination suggest the emergence of an alternative view that looks beyond the ritual circle by virtue of a broader awareness of ethical implications. This avoids or alters both the antinomian implications of formless repentance and the legalistic implications of form repentance by transmuting the dynamic act of repenting into an open-ended commitment to social rectification and responsibility.

One key to this view is that Zen has claimed a contrast between the Christian approach, which is interpreted as a mere apology (*ayamari*) that seeks automatic forgiveness and dispensation from a higher authority in a fashion resembling the deficiencies of *zange metsuzai*, and the genuine Buddhist approach, which is focused on reflection (*hansei*) and self-transformation.[23] East Asia is often referred to as a "shame" culture rather than a "guilt" culture in that Confucian influences stress the importance of peer pressure and social sanctions in curbing misconduct and guiding behavior through external means, whereas a sense of wrongdoing is internalized in Western society. However, Zen at the level of its marrow seeks to reverse this assumption by highlighting the role of internal mechanisms of self-doubt and self-discovery that can be referred to collectively as *jiko hihan* (self-criticism in the authentic sense). Zen's strength lies in disputing alternative approaches—Eastern or Western—that appear reduced to the skin of artificial, superficial, externally induced remedies for complex inner states of mind.

On *Zangedō*

In light of the various meanings listed in an intriguing typology of Buddhist repentance rituals developed by David Chappell, which distinguishes between mechanical and spiritual and between inner- and outer-directed styles, I suggest that the term *zange* can best be understood by making a basic distinction between two forms.[24] One is *zange metsuzai* in the ceremonial, liturgical sense encompassing remorse and punishment for wrongdoing as in the *Uposatha* and *Pravarana* rituals, and the other is a dynamic process of self-reflection and self-renewal referred to as *Zangedō*, to borrow the term which forms the centerpiece of the postwar philosophy of Tanabe Hajime. Ironically, the modern Zen *Shushōgi*, in speaking of *zange metsuzai* as one of the five main sections of the text, seems to suggest a mechanical model of repentance based on devotionalism, whereas Tanabe's Pure Land approach appears more individualistic and intuitive in putting a strong emphasis on a person's change of heart, spiritual "turning," or transformation in the religious quest.

Zangedō, which involves a profound personal sense of self-criticism (*jiko hihan*), implies an existential struggle and coming to terms with one's wrongdoing, which can be applied on both individual and communal levels. In this context, the emphasis on "self" in the compound terms cited above is meant to suggest an internal process of discovery and awakening without a non-Buddhist reification of ego or an exclusive focus on particularity as opposed to universality. The approach of *Zangedō* is at once reclusive in the sense of wholeheartedly exploring interiority yet being socially engaged, transcendent in going beyond the mundane, and trans-descendent in returning to implications in the everyday world, and it also encompasses voluntary and required aspects of repentance.

The distinction between *zange metsuzai* and *Zangedō* further encompasses the distinction between repentance *toward* Buddhism due to preceptual transgressions and repentance *for* Buddhism because of its wrongdoings vis-à-vis society at large. Therefore, the transformation of *zange metsuzai* into *Zangedō* requires an authentic encountering of social problems in a way that demands an abandonment of the traditional Zen deemphasis on form repentance. This leads to a more general, socially oriented sense of repenting *for* Buddhism, especially for its not taking full responsibility for nor correcting its contributions to social discrimination and prewar imperialism. Whereas *zange metsuzai* operates within the closed circle of the monastic institution, *Zangedō* open-endedly extends traditional monastic ritual into the realm of social responsibility and commitment to reform.

Overturning social problems at their roots involves a sustained self-examination based on *Zangedō*, which in contrast to the *Platform Sutra*, stresses the underlying inseparability of form and formless repentance. Understood in its authentic, self-reflective sense rather than as a facile, automatic confession that would constitute Zen skin, repentance as Zen marrow can become the basis of a synthesis of the Zen and Pure Land, Mahayana and Theravada, and Buddhist and Christian world views. Tanabe writes, "The turning point for a new beginning lies in *zange*. Without it, we have no way to rebuild [society]."[25] According to this injunction, authentic repentance covering both the concrete or relative and ideal or absolute realms may not only help to free Zen, including the disparity between the TZN and HCC standpoints, and other sects, but can enable Buddhism to help liberate society as a whole through a genuinely moral call to action. If appropriately interpreted and applied, this provides a key to a dynamic method of adjusting to endless conflicts.

Zangedō in turn responds to the demand of American thinker William James, one of the first commentators on worldwide mystical traditions, who has advocated the inseparability of mysticism and morality and highlighted the inability of mystics to escape from taking credit or blame for social responsibility.

Following James, it is necessary for Zen not only to acknowledge passively but also to foster vigorously and continuously to cultivate the profound connection between meditation and society. In that sense, the ahistorical, amoral attitude of Zen mysticism with its antinomian implications is overcome by a renewed commitment to ethical decision making.[26]

At the same time, it must be noted that intellectual historian and cultural critic Takeuchi Yoshimi makes it clear that a false sense of what appears to be a *Zangedō* type of repentance can result in mere conversion (*tenkō*). This represents a path of equivocation, which is exactly what some of those guilty of wartime excesses did in switching sides, in a way that abandons fundamental principles and allows one to take up any outlook deemed necessary by convenience or social pressure because of a lack of moral foundation. Such an attitude is characterized by "the forced recantation of political beliefs on the part of Marxist and left-wing writers in the 1930s," and by the way Buddhists who sympathized with the imperial regime before and during the war eagerly proclaimed their disavowal for militarism afterward.[27] In these unfortunate instances, it appears that marrow became skin, and similar responses in the future would allow Zen to slip back into a state of moral stagnation by forsaking the difficult, castor oil path of resistance for the easier, snake oil path of reversal.

In conclusion, if Zen is able to avoid the problem Takeuchi depicts and to demonstrate convincingly that it has the capacity within its own cycle of literary writes and ceremonial rites to correct the wrongs it has perpetuated, for which it must be held accountable, it can vigorously pursue a regimen of social rights. From the standpoint of marrow, the abbot would no longer be seen as an autocratic figure prowling the Dharma Hall while making occasional visits to the Samgha Hall within the grounds of the compound, which is a confined and constrained landscape, leaving him naive about and insensitive to the concerns and demands of general society. The corruption and scandal depicted in Mishima Yukio's *Temple of the Golden Pavilion* and evidenced in Zen centers on both sides of the Pacific are then regretted and diminished, if not necessarily altogether overcome. On this basis, the abbot becomes a genuine social leader and reformer who, by virtue of continuously cultivated contemplation, helps to spread and disseminate the dharma, at once for and beyond an ever-expanding samgha.

Notes

CHAPTER I

1. On Buddhism, see Roger-Pol Droit, *The Cult of Nothingness: The Philosophers and the Buddha* (Chapel Hill: University of North Carolina Press, 2003); Gregory Schopen, ed., *Bones, Stones and Buddhist Monks: Collected Papers on the Archaeology, Epigraphy and Texts of Monastic Buddhism in India* (Honolulu: University of Hawaii Press, 1997); Donald Lopez, *Prisoners of Shangri-la: Tibetan Buddhism and the West* (Chicago: University of Chicago Press, 1999); and Bernard Faure, *Chan Insights and Oversights: An Epistemological Critique of the Chan Tradition* (Princeton, NJ: Princeton University Press, 1993). On Taoism, see J. J. Clarke, *The Tao of the West: Western Transformations of Taoist Thought* (London: Routledge, 2000); and for East Asia more generally, see Jonathan Spence, *The Chan's Great Continent: China in Western Minds* (New York: Norton, 1997); and Ian Buruma, *Inventing Japan, 1853–1964* (New York: Modern Library, 2003).

2. See Edward Said, *Orientalism* (New York: Vintage, 1979); and John MacKenzie, *Orientalism: History, Theory and the Arts* (Manchester, England: Manchester University Press, 1995).

3. For example, in the 1970s, post–Vietnam era films such as *Apocalypse Now*, *Enter the Dragon*, *Saint Jack*, and *Yakuza* depicted the demonic side of Asia.

4. Bernard Faure, "The Kyoto School and Reverse Orientalism," in Charles Wei-hsun Fu and Steven Heine, eds., *Japan in Traditional and Postmodern Perspectives* (Albany: State University of New York Press, 1995), pp. 245–281; Ian Buruma and Avishai Margalit, *Occidentalism: The West in the Eyes of Its Enemies* (New York: Penguin, 2004); and Peter N. Dale, *The Myth of Japanese Uniqueness* (New York: St. Martin's, 1986).

5. For example, pre–Cold War era films such as *Lost Horizon* and *Razor's Edge* portrayed Asia as utopian, and *South Pacific* also did so at a time of increased intermarriage in the late 1950s.

6. For example, Edwin Arnold's turn-of-the-century *Light of Asia* (Whitefish, MT: Kessinger, rpt. 1997) on the positive side, and Mishima Yukio's post–World War II *Temple of the Golden Pavilion* on the negative side.

7. Eugen Herrigel, *Zen in the Art of Archery* (New York: Vintage, 1953), p. 8.

8. Ibid., p. 6.

9. See Robert H. Sharf, "Buddhist Modernism and the Rhetoric of Meditative Experience," *Numen* 42/3 (1995): 228–283. Zen seems to have its own special brand of reverse Orientalism, which characterizes other forms of Buddhism and Eastern religions, as well as all forms of mysticism and spirituality as close, but no cigar. See Paul Tillich and Hisamatsu Shin'ichi, "Dialogues, East and West: Paul Tillich and Hisamatsu Shin'ichi (Part One)," *Eastern Buddhist* 4/2 (1971): 89–107, and "Dialogues, East and West: Paul Tillich and Hisamatsu Shin'ichi (Part Two)," *Eastern Buddhist* 5/2 (1972): 107–128. Also, the classic East Asian utopian vision is expressed by Tao Yuanming in his poetry of reclusion and the narrative "Peach Blossom Spring," about a lost village, discovered by a fisherman wandering in the forest, that exudes a spirit of sharing and a capacity for longevity and harmony.

10. Arthur Koestler, *The Lotus and the Robot* (New York: Harper Colophon, 1960), pp. 245–246.

11. Ibid., p. 282.

12. Richard E. Nisbett, *The Geography of Thought: How Asians and Westerners Think Differently...and Why* (New York: Free Press, 2003). See also Kishore Mahbubani, *Can Asians Think? Understanding the Divide between East and West* (London: Steerforth, 2002); and Randolph Schmid, "Asian, Westerners See World Differently: When Shown a Photo, Chinese Pay More Attention to the Background," available at http://www.chron.com/cs/CDA/ssistory.mpl/nation/3320805, which cites Nisbett. The term "post-Orientalism" used here refers to the idea that Nisbett is trying to be neutral and nonjudgmental, but nevertheless implications and agendas can be read between the lines of his and other related studies. Also see "Asian and American Leadership Styles: How Are They Unique?" *Harvard Business School Working Knowledge* (June 27, 2005), available at http://hbswk.hbs.edu/item/4869.html.

13. Leonard Cohen, "There Is a War," on *New Skin for the Old Ceremony* (1974).

14. *Wu-men kuan*, case 3, in *Taishō shinshū daizōkyō*, ed. Takakusu Junjirō and Watanabe Kaigyoku, 100 vols. (Tokyo: Taishō issaikyō kankōkai, 1924–1932), 48:292c–293a.

15. Kagamishima Genryū, Satō Tatsugen, and Kosaka Kiyū, eds., *Yakuchū Zen'en shingi* (Tokyo: Sōtōshū shūmuchō, 1972). For a partial translation, see Yifa, *The Origins of Buddhist Monastic Codes in China: An Annotated Translation and Study of the Chanyuan Qinggui* (Honolulu: University of Hawaii Press, 2002).

16. Herrigel's wife, Gustie Herrigel, published the book *Zen and the Art of Flower Arrangement*, trans. R. F. C. Hull (rpt., London: Souvenir, 1999), which features a foreword by D. T. Suzuki.

17. The main scholarly trends include (1) filling in historical gaps, including the Northern school and the Daruma school, two movements that quickly became defunct but are crucial for understanding early T'ang Chinese Ch'an and early Kamakura Japanese Zen, respectively, and the Ōbaku sect, the so-called third school of Zen in Japan, which was established during the Tokugawa era; (2) deconstructing through modern historiography the "string of pearls" approach to traditional lineages based on pseudohistorical records; (3) emphasizing the evolution of institutional history and the role of monastic codes; and (4) stressing the infusion in Zen rites of popular religious and folklore practices.

18. See, for example, Victor Sōgen Hori, *Zen Sand: The Book of Capping Phrases for Kōan Practice* (Honolulu: University of Hawaii Press, 2003), especially chapter 4, "The Kōan and the Chinese Literary Game," pp. 41–61.

19. See Ian Reader and George J. Tanabe, Jr., *Practically Religious: Worldly Benefits and the Common Religion of Japan* (Honolulu: University of Hawaii Press, 1998); and Tamamuro Taijō, *Sōshiki Bukkyō* (Tokyo: Daihōrinkaku, 1963).

20. Arthur Koestler, "Neither Lotus nor Robot," *Encounter* 16 (1960): 58, cited in Larry A. Fader, "Arthur Koestler's Critique of D. T. Suzuki's Interpretation of Zen," *Eastern Buddhist* 13/2 (1980): 48. Of course, no less a figure than Socrates was similarly attacked in his own lifetime, lampooned by the comic playwright Aristophanes in *Clouds*, and tried and sentenced to death by a court in Athens. Even his foremost advocate, Plato, acknowledged the problematic implications of the philosophy of Socrates, whose refutation of the arguments of a traditional lawgiver

> shakes him from his convictions and makes him believe that the noble is no more noble than shameful, and the same with the just, the good, and the thing he honored most.... Then when he no longer honors and obeys those convictions, and can't discover the true ones, will he be likely to adopt any other way of life than that which flatters him?...And so, I suppose, from being law abiding he becomes lawless.

From *Republic* 538c–539a, as cited in C. D. C. Reeve, ed., *The Trials of Socrates* (Indianapolis, IN: Hackett, 2002), p. 87.

21. Duncan Ryūken Williams, *The Other Side of Zen: A Social History of Sōtō Zen in Tokugawa Japan* (Princeton, NJ: Princeton University Press, 2005).

22. Ibid., p. 4, citing works by Gregory Schopen on Indian Buddhism, John Kieschnick on Chinese Buddhism, and Robert Sharf and Bernard Faure on Ch'an/Zen. Perhaps the first use of the term was by Schopen in an article originally published in 1987, "Burial *Ad Sanctos* and the Physical Presence of the Buddhas in Early Indian Buddhism: A Study in the Archaeology of Religions," included in *Bones, Stones and Buddhist Monks*, pp. 114–147. According to Schopen, the field of religious studies in general, and Buddhist studies in particular, has put too much emphasis on the history of religions (a misnomer in English based on the German term *Religionswissenschaft*), which is a textual approach, and should put more emphasis on archaeological studies examining "religious constructions and architectures, inscriptions, and art historical remains" (p. 114). What Schopen means by an archaeological

approach is extended to encompass ritual and fieldwork studies by other scholars. For example, Robert E. Buswell, while much of his work is classicist in the positive sense, comments in a book based on his own experiences and observations in a Korean temple:

> By ignoring Buddhism's living tradition, scholars of the religion risk succumbing to the Orientalist dogma described by Edward Said, in which "abstractions about the Orient, particularly those based on texts representing a 'classical' Oriental civilization, are always preferable to direct evidence from modern Oriental realities."

From *The Zen Monastic Experience* (Princeton, NJ: Princeton University Press, 1992), p. 11.

23. James W. Heisig and John C. Maraldo, eds., *Rude Awakenings: Zen, the Kyoto School, & the Question of Nationalism* (Honolulu: University of Hawaii Press, 1995); Paul L. Swanson and Jamie Hubbard, eds., *Pruning the Bodhi Tree: The Storm over Critical Buddhism* (Honolulu: University of Hawaii Press, 1997); Brian (Daizen) Victoria, *Zen at War* (New York: Weatherhill, 1997); and Victoria, *Zen War Stories* (London: RoutledgeCurzon, 2003).

24. Christopher Ives, "What's Compassion Got to Do with It? Determinants of Zen Social Ethics in Japan," *Journal of Buddhist Ethics 12 (2005)*: 37–61.

25. See Heisig and Maraldo, eds., *Rude Awakenings*. Also, Koestler says in the preface that the title of the chapter " 'A Stink of Zen' " is "not a rude expression," since it is based on Zen sayings to the effect that that you should "know your own shit stinks" (p. 12). In the debate on the real meaning of Zen, Suzuki says that the phrase applies to Koestler.

26. James P. Carse, *Finite and Infinite Games: A Vision of Life as Play and Possibility* (New York: Ballantine, 1986), p. 12.

27. See Zeff Bjerken, "On Mandalas, Monarchs, and Mortuary Magic: Siting the Sarvadurgatiparisodhana Tantra in Tibet," *Journal of the American Academy of Religion* 73/3 (2005): 813–842.

28. T. Griffith Foulk, "Sung Controversies concerning the 'Separate Transmission' of Ch'an," in Peter N. Gregory and Daniel A. Getz, eds., *Buddhism in the Sung* (Honolulu: University of Hawaii Press, 1999), p. 287.

29. Peter N. Gregory, *Tsung-mi and the Sinification of Buddhism* (rpt., Honolulu: University of Hawaii Press, 2002), p. 251.

30. The persecution was lifted quickly against Buddhism, but not other foreign religions, although they reemerged in China during the Mongol period of the thirteenth century.

31. See Morten Schlütter, " 'Before the Empty Eon' versus 'A Dog Has No Buddha-nature': Kung-an Use in the Ts'ao-tung Tradition and Ta-hui's Kung-an Introspection Ch'an," in Steven Heine and Dale S. Wright, eds., *The Kōan: Texts and Contexts in Zen Buddhism* (New York: Oxford University Press, 2000), pp. 168–199.

32. Michael Pye, trans., *Emerging from Meditation* (Honolulu: University of Hawaii Press, 1990).

33. Mishima Yukio, *Temple of the Golden Pavilion* (New York: Perigee, 1959).

34. *Life of Oharu*, dir. Mizoguchi Kenji (1964).

35. See Steven Heine, "A Critical Survey of Works on Zen after Yampolsky," *Philosophy East and West* 47/4 (2007): 125–142.

36. Paul Reps and Nyogen Senzaki, comps., *Zen Flesh, Zen Bones: A Collection of Zen and Pre-Zen Writings* (Boston: Tuttle, 1957; rpt., 1998).

37. See Robert H. Sharf, "Sanbōkyōdan: Zen and the Way of the New Religions," *Japanese Journal of Religious Studies* 22/3–4 (1995): 417–458.

38. Hu Shih, "Ch'an (Zen) Buddhism in China: Its History and Method," *Philosophy East and West* 3/1 (1953): 3–24; and Daisetz Teitaro Suzuki, "Zen: A Reply to Hu Shih," *Philosophy East and West* 3/1 (1953): 25–46.

39. Bernard Faure, "Chan and Zen Studies: The State of the Field," in Bernard Faure, ed., *Chan Buddhism in Ritual Context* (London: RoutledgeCurzon, 2003), p. 3.

40. The problem with Hu Shih's approach is that it tried to discover in light of the Tun-Huang finds what the real history of Zen was by using what seemed to be early texts; in other words, the assumption was that the earlier the provenance of the text the more reliable it was historically. However, Zen texts from the outset during the T'ang dynasty were in the business of "inventing tradition," so that, as John R. McRae points out, "in attempting to eliminate later fabrications in favor of an earlier kernel of historical truth, [this] failed to recognize that the true history of Ch'an was to be found in those very processes of creative fabrication. The irony was…that Ch'an texts comprised over a third of all Chinese Buddhist literature," in "Yanagida Seizan's Landmark Work on Chinese Ch'an," *Cahiers d'Extrême-Asie* 7 (1993–1994): 80.

41. Yanagida Seizan, *Shoki zenshū shisho no kenkyū* (Kyoto: Hōzōkan, 1967); and Philip B. Yampolsky, trans., *The Platform Sutra of the Sixth Patriarch: The Text of the Tun-Huang Manuscript* (New York: Columbia University Press, 1967).

42. See the criticism proffered by Critical Buddhism (*Hihan Bukkyō*), in Swanson and Hubbard, eds., *Pruning the Bodhi Tree*.

43. See John R. McRae, *Seeing through Zen: Encounter, Transformation, and Genealogy in Chinese Chan Buddhism* (Berkeley: University of California Press, 2003), especially the chapter "Zen and the Art of Fund-Raising," pp. 101–118.

44. Also see Koestler, "The Lotus and the Robot," *Encounter* 15 (1959): 13–32, a reprint of one of the chapters from the book, and "Neither Lotus nor Robot," *Encounter* 16 (1960): 58–59, which continues the debate with Suzuki. For a more sophisticated critique of Herrigel, see Sharf, "Buddhist Modernism and the Rhetoric of Meditative Experience," esp. pp. 233–235.

45. Koestler points out that the "inevitable Introduction by Professor Suzuki" does not mention Herrigel's Nazi affiliation.

46. See Carlos Castaneda, *The Teachings of Don Juan: A Yaqui Way of Knowledge* (Berkeley: University of California Press, 1968).

47. Herrigel, *Zen in the Art of Archery*, p. 42.

48. Heinrich Dumoulin, *A History of Zen Buddhism* (Boston: Beacon, 1963), p. 290, citing the Gospel of John 1:19. This book was originally published in German

in 1959, and Dumoulin spent the next thirty years more or less rewriting the work until he completed the monumental two-volume study *Zen Buddhism: A History I (India and China)* (New York: Macmillan, 1987) and *Zen Buddhism: A History II (Japan)* (New York: Macmillan, 1990).

49. Koestler, *The Lotus and the Robot*, p. 246.

50. Ibid., p. 274.

51. Khazaria was an early medieval empire in Eastern Europe in which the rulers converted to Judaism, making it necessary to see that most of the world's Jews today are actually descendants of these people, who were forced converts rather than Semites, according to Koestler's controversial thesis.

52. Yamada Shōji, "The Myth of Zen in the Art of Archery," *Japanese Journal of Religious Studies* 28/1–2 (2001): 1–30, derived from an article published in 1999 as "Shinwa toshite no yumi to Zen."

53. *Lost in Translation*, dir. Sofia Coppola (2003).

54. Of course, creative misunderstandings based in part on language gaps have happened before in the history of Zen, such as the example of Dōgen's changing his Chinese mentor's saying "casting off the dust from the mind" to "casting off body-mind," as the phrases are homophones in Japanese pronunciation.

55. Cited in Yamada, "The Myth of Zen in the Art of Archery," p. 24, who notes that this was in a foreword to the German edition that was not included in the 1953 English version. The original German "Es geschossen" appeared in Herrigel's 1948 book but not in the original 1936 essay. Another, more literal Japanese rendering could be "sore ga iru," but we have no way of knowing whether Awa ever used an equivalent to "it" (*sore*), or whether this was fabricated or at least part of a miscommunication or misunderstanding that got created between teacher and student lacking an interpreter and was compounded over the years by a kind of "whispering down the lane" effect.

56. McRae, *Seeing through Zen*, p. xix.

57. The original is in the fifth fascicle of the *Ching-te chuan-teng lu* (*Taishō* 51:240), and the Dōgen passage from *Shōbōgenzō* "Kattō" is in *Dōgen zenji zenshū*, ed. Kawamura Kōdō et al., 7 vols. (Tokyo: Shunjūsha, 1988–1993), 1:416.

58. Ishii Shūdō, *Sōdai zenshū shi no kenkyū* (Tokyo: Daitō shuppansha, 1987), pp. 105–108.

59. *Taishō* 51:196–467.

60. It is important to note that according to the *Leng-chia shih-tzu chi* of the early eighth century, the first patriarch of Ch'an was Gunabhadra, a Mahayana priest from central India who arrived by boat in Canton, with Bodhidharma listed as the second and Hui-k'o as the third patriarch who received transmission via obtaining four scrolls of the *Lankavatara Sutra*. See Yampolsky, trans., *The Platform Sutra of the Sixth Patriarch*, pp. 19–21. Yampolsky points out that no connection between Gunabhadra and Bodhidharma could be found by Hu Shih's historical studies, so that the account is "obviously fictional" and "its absurdity" led it to be dropped from the records for "Ch'an has tended to reject any attributions that were completely untenable."

61. Foulk, "Sung Controversies concerning the 'Separate Transmission' of Ch'an," p. 260.

62. *Dōgen zenji zenshū*, I:418.

63. Reps and Nyogen, *Zen Flesh, Zen Bones*, p. 13.

64. It is interesting to note another example of reification in the modern translation/commentary of case 16 in the *Wu-men kuan* (*Taishō* 48:295a), "The Sound of the Bell and the 7-Piece [Robe]," by Zenkei Shibayama and translated into English by Sumiko Kudo. The verse comment by monk Wu-men is rendered as "If you understand 'it,' all things are One," even though the original literally says "Understand, and all things are one"; in *Zen Comments on the Mumonkan* (New York: Mentor, 1974), p. 125.

65. See Masao Abe, *A Study of Dōgen: His Philosophy and Religion* (Albany: State University of New York Press, 1994), p. 92.

66. *Chan-men kuei-shih* (J. *Zenmon kishiki*, a very short but crucial text also known as *Pai-chang ch'ing-kuei*, J. *Hyakujō shingi*) in *Taishō* 51:250c–251b; all citations throughout the book are from this source. There are several English translations, including Steven Heine, *Shifting Shape, Shaping Text: Philosophy and Folklore in the Fox Kōan* (Honolulu: University of Hawaii Press, 1999), pp. 220–222. It first appeared in a version in 988 in the *Sung kao-seng chuan*, but the common version was first published in 1004 as part of the *Ching-te chuan-teng lu*. Probably falsely attributed to Pai-chang, it nevertheless is claimed by tradition to be the precursor of the lengthy and tremendously influential *Ch'an-yüan ch'ing-kuei* of 1103, which is used to guide behavior in all Zen temples.

67. See *Zengaku daijiten* (Tokyo: Taishūkan shoten, 1985), first appendix, pp. 10–32; Martin Collcutt, *Five Mountains: The Rinzai Zen Institution in Medieval Japan* (Cambridge, MA: Harvard University Press, 1981), pp. 171–220; and T. Griffith Foulk, "Myth, Ritual, and Monastic Practice in Sung Ch'an Buddhism," in Patricia B. Ebrey and Peter N. Gregory, eds., *Religion and Society in T'ang and Sung China* (Honolulu: University of Hawaii Press, 1993), pp. 147–208.

68. Four additional mainstays included at Eiheiji and other Zen temples are the Abbot's Quarters, known as the "ten-foot square hut" (*hōjō*), following a passage in the *Vimalakirti Sutra* in which an informed layman holds forth in a humble abode with the ability to outsmart bodhisattvas; the hall to commemorate the local earth deity (*dojishin*) associated with protection of the temple grounds; a Bell Tower (*bonshō*) that houses a large bronze bell rung at New Year's and other festivals and at purification ceremonies; and a Reading Room (*shuryō*) for the study of sutras and related Buddhist and literary works. The Abbot's Quarters is usually located north of the Dharma Hall, with the Earth Deity Hall and Bell Tower to the right, and Reading Room to the left. In addition, the temple compounds frequently housed numerous other halls, depending on size, function, and financial strength, as Foulk points out in "The 'Rules of Purity' in Japanese Zen," in Steven Heine and Dale S. Wright, eds., *Zen Classics: Formative Texts in the History of Zen Buddhism* (New York: Oxford University Press, 2005), pp. 137–169.

69. Kagamishima et al., eds., *Yakuchū Zen'en shingi*; and Yifa, *The Origins of Buddhist Monastic Codes in China*.

70. Heine, *Shifting Shape, Shaping Text*, p. 218.

71. Collcutt, *Five Mountains*, pp. 186, 183.

CHAPTER 2

1. For example, see Dōgen's group of five poems on the *Lotus Sutra*, which includes "Colors of the mountains / Streams in the valleys / One in all, all in one / The voice and body of / Our Sakyamuni Buddha," in Steven Heine, trans., *The Zen Poetry of Dōgen: Verses from the Mountain of Eternal Peace* (Mt. Tremper, NY: Dharma Communications, 2005), p. 109. This is based on a traditional verse cited in *Shōbō-genzō*, "Keisei sanshoku" by Chang-tsung, "The sounds of the valley stream his long tongue / The changing colors of the mountains his blissful body / Since last night I have heard 84,000 hymns / But how can I explain them all to people the following day?"

2. See Steven Katz, *Mysticism and Philosophical Analysis* (New York: Oxford University Press, 1978). Katz begins on p. 1 by considering, "Mystics do not say what they mean and do not mean what they say," and then cites Rumi, "When you say, 'words are of no account,' you negate your own assertion through your words. If words are of no account, why do we hear you say that words are of no account? After all, you are saying this in words."

3. John R. McRae, *The Northern School and the Formation of Early Ch'an Buddhism* (Honolulu: University of Hawaii Press, 1986), p. 257. Also:

> Although one may be able to ascend heaven in broad daylight [by this method], if one relies [only] on the blue words of the jade-[encrusted] books, [one's efforts] will ultimately come to naught. This is merely one conditioned activity of this world, and even here [personal instruction is absolutely] necessary. How much more so the unsurpassable, true teaching [of Bodhidharma]—how could it possibly be explained in words?

The *Chuan fa-pao chi* was perhaps the first in a series of transmission of the lamp texts that continued with the *Pao-lin chuan* of 801 and of 952. Beginning with the *Ching-te chuan-teng lu* of 1004, there were several dozen texts in this genre produced in the eleventh through thirteenth centuries. See Albert Welter, *Monks, Rulers, and Literati: The Political Ascendancy of Chan Buddhism* (New York: Oxford University Press, 2006).

4. *Taishō shinshū daizōkyō*, ed. Takakusu Junjirō and Watanabe Kaigyoku, 100 vols. (Tokyo: Taishō issaikyō kankōkai, 1924–1932), 47:502c.

5. William M. Bodiford, *Sōtō Zen in Medieval Japan* (Honolulu: University of Hawaii Press, 1993), p. 143. See also Ishikawa Rikizan, "Transmission of *Kirigami* (Secret Initiation Documents): A Sōtō Practice in Medieval Japan," in Steven Heine and Dale S. Wright, eds., *The Kōan: Texts and Contexts in Zen Buddhism* (New York: Oxford University Press, 2000), pp. 233–243; and Andō Yoshinori, *Chūsei Zenshū bunseki no kenkyū* (Tokyo: Kokusho inkōkai, 2000).

6. This is included as the sixth case of the *Wu-men kuan* (*Taishō* 48:293c). The third and fourth lines of the motto are "Pointing directly to the human mind, / Seeing

into one's own nature and becoming a Buddha." According to T. Griffith Foulk, these words were even put into the mouth of Sakyamuni Buddha in some texts; see "Sung Controversies concerning the 'Separate Transmission' of Ch'an," in Peter N. Gregory and Daniel A. Getz, eds., *Buddhism in the Sung* (Honolulu: University of Hawaii Press, 1999), p. 268.

7. See Albert Welter, "Mahakasyapa's Smile: Silent Transmission and the Kung-an (Kōan) Tradition," in Heine and Wright, eds., *The Kōan*, pp. 75–109. Also according to Welter, "In the early Song, the meaning of Bodhidharma's coming from the west increasingly came to be understood also in terms of 'a separate transmission outside the teaching' " (*kyōge betsuden*), in *Monks, Rulers, and Literati*, p. 201.

8. See Mario Poceski, *The Hongzhou School and the Development of Tang Dynasty Chan* (New York: Oxford University Press, 2007).

9. See Ludwig Wittgenstein, "My propositions serve as elucidations in the following way: Only he who understands me, eventually recognizes them as nonsense," in *Tractatus Logico-Philosophicus*, trans. D. F. Pears and B. E. McGuinness (New York: Humanities, 1961), 6.54; see discussion in Henry Ruf, *Postmodern Rationality, Social Criticism, and Religion* (St. Paul, MN: Paragon, 2005), p. 94. Another prominent example would be Theater of the Absurd playwright Eugène Ionesco, whose works such as *Rhinoceros* tended to deconstruct into wild caricature and parody, with language itself disintegrating into disjointed fragments of words.

10. Heinrich Dumoulin, *Zen Buddhism: A History I (India and China)* (New York: Macmillan, 1987), p. 249.

11. *Wu-men kuan*, case 13 (*Taishō* 48:294b–c), and *Tsung-jung lu*, case 55 (*Taishō* 48:189a–190a).

12. T. Griffith Foulk, "Myth, Ritual, and Monastic Practice in Sung Ch'an Buddhism," in Patricia B. Ebrey and Peter N. Gregory, eds., *Religion and Society in T'ang and Sung China* (Honolulu: University of Hawaii Press, 1993), p. 180.

13. Welter, *Monks, Rulers, and Literati*, p. 126.

14. Dale S. Wright, *Philosophical Meditations on Zen Buddhism* (New York: Cambridge University Press, 1998), p. 17n.41.

15. Ibid.

16. Foulk, "Myth, Ritual, and Monastic Practice," p. 176. See Martin Collcutt, *Five Mountains: The Rinzai Zen Institution in Medieval Japan* (Cambridge, MA: Harvard University Press, 1981), p. 195.

17. Dōgen mentions this in several places, including *Shōbōgenzō zuimonki*, fascicle 3 (in traditional edition), *Shōbōgenzō*, "Shohō jissō," and *Eihei kōroku* 2.128. Although it is difficult to determine whether this practice was as unique and extraordinary as he claims, Dōgen had traveled to several of the Chinese Five Mountains temples and therefore had a comparative perspective.

18. See Taigen Dan Leighton and Shohaku Okumura, trans., *Dōgen's Extended Record: A Translation of the Eihei Kōroku* (Boston: Wisdom, 2004).

19. The Japanese Zen version was somewhat different from the earlier seven-hall style dating back to the period of Nara Buddhism, which included the pagoda (*tō*), golden Buddha Hall (*kondō*), Lecture Hall (*kōdō*), Bell Tower (*shōrō*), sutra repository

(*kyōzō*), monks' dormitories (*sōbō*), and refectory (*jikidō*). This was because of a new emphasis on several key facilities, including the Dharma Hall and Samgha Hall, as well as the Abbot's Quarters (although this was not considered one of the seven main halls), and the elimination of the pagoda, Bell Tower, and sutra repository as main buildings, although the latter two were often included. Also, Dōgen was apparently offered by Hōjō Tokiyori the opportunity to lead Kenchōji in the then-capital city of Kamakura, but he declined, preferring instead to stay at Eiheiji in the remote mountains.

20. Foulk, "Myth, Ritual, and Monastic Practice," pp. 163–164. Also: "The elite ranks of Zen masters in the Sung included not only meditation specialists but also Pure Land devotees, Tantric ritualists, experts on monastic discipline, exegetes of sutra and philosophical literature, poets, artists, and even monks with leanings toward Neo-Confucianism" (p. 161).

21. In China, where there was a limited sense of sectarian identity, in many cases Ch'an temples were closely affiliated or the abbacies rotated back and forth with the Lü and T'ien-t'ai schools. But in Japan, there was an either-or situation, and as the Tendai and Shingon sects began dying out in some areas in the medieval period, many of the temples were converted to Zen, especially the Sōtō sect in the northern provinces outside of Kyoto.

22. Thomas Cleary, trans., *Book of Serenity: One Hundred Zen Dialogues* (Hudson, NY: Lindisfarne, 1990).

23. Wright, *Philosophical Meditations on Zen Buddhism*, p. 10.

24. Cited from "A History of the Religious Beliefs and Philosophical Opinions in China from the Beginning to the Present Time," in Bernard Faure, *Chan Insights and Oversights* (Princeton, NJ: Princeton University Press, 1993), p. 42. Faure notes that Wieger was a former Protestant turned Jesuit who showed contempt for Chinese "paganism" and saw Ch'an as an offshoot of Vedantism, citing the oracles of Brahman.

25. Mishima Yukio, *Temple of the Golden Pavilion* (New York: Perigee, 1959), pp. 244 and 245.

26. Alan Cole, *Patriarchs on Paper: The Gradual Birth of Chinese Buddhas in Tang-Era Literature* (Berkeley: University of California Press, forthcoming), p. 357, in typescript version.

27. Burton Watson, trans., *The Complete Works of Chuang Tzu* (New York: Columbia University Press, 1968), p. 302. Wittgenstein ends the *Tractatus*: "Whereof one cannot speak, thereof one must be silent."

28. Cited in Zhang Longxi, *The Tao and the Logos: Literary Hermeneutics, East and West* (Durham, NC: Duke University Press, 1992), p. 124 (with some modifications).

29. Victor Sōgen Hori, *Zen Sand: The Book of Capping Phrases for Kōan Practice* (Honolulu: University of Hawaii Press, 2003), p. 56.

30. Mark C. Taylor, *Erring: A Postmodern A/theology* (Chicago: University of Chicago Press, 1987), p. 103.

31. http://home.wlv.ac.uk/~fa1871/surrext.html (accessed August 28, 2006).

32. Because of Carroll's personal predilections, a Freudian reading of his nonsense writings as a way of suppressing socially unacceptable thought patterns in childlike syntax probably carries weight.

33. Lewis Carroll, *Alice's Adventures in Wonderland and Through the Looking-Glass*, ed. Hugh Haughton (New York: Penguin, 1998), p. xiv. See also Jackie Wullschlager, *Inventing Neverland: The Lives and Fantasies of Lewis Carroll, Edward Lear, J. M. Barrie, Kenneth Grahame and A. A. Milne* (New York: Free Press, 1995); and John F. Lehmann, *Lewis Carroll and the Spirit of Nonsense* (Nottingham, England: University of Nottingham Press, 1972). Haughton points out that Alice, who asks, "Who in the world am I? That's the great puzzle!" while the Cheshire Cat grins, "We're all mad here," consistently and matter-of-factly dismisses her interlocutors as nonsensical, but this does not mean their wild disorder has no impact or intrusion on her.

34. Haughton, "Introduction," in Carroll, *Alice's Adventures in Wonderland*, p. 1.

35. Carroll, *Alice's Adventures in Wonderland*, p. 186. Humpty also says he "pays" words to work for him and that he can "explain all the poems that were invented—and a good many that haven't been invented just yet" (p. 187).

36. Carroll, *Alice's Adventures in Wonderland*, p. 83.

37. Quotes in this paragraph are from T. S. Eliot, *The Waste Land and Other Poems* (New York: Barnes & Noble Classics, 2005), p. xxi.

38. John Cage, *Silence: Lectures and Writings* (Middletown, CT: Wesleyan University Press, 1961), p. xi.

39. Welter, *Monks, Rulers, and Literati*, p. 186.

40. Foulk, "Sung Controversies concerning the 'Separate Transmission' of Ch'an," p. 260.

41. Victor Sōgen Hori adopts and applies a term first used by Hee-Jin Kim regarding Dōgen's use of the kōan, which was used in many ways in contrast to the Lin-chi/Rinzai school approach to the Rinzai Zen monastic curriculum. Both Hori and Kim agree in their critique of "the instrumentalist idea that a kōan is merely a nonrational instrument for a breakthrough to a noncognitive pure consciousness," according to "Kōan and *Kenshō* in the Rinzai Zen Curriculum," in Heine and Wright, eds., *The Kōan*, p. 281. Hori cites Hee-Jin Kim, "The Reason of Words and Letters: Dōgen and *Kōan* Language," in William R. LaFleur, ed., *Dōgen Studies* (Honolulu: University of Hawaii Press, 1985), pp. 54–82.

42. Watson, trans., *The Complete Works of Chuang Tzu*, p. 304.

43. Bernard Faure, "Fair and Unfair Language Games in Chan/Zen," in Steven T. Katz, ed., *Mysticism and Language* (New York: Oxford University Press, 1992), p. 173.

44. *Pi-yen lu*, case 73 (*Taishō* 48:200c–201c).

45. Katsuki Sekida, trans., *Two Zen Classics: Mumonkan and Hekiganroku* (New York: Weatherhill, 1977), p. 338.

46. Ōgawa Takashi, "Hekiganroku zōkō (5)," *Zen bunka* 179 (2003): 23–31.

47. John C. H. Wu, *The Golden Age of Zen* (Taipei: United Publishing Center, 1975), p. 103.

48. See Steven Heine, *Opening a Mountain: Kōans of the Zen Masters* (New York: Oxford University Press, 2002); and Heine, *White Collar Zen: Using Zen Principles to Overcome Obstacles and Achieve Your Career Goals* (New York: Oxford University Press, 2005), pp. 107–116.

49. *Wu-men kuan*, case 40 (*Taishō* 48:298a); also Nishimura Eshin, ed., *Mumonkan* (Tokyo: Iwanami bunko, 1994), pp. 152–155.

50. *Pi-yen lu*, case 25 (*Taishō* 48:165c–166c); also Iriya Yoshitaka et al., eds., *Hekiganroku*, 3 vols. (Tokyo: Iwanami shoten, 1992–1996), I:321–332.

51. See Bernard Faure, *The Rhetoric of Immediacy* (Princeton, NJ: Princeton University Press, 1991); and T. Griffith Foulk, "The Form and Function of Kōan Literature," in Heine and Wright, eds., *The Kōan*, pp. 15–45.

52. *Taishō* 48:294b–c and *Taishō* 48:262a–c, respectively. The translation is, with minor stylistic changes, taken from Cleary, *Book of Serenity*, pp. 233–236; the *Wu-men kuan* version is taken from *Ching-te chuan-teng lu*, vol. 16, under the heading of Yen-t'ou, who is also referenced in the *Tsu-t'ang chi*, vol. 7; and the *Tsung-jung lu* version is from *Wu-teng hui-yüan*, vol. 6. Te-shan is referenced in *Tsu-t'ang chi*, vol. 5, and *Ching-te chuan-teng lu*, vol. 15.

53. Yifa, *The Origins of Buddhist Monastic Codes in China: An Annotated Translation and Study of the Chanyuan Qinggui* (Honolulu: University of Hawaii Press, 2002), p. 124. In addition, "After the midday meal, the bell is struck in front of the Samgha hall. Everyone is seated, and the person who presides over the Dharma stands on the south side of the front gate, facing the Holy Monk" (p. 183).

54. See discussion in Robert Aitken, trans., *The Gateless Barrier: The Wu-Men Kuan (Mumonkan)* (New York: North Point, 1991), pp. 91–92.

55. *Taishō* 48:235c–236a.

56. See Steven Heine, *Shifting Shape, Shaping Text: Philosophy and Folklore in the Fox Kōan* (Honolulu: University of Hawaii Press, 1999).

57. Cited in Thomas Cleary, *No Barrier: Unlocking the Zen Koan* (New York: Bantam, 1993), p. 63. Also Bao-en said:

> If you accept unrealities and take in echoes, you miss [Te-shan]. If you suppress the strong and help the weak, you bury [Yen-t'ou]. I tell you frankly, for an example of the proverb, "When the teacher is excellent, the apprentices are strong," credit goes to [Te-shan] and his disciples [Hsüeh-feng] and [Yen-t'ou]. Expertise is demonstrated in the hands of experts; who knows beyond the knowledge of connoisseurs?

CHAPTER 3

1. Zen temples, which are often built in reclusive mountain landscapes or featuring an appropriate natural setting with trees, streams, and ponds or a constructed rock garden or bridges within the compound, further highlight the value of using monastic grounds as a contemplative space that offers a reprieve and release from worldly affairs. See the following book for a presentation of the TZN view: Seiko Goto, *The Japanese Garden: Gateway to the Human Spirit* (New York: Peter Lang, 2003). The most prominent example of a medieval rock garden is Ryōanji temple in Kyoto, which was perhaps designed by the painter Sōami (1472–1525). A classic of the "dry mountains-rivers" (*kare sansui*) style that contains only rocks and sand constructed in

patterns but no living form except moss, the Ryōanji garden is surrounded by earthen walls in three directions and faced with the corridor of the Abbot's Quarters. In the rectangular space, measuring thirty meters from east to west and ten meters from north to south, fifteen rocks of various sizes are arranged on white sand in five groups, comprising five, two, three, two, and three rocks. The most popular explanation of this garden is that the rocks represent a mother tiger and her cubs swimming in the river of white sand toward a fearful dragon. The asymmetrical composition achieves a certain balance and harmony that creates energy and rhythm in the midst of subtlety and simplicity. However, some critics argue that the connection between gardens and Zen is one more example of modern, especially postwar, elaborations.

2. D. T. Suzuki has referred to all ritual and devotional practices as "artificialities in the eyes of Zen," in *An Introduction to Zen Buddhism* (rpt., New York: Grove, 1964), p. 39; cited in T. Griffith Foulk, "Ritual in Japanese Zen Buddhism," in Steven Heine and Dale S. Wright, eds., *Zen Ritual* (New York: Oxford University Press, 2007). See also Catherine Bell, *Ritual: Perspectives and Dimensions* (New York: Oxford University Press, 1997), for a discussion of the diverse functions of ritual other than the instrumentalist approach indicated here, but still acting as an intermediary or stepping-stone between secular and sacred realms, an approach seemingly denied by the ideology of Zen as a silent, immediate (or unmediated) transmission.

3. T. Griffith Foulk, "Myth, Ritual, and Monastic Practice," in Patricia Buckley Ebrey and Peter N. Gregory, eds., *Religion and Society in T'ang and Sung China* (Honolulu: University of Hawaii Press, 1993), p. 193.

4. See Umehara Takeshi, *Rakan: Hotoke to hito no aida* (Tokyo: Kodansha, 1977).

5. There are two kinds of Tengu, generally, with both found at Daiyūzan, one modeled on the *yamabushi* style of appearance and the other on the image of the crow.

6. Ian Reader and George F. Tanabe, Jr., *Practically Religious: Worldly Benefits and the Common Religion of Japan* (Honolulu: University of Hawaii Press, 1998), esp. pp. 9–10.

7. Ian Reader, "Zazenless Zen? The Position of Zazen in Institutional Zen Buddhism," *Japanese Religions* 14/3 (1986): 7–27.

8. According to Jacques Gernet, "The Robe is only the replica and the double of the Law. Whoever possesses the one possesses the other"; cited in Bernard Faure, "*Quand l'habit fait le moine*: The Symbolism of the *Kasaya* in Sōtō Zen," in Bernard Faure, ed., *Chan Buddhism in Ritual Context* (London: RoutledgeCurzon, 2003), p. 215.

9. Duncan Ryūken Williams, *The Other Side of Zen: A Social History of Sōtō Zen Buddhism in Tokugawa Japan* (Princeton, NJ: Princeton University Press, 2005); see especially the first chapter, "Toward a Social History of Sōtō Zen," pp. 1–12. For other examples of positive evaluations of popular religiosity in Zen, see William M. Bodiford, "Sōtō Zen in a Japanese Town: Field Notes on a Once-Every-Thirty-Three-Years Kannon Festival," *Japanese Journal of Religious Studies* 22/1 (1994): 3–36; and H. Neill McFarland, *Daruma: The Founder of Zen in Japanese Popular Culture* (Tokyo: Kodansha, 1987).

10. Martin Collcutt notes the Zen iconoclastic turn to self-reliance, as well as the "fear that, through these ceremonies, dependence on the state and the patrons who

sponsored Buddha hall ceremonies and memorial services would be unduly in-creased," in *Five Mountains: The Rinzai Zen Monastic Institution in Medieval Japan* (Cambridge, MA: Harvard University Press, 1981), p. 140.

11. Yifa, *The Origins of Buddhist Monastic Codes in China: An Annotated Transla-tion and Study of the Chanyuan Qinggui* (Honolulu: University of Hawaii Press, 2002), p. 270.

12. Foulk, "Myth, Ritual, and Monastic Practice," pp. 193 and 170–171.

13. See *Hōkyōki* in Kawamura Kōdō et al., eds., *Dōgen zenji zenshū*, 7 vols. (Tokyo: Shunjūsha, 1988–1993), vol. V.

14. Kenneth Kraft, *Eloquent Zen: Daitō and Early Japanese Zen* (Honolulu: Uni-versity of Hawaii Press, 1992).

15. Collcutt, *Five Mountains*, p. 194.

16. Foulk, "Myth, Ritual, and Monastic Practice," p. 193.

17. Ibid., 196.

18. See Nancy Shatzman Steinhardt, *Chinese Imperial City Planning* (Honolulu: University of Hawaii Press, 1990); Nancy Shatzman Steinhardt, ed., *Chinese Archi-tecture* (New Haven, CT, and London: Yale University Press, 2002); and Stephen Little with Shawn Eichman, eds., *Taoism and the Arts of China* (Chicago: Art Institute of Chicago, 2000).

19. Kagamishima Genryū, Satō Tatsugen, and Kosaka Kiyū, eds., *Yakuchū Zen-en shingi* (Tokyo: Sōtōshū shūmuchō, 1972), pp. 76–77 and 256; and Foulk, "Myth, Ritual, and Monastic Practice," pp. 177–178.

20. T. Griffith Foulk and Robert H. Sharf, "On the Ritual Use of Ch'an Por-traiture in Medieval China," *Cahiers d'Extrême-Asie* 7 (1993–1994): 184.

21. Ibid.

22. Collcutt, *Five Mountains*, p. 191.

23. Bernard Faure, *Chan Insights and Oversights: An Epistemological Critique of the Chan Tradition* (Princeton, NJ: Princeton University Press, 1993), p. 158; see also Iriya Yoshitaka, ed., *Baso goroku* (Kyoto: Zen bunka kenkyūjō, 1974), pp. 120–129 (Pinyin changed to Wade-Giles).

24. See Foulk and Sharf, "On the Ritual Use of Ch'an Portraiture in Medieval China"; Bernard Faure, *The Rhetoric of Immediacy: A Cultural Critique of Chan/Zen Buddhism* (Princeton, NJ: Princeton University Press, 1991), pp. 169–175; and Wendi Adamek, "Imagining the Portrait of a Chan Master," in Faure, ed., *Chan Buddhism in Ritual Context*, pp. 36–73.

25. *Tsung-jung lu*, case 10, in *Taishō shinshū daizōkyō*, ed. Takakusu Junjirō and Watanabe Kaigyoku, 100 vols. (Tokyo: Taishō issaikyō kankōkai, 1924–1932), 48:233a–c.

26. Ishikawa Rikizan, "Chūsei Zenshū to shinbutsu shūgō," *Nihon Bukkyō* 60–61 (1984): 51. Some of the developments in Japan are foreshadowed by early Buddhist myths in which the mischievous Naga dragons come to protect and get transformed into the Buddha (or vice versa); see the image from Lowell Bloss, "The Buddha and the Naga: A Study in Buddhist Folk Religiosity," *History of Religions* 13/1 (1973): 36–51.

27. William M. Bodiford, "The Enlightenment of Kami and Ghosts: Spirit Ordinations in Japanese Sōtō Zen," in Bernard Faure, ed., *Chan Buddhism in Ritual
Context* (London: RoutledgeCurzon, 2003), p. 253. This is true not only for the Sōtō
sect, as there are also numerous prominent cases in Rinzai Zen.

28. Of the 15,000 Sōtō temples, only about 1 in 500 (or 31) are considered
monastic training centers.

29. Azuma Ryūshin, *Sōtōshū: Waga ie no shūkyō* (Tokyo: Daihōrinkaku, 1983),
pp. 82-88; see Faure, *The Rhetoric of Immediacy*, p. 282n.46. For a partial list of Sōtō
temples, see Ishikawa, "Chūsei Zenshū to shinbutsu shūgō," pp. 44-45.

30. Bodiford, *Sōtō Zen in Medieval Japan*, p. 88. See a translation of his meditation manual *Zazenyōjinki*, a follow-up to Dōgen's *Fukanzazengi*, in Steven Heine,
trans., "Advice on the Practice of Zazen: Taishō Volume 82, Number 2586," in *Zen
Texts* (BDK English Tripitaka 73-III, 98-VIII, 98-IX, 104-I) (Berkeley, CA: Numata
Center for Buddhist Translation and Research, 2005), pp. 263-275.

31. Heinrich Dumoulin, *Zen Buddhism: A History II (Japan)* (New York: Macmillan, 1990), p. 213.

32. Faure, *Chan Insights and Oversights*, p. 166n.27.

33. Ōtani Teppu, ed., "Daijōji hihon 'Tōkokuki,'" *Shūgaku kenkyū* 16 (1974): 233.

34. Bernard Faure, *Visions of Power: Imagining Medieval Japanese Buddhism*
(Princeton, NJ: Princeton University Press, 1996).

35. Also, leading Rinzai temples in the town of Kamakura, such as Kenchōji and
Engakuji, serve as stops on a twenty-four-site Jizō pilgrimage route.

36. A kōan case on this topic is *Pi-yen lu*, case 26, known as Pai-chang's "Sitting
Alone atop Ta-hsiung Peak" (*Taishō* 51:250c-251b).

37. Legend is that bending backward is good for childbirth, and thus the wooden
shoes causing this posture have become a kind of fertility symbol, especially for
childless couples or women who have had miscarriages.

38. Yamaoka Takaaki, "Daiyūzan Saijōji ni okeru Bukkyōteki fukugō ni tsuite,"
Shūgaku kenkyū 25 (1983): 115-136.

39. *Daiyūzan: Daiyūzan Saijōji kaisō roppyakunen hōzan* (Kanagawa-ken, Japan:
Daiyūzan Saijōji kaisō roppyakunen hōzan jimuchō, 1994), p. 77. According to
Williams in *The Other Side of Zen*, this was performed traditionally by monks who
were masked and walking backward up the steps.

40. There are other neighborhoods in Tokyo with temples that claim special
healing powers for various kinds of ailments and afflictions, including the area around
Meguro station on the Yamanote line in Meguro ward and locations in Bunkyō,
Sumida, and Arakawa wards; see Reader and Tanabe, *Practically Religious*, pp. 249-
250. There are handbooks, such as the *Tokyo goriyaku sanjo*, that document sacred
sites around town where there have been examples of miraculous events (*reigen*) or
marvelous efficacy (*reigen arataka*); see ibid., p. 244.

41. As with other examples of the Inari cult, including Fushimi Inari, the head
temple charges the off-site locations for the privilege of being awarded a spirit; see
Reader and Tanabe, *Practically Religious*, esp. pp. 145-146.

42. This institution enshrines at least three forms of the fox/rice deity, which are considered mutually supportive as protector gods for the temple-shrine complex and its followers: the Buddhist deity Dakini-shinten, depicted as a female bodhisattva sitting astride a flying white fox, enshrined in the Dharma Hall; the indigenous Inari fertility deity known as Toyokawa Inari, which is held in the Shrine Hall; and a variety of small fox icons which are guardians of these primary images. See Steven Heine, *Shifting Shape, Shaping Text: Philosophy and Folklore in the Fox Kōan* (Honolulu: University of Hawaii Press, 1999).

43. Karen Smyers, "The Jewel and the Fox: A Study of Shared and Private Meanings in *Inari* Worship," Ph.D. diss., Princeton University, 1993, pp. 160–162. See also Smyers, *The Fox and the Jewel: Shared and Private Meanings in Contemporary Japanese Inari Worship* (Honolulu: University of Hawaii Press, 1998).

44. *Zengaku daijiten* (Tokyo: Taishūkan shoten, 1985), p. 1190. A rich source of information is a 1993 NHK documentary entitled *Toyokawa Inari: Myōgonji ni tsutaerareta shinkō.*

45. I am avoiding using the term "Shinto" to categorize Inari because, as explained below, the cult is not officially recognized as such and exists in a more diffused network of associations than "sect Shinto." Or, as Thomas Kasulis writes:

> Shinto generally functions as a folk religion: each locality has its special *kami*, distinctive festivals, and sacred objects. Shinto is more a set of somatically enacted feelings about purification, renewal, regionality, and communal spirit than it is any kind of philosophical or doctrinal system.

From "Researching the Strata of the Japanese Self," in Roger T. Ames and Wimal Dissanayake, eds., *Self as Person in Asian Theory and Practice* (Albany: State University of New York Press, 1994), p. 99.

46. Alan L. Miller, "Religions of Japan," in *Religions of the World* (New York: St. Martin's, 1983), pp. 336–338. The Ukemochi myth seems to conform to the pattern of the Pacific island Hainuwele mythic cycle, which has affinities with myths from India and other cultures.

47. The notion of *suijaku* is similar to *gongen* in highlighting the role of a localized spiritual force, but the latter generally refers to a Buddhist manifestation rather than to an indigenous god.

48. On the remarkable number of syncretistic temples and deities, see Gorai Shigeru, ed., *Inari shinkō no kenkyū* (Tokyo: Sanin shinbunsha, 1985), pp. 75–170 (on Buddhist sects generally) and pp. 541–638 (on Zen, especially Sōtō, temples). Sōtō Zen temples also have extensive syncretisms with a variety of indigenous deities and deities imported from India, both Buddhist and Hindu.

49. Gorai, ed., *Inari shinkō no kenkyū*, pp. 541–638.

50. In many legends, Buddhist sorcerers use the power of this image associated with the demonic side of Dakini for ulterior motives and personal gain. It is likely that in the popular imagination these legends are mixed and conflated, so that the Buddhist deity Dakini-shinten (*shinten* means "true deity") riding on a white fox while carrying rice holds at least some demonic connotations and is associated in the

popular imagination with sorcery and uncanny witchcraft. For an example of a folktale about the demonic Dakini, see Royall Tyler, trans., *Japanese Tales* (New York: Pantheon, 1988), pp. 63–66; and Yamada Yoshino et al., eds., *Nihon koten bungaku taikei* (Tokyo: Iwanami shoten, 1961–1963), 84:214–219.

51. Tyler, trans., *Japanese Tales*, p. 118; Yamada et al., eds., *Nihon koten bungaku taikei*, 84:58.

52. Kiyoshi Nozaki, *Kitsune: Japan's Fox of Mystery, Romance and Humor* (Tokyo: Hokuseido, 1961), p. 204.

53. See Anne-Marie Bouchy, "Le Renard: Element de la conception du monde dans la tradition japonaise," in Marie-Lise Befa and Roberte Hamayon, eds., *Le Renard: Tours, detours et retours*, special issue of *Etudes mongoles... et sibeeriennes* 15 (1984): 9–70; William M. Bodiford, *Sōtō Zen in Medieval Japan* (Honolulu: University of Hawaii Press, 1993), p. 173; and Faure, *The Rhetoric of Immediacy*, p. 281. There are many such accounts in vols. 16 and 17 (*Shiden* 1 and 2) of *Sōtōshū zensho*, 18 vols. (Tokyo: Sōtōshu shūmuchō, 1970–1973), esp. 17:278a, as discussed in Hirose Ryōko, "Sōtō zensō ni okeru shinjin kado-akurei chin'atsu," *Indogaku Bukkyōgaku kenkyū* 21/2 (1983): 233–236.

54. Dorothy Britton, trans., *A Haiku Journey: Bashō's Narrow Road to a Far Province* (Tokyo: Kodansha, 1980), p. 39; and Koizuka Minoru, *Kitsune monogatari* (Tokyo: Sanichi shobō, 1982), pp. 102–115.

55. The term *genjōkōan*, an important concept in Dōgen's thought which serves as the title of the first chapter of his *Shōbōgenzō* text dealing with the philosophy of time, death, and illusion, is used here for its talismanic effect, much as the term *shinjin datsuraku* (casting off body-mind), which refers to Dōgen's enlightenment experience under the tutelage of Chinese mentor Ju-ching, is used in popular lore, including contemporary media representations of his life.

56. Allan Grapard, *The Protocol of the Gods: A Study of the Kasuga Cult in Japanese History* (Berkeley: University of California Press, 1992), p. 11.

57. See Faure, *The Rhetoric of Immediacy*, pp. 305–306, on this fault line, which "has been usually silenced or explained away—both by the tradition itself and by its scholarly replication—by means of notions such as the Two Truths.... This leaves us with plural, multivocal, differential traditions on both sides of the earlier divide, a divide that retains only a provisional validity."

58. *Wu-men kuan*, case 2 (*Taishō* 48:293a–b); and *Tsung-jung lu*, case 8 (*Taishō* 48:231c–232b).

59. Dōgen, *Shōbōgenzō*, in *Dōgen zenji zenshū*, I:318.

60. The Zen masters are one-upped spiritually by women in *Pi-yen lu* (J. *Hekiganroku*), case 4 (*Taishō* 48:143b–144c), and *Wu-men kuan*, case 31 (*Taishō* 48:297a).

61. Other *Shōbōgenzō* passages are more skeptical or negative in regard to folk beliefs, especially in the "Kie-buppōsōbō" fascicle of the twelve-fascicle *Shōbōgenzō* from late in Dōgen's life.

62. Michael Kelsey, "Salvation of the Snake, the Snake of Salvation: Buddhist-Shinto Conflict and Resolution," *Japanese Journal of Religious Studies* 8/1–2 (1981): 110.

Tyler points out how Kannon can take various forms, including a voracious snake, to save people, in *Japanese Tales*, p. xli.

63. Whalen Lai, "The *Chan-ch'a ching*: Religion and Magic in Medieval China," in Robert Buswell, ed., *Chinese Buddhist Apocrypha* (Honolulu: University of Hawaii Press, 1990), p. 175, which mentions criticism of Hume by Peter Brown, *The Cult of Saints: Its Rise and Function in Latin Christianity* (Chicago: University of Chicago Press, 1981), pp. 12–22.

64. In Burton Watson, trans., *Basic Writings of Mo-tzu, Hsun-Tzu, Han Fei-tzu* (New York: Columbia University Press, 1967), p. 85, slightly modified.

65. Jean-Claude Schmitt, *The Holy Greyhound: Guinefort, Healer of Children since the Thirteenth Century*, trans. Martin Thom (Cambridge: Cambridge University Press, 1979), p. 4.

66. Ibid., p. 16.

67. Aron Gurevich, *Medieval Popular Culture: Problems of Belief and Perception* (Cambridge: Cambridge University Press, 1988), p. 97.

68. Janet R. Goodwin, *Alms and Vagabonds: Buddhist Temples and Popular Patronage in Medieval Japan* (Honolulu: University of Hawaii Press, 1994), p. 126.

69. Reader and Tanabe, *Practically Religious*, p. 10.

70. Ibid., p. 99.

71. Ibid., p. 100. This question is asked of the approach to reconciling Sōtō Zen's puritanical theory that reflects transcendental (Skt. *lokattara*) Buddhism with miscellaneous practices that reflect cultural influences comprising folk magic, as proposed by Yasuaki Nara in "May the Deceased Get Enlightenment! An Aspect of the Enculturation of Buddhism in Japan," *Buddhist-Christian Studies* 15 (1995): 19–42.

72. For this issue, see Kyoko Motomichi Nakamura, trans., *Miraculous Stories from the Japanese Buddhist Tradition: The Nihon Ryōiki of the Monk Kyōkai* (Cambridge, MA: Harvard University Press, 1971), p. 78n.121; and also see Hakamaya Noriaki, *Hihan Bukkyō* (Tokyo: Daizō shuppan, 1990), pp. 275–304, for pressing the case against the ethics of Zen syncretism.

CHAPTER 4

1. A detailed discussion of the role of women is beyond the scope of this book, but is worthy of examination. Paula Arai has noted that one of the features of medieval Sōtō Zen was the role played at several nunneries by female monastics, who sought to keep alive the integrity of the tradition of clerical discipline espoused by Dōgen and who also developed unique rituals for healing and purification; see Arai, "Women and Dōgen: Rituals Actualizing Empowerment and Healing," in Steven Heine and Dale S. Wright, eds., *Zen Ritual* (New York: Oxford University Press, 2007), pp. 185–204. It is unclear, however, whether and to what extent Dōgen himself endorsed the equality of women because there are several seemingly contradictory passages in his writings on this topic, although the "Raihaitokuzui" fascicle of the *Shōbōgenzō* seems particularly positive.

2. Cited in Brian (Daizen) Victoria, *Zen War Stories* (London: RoutledgeCurzon, 2003), pp. 66–67. Elsewhere (pp. 19–23), Victoria shows that the Japanese military borrowed ritual and practice patterns from Zen temples, in particular Kenchōji temple in Kamakura, to guide the internal regulations and system of discipline for training soldiers.

3. Takuan Sōhō, *The Unfettered Mind: Writings of the Zen Master to the Sword Master*, trans. William Scott Wilson (New York: Kodansha, 1986), p. 82.

4. James W. Heisig and John C. Maraldo, eds., *Rude Awakenings: Zen, the Kyoto School, & the Question of Nationalism* (Honolulu: University of Hawaii Press, 1995); Paul L. Swanson and Jamie Hubbard, eds., *Pruning the Bodhi Tree: The Storm over Critical Buddhism* (Honolulu: University of Hawaii Press, 1997); Brian Victoria, *Zen at War* (New York: Weatherhill, 1997); and Victoria, *Zen War Stories*. In *Rude Awakenings*, debunkers and defenders alike are mixed and matched, but no clear outcome or even conclusion in the case of some of the chapters emerges, because the material is complex and commentators seem to hedge their bets in trying to be provocative yet, conversely, not overly unkind to their antagonists. For example, Jan Van Bragt writes:

> I am persuaded that a calm reading of the texts of the principal Kyoto philosophers at the height of the critical years of the war will show them to have been utterly sincere in departing from the official nationalist ideology to stress the importance of the individual as a creative agent, to urge an international, world-historical outlook, and to relativize the position of state Shinto.

From "Kyoto Philosophy—Intrinsically Nationalistic?" in Heisig and Maraldo, eds., *Rude Awakenings*, p. 250.

5. Robert H. Sharf, "Whose Zen? Zen Nationalism Revisited," in Heisig and Maraldo, eds., *Rude Awakenings*, p. 48. See also Sharf, "The Zen of Japanese Nationalism," in Donald S. Lopez, ed., *Curators of the Buddha: The Study of Buddhism under Colonialism* (Chicago: University of Chicago Press, 1995), pp. 107–160 (which also appeared in *History of Religions* 33/1 [1993]: 1–43).

6. Sharf, "Whose Zen? Zen Nationalism Revisited," p. 50.

7. Kirita Kiyohide, "D. T. Suzuki on Society and the State," in Heisig and Maraldo, eds., *Rude Awakenings*, p. 73.

8. Cited in Horio Tsutomu, "The *Chūōkōron* Discussions: Their Background and Meaning," in Heisig and Maraldo, eds., *Rude Awakenings*, p. 291.

9. There are examples of constructive attempts at achieving a balanced view, such as Christopher Ives, *Zen Awakening and Society* (Honolulu: University of Hawaii Press, 1991); and Steve Odin, *The Social Self in Zen and American Pragmatism* (Albany: State University of New York Press, 1996).

10. Yifa, *The Origins of Buddhist Monastic Codes in China* (Honolulu: University of Hawaii Press, 2002), p. 69.

11. Kenninji, the first Zen temple built in Kyoto in 1202, did not have such a building, as it still featured the integration of esoteric (Taimitsu) practices; see Steven

Heine, *Did Dōgen Go to China? What He Wrote and When He Wrote It* (New York: Oxford University Press, 2006).

12. See Martin Collcutt, *Five Mountains: The Rinzai Zen Monastic Institution in Medieval Japan* (Cambridge, MA: Harvard University Press, 1981), p. 207; and T. Griffith Foulk, "Myth, Ritual, and Monastic Practice in Sung Ch'an Buddhism," in Patricia B. Ebrey and Peter N. Gregory, eds., *Religion and Society in T'ang and Sung China* (Honolulu: University of Hawaii Press, 1993), pp. 183–187.

13. In other manifestations, Manjusri appears as a golden lion flying in the sky or as an impoverished beggar, depending on the karmic needs of those he encounters.

14. This admonition is perhaps the most famous passage in the text, whether or not it was ever carried out.

15. Although this passage seems to suggest that Zen is unbound by either Hinayana's 250 or Mahayana's 48 precepts, in fact, like some forms of Chinese Buddhism, Zen adhered to both sets of precepts. At first, only the Mahayana precepts were accepted in Japan, where Dōgen proposed a modified system of 16 precepts in *Shōbōgenzō* "Jukai," but eventually the Rinzai Zen school followed both sets of precepts, following Eisai, who insisted on combining the Hinayana and Mahayana approaches based on the model he had experienced in China.

16. Yifa, *The Origins of Buddhist Monastic Codes in China*, p. 139.

17. Ibid., p. 153.

18. *Dōgen zenji zenshū*, ed. Kawamura Kōdō et al., 7 vols. (Tokyo: Shunjūsha, 1988-1993), VI:16; translation in Kazuaki Tanahashi, ed., *Moon in a Dewdrop: Writings of Zen Master Dōgen* (New York: North Point, 1985), p. 61.

19. According to Sukumar Dutt, the *Uposatha*, which is based on cyclical householder purification rites, was developed long after the *Pratimoksha* code, "a symbolical expression of the unity (*samaggata*) of the *sangha*," and the incorporation of the repentance model "was the final reaffirmation of the character of the Sangha as an Order," in Dutt, *Buddhist Monks and Monasteries of India: Their History and Their Contribution to Indian Culture* (rpt., Delhi: Motilal Banarsidass, 1988), pp. 67, 73.

20. In Philip Yampolsky, trans., *The Platform Sutra of the Sixth Patriarch: The Text of the Tun-Huang Manuscript* (New York: Columbia University Press, 1967), pp. 144–145 (Chinese version, p. 10; translation altered).

21. Matsuo Kenji, "What Is Kamakura New Buddhism? Official Monks and Reclusive Monks," *Japanese Journal of Religious Studies* 24/1–2 (1997): 183. However, William M. Bodiford points out that the Burakumin Liberation League

> attack[s] not just individual acts of discrimination but also basic Sōtō social attitudes, charging that the roots of later Sōtō institutional abuses must be traced back to Dōgen. In their view the Sōtō founder lacked the social vision of other contemporaneous Buddhist leaders . . . who organized campaigns to help lepers and people of "nonhuman" (*hinin*) status [the same group Matsuo Kenji mentions].

From "Zen and the Art of Religious Prejudice: Efforts to Reform a Tradition of Social Discrimination," *Japanese Journal of Religious Studies* 23/1–2 (1996): 21.

22. Kazuo Kasahara, ed., *A History of Japanese Religion* (Tokyo: Kosei, 2001), p. 252. Gozan Zen sect refers to mainly Rinzai temples associated with the powerful social strata in the capital cities of Kyoto and Kamakura, which was borrowed from a similar temple system used in China.

23. Susan Moon, ed., *Not Turning Away: The Practice of Engaged Buddhism* (Boston: Shambhala, 2004).

24. Masao Abe, *Buddhism and Interfaith Dialogue* (Honolulu: University of Hawaii Press, 1995), p. 237.

25. See Donald Mitchell, ed., *Masao Abe: A Zen Life of Dialogue* (New York: Tuttle, 1998).

26. Additional recent examples which assert the value of Zen in today's society include the movement of socially engaged Buddhism, originated by the contemporary Vietnamese master Thich Nhat Hanh, and the Buddhist Peace Fellowship, a largely Western movement.

27. See Masao Abe, *Zen and the Modern World*, ed. Steven Heine (Honolulu: University of Hawaii Press, 2003), pp. 29–33.

28. Steven Heine, "Postwar Issues in Japanese Buddhism," in Charles W. Fu and Gerhard Spiegler, eds., *Religious Issues and Interreligious Dialogues: An Analysis and Sourcebook of Developments since 1945* (Westport, CT: Greenwood, 1989), pp. 258 and 261–263.

29. Nishitani Keiji, *Religion and Nothingness*, trans. Jan Van Bragt (Berkeley: University of California Press, 1982), pp. 215–216.

30. Ibid., p. 272.

31. Nishitani Keiji, "Science and Zen," in Frederick Franck, ed., *The Buddha Eye: An Anthology of the Kyoto School* (New York: Crossroad, 1982), p. 123 (emphasis in original).

32. Odin, *The Social Self in Zen and American Pragmatism*, p. 453.

33. Ibid., p. 437.

34. Ibid., p. 39.

35. Peter N. Dale, *The Myth of Japanese Uniqueness* (New York: St. Martin's, 1986).

36. Some of the sources include Simon P. James, *Zen Buddhism and Environmental Ethics* (Hampshire, England: Ashgate, 2004); and Mary Evelyn Tucker and Duncan Ryūken Williams, eds., *Buddhism and Ecology: The Interconnection of Dharma and Deeds* (Cambridge, MA: Harvard Center for World Religions, 1998).

37. According to Nara Yasuaki:

> With the Sōtō school, its "Green Plan" has highlighted the importance of environmental preservation to the general lay membership through activities (including the publications of pamphlets, short books, and calendars) sponsored by individual temples, youth groups, and women's groups. From a Buddhist perspective, the environmental issue also requires careful doctrinal reflection in addition to action. In the West, this type of work has already begun in earnest.

From "The Sōtō Zen School in Modern Japan," paper presented at Dōgen Zen and Its Relevance for Our Time (symposium at Stanford University, October 1999).

38. See Susan B. Hanley, *Everyday Things in Premodern Japan: The Hidden Legacy of Material Culture* (Berkeley: University of California Press, 1999).

39. E. F. Schumacher, *Small Is Beautiful: Economics as if People Mattered* (rpt., New York: Harper, 1989), originally published in the 1970s.

40. *Dōgen zenji zenshū*, VI:24; translation is in Tanahashi, ed., *Moon in a Dewdrop*, p. 65. On the notion of cosmocentrism, see Ives, *Zen Awakening and Society*, pp. 136–138.

41. This notion is expressed in Dōgen's *Shōbōgenzō* "Bendōwa" fascicle in *Dōgen zenji zenshū*, vol. I.

42. See Richard Jaffe, *Neither Monks nor Laymen* (Princeton, NJ: Princeton University Press, 2002).

43. Tamamuro Taijō, *Sōshiki Bukkyō* (Tokyo: Daihōrinkaku, 1963). A popular movie released in the 1980s, *The Funeral* directed by Itami Jūzō, portrayed a Buddhist priest unable to conceal that his only interest was in collecting a donation at the funeral of an old man whose family's turmoil and scandals were also being revealed.

44. Tanabe Hajime wrote *Zangedō toshite no tetsugaku* (Philosophy as Repentance, or Metanoetics) at the end of the war, and Ienaga Saburō, beginning in the 1950s, protested Japanese history textbooks for their dishonesty and duplicity on Nanking and related topics. See Tanabe, *Philosophy as Metanoetics*, trans. Takeuchi Yoshinori (Berkeley: University of California Press, 1990).

45. See *Bukkyō, tokushū: Sabetsu* [Buddhism: Special Issue on Discrimination] 15/4 (1991); and Nakao Shunbaku, *Bukkyō to sabetsu* [Buddhism and Discrimination] (Kyoto: Nagata bunshodō, 1985).

46. Ueda Shizuteru, "Nishida, Nationalism, and the War in Question," in Heisig and Maraldo, eds., *Rude Awakenings*, p. 82.

47. Matsuo, "What Is Kamakura New Buddhism?" p. 180.

48. Christopher Ives, "What's Compassion Got to Do with It? Determinants of Zen Social Ethics in Japan," *Journal of Buddhist Ethics* 12 (2005): 47.

49. Brian (Daizen) Victoria, "Japanese Corporate Zen," in E. Patricia Tsurumi, ed., *The Other Japan: Postwar Realities* (Armonk, NY: Sharpe, 1988), p. 137.

50. Albert Welter, *Monks, Rulers, and Literati: The Political Ascendancy of Chan Buddhism* (New York: Oxford University Press, 2006), p. 37. Also, "Throughout the course of Chan history, as with the history of Buddhism in China as a whole, the fate of the religion was intricately bound to official favor" (p. 174).

51. Ibid., p. 26.

52. See Foulk, "Myth, Ritual, and Monastic Practice."

53. Ichikawa Hakugen, *Bukkyōsha no sensō-sekinin* (Tokyo: Shunjūsha, 1970).

54. Bernard Faure, *Chan Insights and Oversights: An Epistemological Critique of the Chan Tradition* (Princeton, NJ: Princeton University Press, 1993), p. 82 ("auto-identity" in the original is changed here to "self-identity"). Faure points out that the sentence was excised from a translation of Nishida's *Nihon bunka no mondai* (The Problem of Japanese Culture), from 1940, as translated and included in Ryusaku

Tsunoda, Wm. Theodore de Bary, and Donald Keene, comps., *Sources of Japanese Tradition*, 2 vols. (New York: Columbia University Press, 1964), 2:350–365, see p. 362, apparently to make the passage sound more benign. The phrase about accountability appears in Faure, "The Kyoto School and Reverse Orientalism," in Charles Wei-hsun Fu and Steven Heine, eds., *Japan in Traditional and Postmodern Perspectives* (Albany: State University of New York Press, 1995), p. 272. Another problematic Nishida essay is *Kokutai* (The National Polity) from 1944.

55. Faure, "The Kyoto School and Reverse Orientalism," p. 248.

56. For a discussion of the "empty center" of Tokyo from a postmodern semiotic perspective, see Roland Barthes, *Empire of Signs* (New York: Hill and Wang, 1982).

57. Ives, *Zen Awakening and Society*, pp. 91–95; this is juxtaposed with Thich Nhat Hanh's reworking of the traditional ten precepts, pp. 95–96.

58. This list includes eminent Zen historians Yanagida Seizan of Kyoto University and the Rinzai sect and Masunaga Reihō of the Sōtō sect's Komazawa University.

59. Graham Parkes, "The Putative Fascism of the Kyoto School and the Political Correctness of the Modern Academy," *Philosophy East and West* 47/3 (1997): 305, 307, 327. While acknowledging that "some of the utterances of members of the Kyoto School are highly problematic" (p. 328), this article becomes dubious when it tries to salvage nearly all aspects of the wartime writings, including finding a way to put Nishitani's musings on the pros and cons of Hitler in "historical context." See also Michiko Yusa, *Zen & Philosophy: An Intellectual Biography of Nishida Kitarō* (Honolulu: University of Hawaii Press, 2002), for a cogent explanation and defense of Nishida's intellectual development. It is interesting that while Parkes criticizes Faure's critique of the Kyoto school in the above article, Faure labels critical Buddhism a form of "intellectual terrorism," in "The Kyoto School and Reverse Orientalism," p. 269.

60. In *Zen at War*, Victoria shows that Sōtō Zen priest Uchiyama Gudō and other politically radical Buddhist priests are highly praised. Uchiyama was a martyr who along with others was convicted and executed in the high treason incident (*taigyaku jiken*) of 1910, which was used as an excuse for suppressing individual freedoms (pp. 30–48).

61. Victoria, *Zen War Stories*, p. 68.

62. Ibid., p. 179. General Tōjō Hideki kept ties with Pure Land, and for Itagaki Seishiro the Nichiren school provided comfort.

63. Robert H. Sharf, "The Idolization of Enlightenment: On the Mummification of Ch'an Masters in Medieval China," *History of Religions* 32/1 (1992): 1–31.

64. Shimada Hiromi, *Kaimyō: Naze shigo ni namae o kaeru no ka* [Posthumous Initiation Names: Why Are Names Changed Posthumously?] (Kyoto: Hōzōkan, 1991), pp. 67–71. For a detailed discussion in English, see Stephen G. Covell, *Japanese Temple Buddhism: Worldliness in a Religion of Renunciation* (Honolulu: University of Hawaii Press, 2006), pp. 165–169.

65. Bodiford, "Zen and the Art of Religious Prejudice," pp. 8–9.

66. A prime example, as shown in Figure 4.4, is using two kanji, *gen* and *da*, which, when written as a single kanji becomes *chiku*, beasts. Also, the *kaimyō* rite is

not the only aspect of discrimination; other rituals, such as *nanoka-gyō*, which memorializes the deceased for forty-nine days after death, are similarly affected.

67. Noma Hiroshi and Okiura Kazuteru, *Sei to sen* [Sacred and Profane], 4 vols., *Ajia, Nihon no chūsei, kinsei, kindai* (Tokyo: Ninbun shoin, 1983–1986).

68. This category is discussed in the *Lotus Sutra*, chapter 14 ("Peaceful Practices"), and in Dōgen's *Shōbōgenzō* "Sanjigo" fascicle and in his *Eihei kōroku* (3.66, 6.24, 7.47).

69. See Nagahara Keiji, "The Medieval Origins of the Eta-Hinin," *Journal of Japanese Studies* 5/2 (1979): 385–403; and Leslie D. Alldritt, "The *Burakumin*: The Complicity of Japanese Buddhism in Oppression and an Opportunity for Liberation," *Journal of Buddhist Ethics* 7 (2000), available at http://jbe.gold.ac.uk/7/alldritt001 .html.

70. "Sendara mondai senmon i'inkai hokoku" [Report of the Research Group on the Problem of Candala], no. 10, ed. Eiheiji Sendara Mondai Senmon I'inkai, *Sanshō* 606 (1994): 8–31; see esp. p. 14.

71. Hakamaya Noriaki, *Hongaku shisō hihan* (Tokyo: Daizō shuppan, 1989), p. 142.

72. Sallie King, *Buddha Nature* (Albany: State University of New York Press, 1991), p. 170.

73. In a similar vein, during the *Suiheisha* equal rights movement in the 1920s, members of the Jōdo Shinshū sect made an appeal for egalitarianism based on a notion that conflated Buddha-nature theory with the imperial ideology that all followers of the emperor are indistinguishable.

74. Ichikawa, *Bukkyōsha no sensō-sekinin*.

EPILOGUE

1. I am highlighting a connection between apparent compromises of principle involved in fostering Zen rites that open the door to excesses and deficiencies in Zen rights. However, it is important to point out that the T'ang dynasty commentator Tsung-mi had already anticipated many of the contemporary arguments by drawing a link between the problematics of Zen writes, especially in the discourse of Ma-tsu's Hung-chou lineage known for defying convention and common sense, and the matter of rights. As Peter N. Gregory notes, "Tsung-mi was highly critical of the antinomian implications of Hung-chou Ch'an's radical rhetoric"; in *Tsung-mi and the Sinification of Buddhism* (rpt., Honolulu: University of Hawaii Press, 2002), p. 305.

2. George Orwell, *1984* (New York: Signet, 1949), p. 214. Orwell notes in the same passage the mind control technique which "lies at the very heart" of the government "since the essential act of the Party is to use conscious deception while retaining the firmness of purpose that goes with complete honesty," and "[e]ven in using the word *doublethink* it is necessary to exercise *doublethink*. For by using the word one admits that one is tampering with reality; by a fresh act of *doublethink* one erases this knowledge; and so on indefinitely with the lie always one leap ahead of the truth."

3. Micha F. Lindemans, "Janus," available at http://www.pantheon.org/articles/j/janus.html (accessed August 28, 2006).

4. Laura Victoria Leven, "Introduction," in Robert Louis Stevenson, *Dr. Jekyll and Mr. Hyde* (New York: Barnes and Noble, 2001), p. xii.

5. Based on a conversation with Morten Schlütter. The situation in regard to understanding Zen seems parallel to intellectual debates (or lack of same, in the sense that a debate requires a two-way dialogue) involving far different areas of inquiry, such as the following remarks on contemporary education theory:

> In the first few years of this decade, two parallel debates about the achievement gap have emerged. The first is about causes; the second is about cures. The first has been taking place in academia, among economists and anthropologists and sociologists who are trying to figure out exactly where the gap comes from, why it exists and why it persists. The second is happening among and around a loose coalition of schools, all of them quite new, all established with the goal of wiping out the achievement gap altogether. The two debates seem barely to overlap—the principals don't pay much attention to the research papers being published in scholarly journals, and the academics have yet to study closely what is going on in these schools. Examined together, though, they provide a complete and nuanced picture, sometimes disheartening, sometimes hopeful, of what the president and his education officials are up against as they strive to keep the promise[s] they have made.

From Paul Tough, "What It Takes to Make a Student," *New York Times Sunday Magazine* (November 26, 2006).

6. Leven, "Introduction," p. xiv.

7. Mark Rowe refers to the impact of the larger issue of what he terms the "funeral problem" (*sōsai mondai*) as "a catchall term for a broad range of doctrinal, historical, social, institutional, and economic issues confronting the traditional sects of Japanese Buddhism," in "Where the Action Is: Sites of Contemporary Sōtō Buddhism," *Japanese Journal of Religious Studies* 31/2 (2004): 357–388, esp. p. 358.

8. "Sendara mondai senmon i'inkai hokoku" [Report of the Research Group on the Problem of Candala], no. 10, ed. Eiheiji Sendara Mondai Senmon I'inkai, *Sanshō* 606 (1994): 32.

9. Nam-lin Hur, "The Sōtō Sect and Japanese Military Imperialism in Korea," *Japanese Journal of Religious Studies* 26/1–2 (1999): 107–134.

10. Yasuaki Nara, "The Sōtō Zen School in Modern Japan," paper presented at Dōgen Zen and Its Relevance for Our Time, symposium at Stanford University (October 23–24, 1999), available at http://www.stanford.edu/group/scbs/calendar/1999–00/dogen_zen/papers/nara.html (accessed August 2, 2006). Also, among other lineages, the Myōshinji faction, the single largest subgroup of the Rinzai sect's temple networks, has undertaken similar exercises. There have been changes in the way funerals are conducted in response to issues such as insufficient space for graves, changing family organizational structures and temple affiliations in an increasingly mobile society, and the role of funeral parlors (*sōgiya*) and motorized hearses

(*reikyūsha*) in addition to so-called natural funerals (*shizensō*) in which ashes are cast in the water rather than buried. See Mark Rowe, "Stickers for Nails: The Ongoing Transformation of Roles, Rites, and Symbols in Japanese Funerals," *Japanese Journal of Religious Studies* 27/3–4 (2000): 353–378. In addition, Stephen G. Covell, dealing mainly with the Tendai sect, discusses the difficulties in revamping the system in contemporary Buddhist temples, in *Japanese Temple Buddhism: Worldliness in a Religion of Renunciation* (Honolulu: University of Hawaii Press, 2006), pp. 183–190. Furthermore, Rowe depicts new, innovative approaches to funeral rites developed within the Sōtō sect, such as Tōchōji temple's stylish facilities and a cost-saving "burial society" (*en no kai*).

11. See Daniel Stevenson, "The Four Kinds of Samadhi in Early T'ien-t'ai Buddhism," in Peter N. Gregory, ed., *Traditions of Meditation in Chinese Buddhism* (Honolulu: University of Hawaii Press, 1986), pp. 45–97. For other sources on East Asian Buddhism, see Jacqueline Stone, *Original Enlightenment and the Transformation of Medieval Japanese Buddhism* (Honolulu: University of Hawaii Press, 1999); Pei-yi Wu, "Self-Examination and Confession of Sins in Traditional China," *Harvard Journal of Asiatic Studies* 39/1 (1978): 5–38; and Chün-fang Yü, *The Renewal of Buddhism in China: Chu-hung and the Late Ming Synthesis* (New York: Columbia University Press, 1990).

12. Adapted from Philip Yampolsky, trans., *The Platform Sutra of the Sixth Patriarch: The Text of the Tun-Huang Manuscript* (New York: Columbia University Press, 1967), p. 141.

13. As cited in Jinhua Jia, *The Hongzhou School of Chan Buddhism in Eighth-through Tenth-Century China* (Albany: State University of New York Press, 2006), p. 69.

14. Steven Heine, "Dōgen and the Precepts, Revisited," in Damien Keown, ed., *Buddhist Studies from India to America: Essays in Honor of Charles S. Prebish* (London: RoutledgeCurzon, 2005), pp. 11–31.

15. *Dōgen zenji zenshū*, ed. Kawamura Kōdō et al., 7 vols. (Tokyo: Shunjūsha, 1988–1993), VII:66.

16. This is one of countless examples in Japanese religions in which a simple pun or wordplay creates a complex sacred association. Other examples occur at Saijōji, the Sōtō temple discussed in chapter 3, in which a talisman described as "a tree that makes money" (*kane no naru ki*) contains bells that are shaken because money and bell are both pronounced "kane," and at Tako Yakushi Hall at Jōjuin temple in Meguro, Tokyo, which venerates a sacred octopus that can cure bodily protrusions as both the words octopus and corn (as on the foot) are pronounced "tako." See Ian Reader and George J. Tanabe, Jr., *Practically Religious: Worldly Benefits and the Common Religion of Japan* (Honolulu: University of Hawaii Press, 1998), pp. 119 and 249.

17. Steven Heine, "Abbreviation or Aberration: The Role of the *Shushōgi* in Modern Sōtō Zen Buddhism," in Steven Heine and Charles S. Prebish, eds., *Buddhism and the Modern World: Adaptations of an Ancient Tradition* (New York: Oxford University Press, 2003), pp. 161–219.

18. See Ian Reader, "Zazenless Zen? The Position of Zazen in Institutional Zen Buddhism," *Japanese Religions* 14/3 (1986): 7–27.

19. Christopher Ives, *Zen Awakening and Society* (Honolulu: University of Hawaii Press, 1991), p. 109.

20. See Simon P. James, *Zen Buddhism and Environmental Ethics* (Hampshire, England: Ashgate, 2004).

21. Lin Jensen, "An Ear to the Ground: Uncovering the Living Source of Zen Ethics," *Tricycle* 15/4 (2006): 37.

22. I wish to point out parallels in the debate with a more general discussion of modern—or postmodern—society in which the approach of relativism encounters absolutism. According to commentary on Pope Benedict XVI's lecture at the University of Regensburg, which contained supposedly offensive comments about Islam:

> On the pope's third point—If the West's high culture keeps playing in the sandbox of postmodern irrationalism—in which there is "your truth" and "my truth" but nothing such as "the truth"—the West will be unable to defend itself. Why? Because the West won't be able to give reasons why its commitments to civility, tolerance, human rights and the rule of law are worth defending. A Western world stripped of convictions about the truths that make Western civilization possible cannot make a useful contribution to a genuine dialogue of civilizations, for any such dialogue must be based on a shared understanding that human beings can, however, imperfectly, come to know the truth of things.

From George Weigel, "Pope Places Large Questions on Our Agenda," *Miami Herald* (September 24, 2006).

23. Rowe, "Where the Action Is," p. 376.

24. According to David Chappell's typology, five kinds of repentance are (1) communal repentance to the samgha to ensure monastic conformity; (2) personal repentance of karmic history; (3) mythological repentance to a supermundane Buddha; (4) meditation repentance of incorrect perceptions and attachments; and (5) philosophical repentance of wrong concepts and discrimination; see Chappell, "Formless Repentance in Comparative Perspective," in *Report of International Conference on Ch'an Buddhism* (Taiwan: Fo Kuang Shan, 1990), pp. 251–267, esp. p. 253.

25. Tanabe Hajime, *Philosophy as Metanoetics*, trans. Takeuchi Yoshinori (Berkeley: University of California Press, 1990), p. 296. However, it is important to keep in mind that Tanabe's message was directed to the nation as well as to his fellow philosophers whose prewar writings contributed to a militarist ideology, which suffered defeat and humiliation in the war.

26. Interestingly, it was Henry James, Sr., who provided the classic rationale for detachment from ethical concerns. Of William James's father, it was said, "As a Platonist and follower of Swedenborgian doctrine, he believed that there are two realms: a visible and an invisible, named Divine Love, the real one." According to Louis Menand:

James therefore claimed to have no use for morality, a concept he regarded as bound up with the pernicious belief that people are responsible for the good or evil of their actions. People who believe this are people who think they can make themselves worthier than other people by their own exertions. But this is to worship the false god of selfhood. "All conscious virtue is spurious," James insisted.

From Menand, *The Metaphysical Club: A Story of Ideas in America* (New York: Farrar, Straus and Giroux, 2001), pp. 85–86.

27. See Takeuchi Yoshimi, *What Is Modernity? Writings of Takeuchi Yoshimi*, ed. and trans. Richard F. Calichman (New York: Columbia University Press, 2005), pp. 75 and 175.

Bibliography

Abe, Masao. *A Study of Dōgen: His Philosophy and Religion*. Albany: State University of New York Press, 1994.

———. *Buddhism and Interfaith Dialogue*. Honolulu: University of Hawaii Press, 1995.

———. *Zen and the Modern World*, ed. Steven Heine. Honolulu: University of Hawaii Press, 2003.

Adamek, Wendi. "Imagining the Portrait of a Chan Master," in Bernard Faure, ed., *Chan Buddhism in Ritual Context*. London: Routledge, 2003, pp. 36–73.

Aitken, Robert, trans. *The Gateless Barrier: The Wu-Men Kuan (Mumonkan)*. New York: North Point, 1991.

Akizuki Ryūmin. *Zen mondō*. Tokyo: Sōbunsha, 1976.

Alldritt, Leslie D. "The *Burakumin*: The Complicity of Japanese Buddhism in Oppression and an Opportunity for Liberation," *Journal of Buddhist Ethics* 7 (2000), available at http://jbe.gold.ac.uk/7/alldritt001.html.

Andō Yoshinori. *Chūsei Zenshū bunseki no kenkyū*. Tokyo: Kokusho inkōkai, 2000.

Arai, Paula. "Women and Dōgen: Rituals Actualizing Empowerment and Healing," in Steven Heine and Dale S. Wright, eds., *Zen Ritual*. New York: Oxford University Press, 2007, pp. 185–204.

"Asian and American Leadership Styles: How Are They Unique?" *Harvard Business School Working Knowledge* (June 27, 2005). Available at http://hbswk.hbs.edu/item/4869.html.

Azuma Ryūshin. *Sōtōshū: Waga ie no shūkyō*. Tokyo: Daihōrinkaku, 1983.

Barthes, Roland. *Empire of Signs*. New York: Hill and Wang, 1982.

Bell, Catherine. *Ritual: Perspectives and Dimensions*. New York: Oxford University Press, 1997.

Bjerken, Zeff. "On Mandalas, Monarchs, and Mortuary Magic: Siting the Sarvadurgatiparisodhana Tantra in Tibet," *Journal of the American Academy of Religion* 73/3 (2005): 813–842.

Bloss, Lowell. "The Buddha and the Naga: A Study in Buddhist Folk Religiosity," *History of Religions* 13/1 (1973): 36–51.

Bodiford, William M. *Sōtō Zen in Medieval Japan.* Honolulu: University of Hawaii Press, 1993.

———. "Sōtō Zen in a Japanese Town: Field Notes on a Once-Every-Thirty-Three-Years Kannon Festival," *Japanese Journal of Religious Studies* 22/1 (1994): 3–36.

———. "Zen and the Art of Religious Prejudice: Efforts to Reform a Tradition of Social Discrimination," *Japanese Journal of Religious Studies* 23/1–2 (1996): 1–27.

———. "The Enlightenment of Kami and Ghosts: Spirit Ordinations in Japanese Sōtō Zen," in Bernard Faure, ed., *Chan Buddhism in Ritual Context.* London: RoutledgeCurzon, 2003, pp. 250–265.

Bouchy, Anne-Marie. "Le Renard: Element de la conception du monde dans la tradition japonaise," in Marie-Lise Befa and Roberte Hamayon, eds., *Le Renard: Tours, detours et retours.* Special issue of *Etudes mongoles ... et sibeeriennes* 15 (1984): 9–70.

Brinker, Helmut, and Hiroshi Kanazawa. *Zen: Masters of Meditation and Writings.* Zurich: Artibus Asiae, 1996.

Britton, Dorothy, trans. *A Haiku Journey: Bashō's Narrow Road to a Far Province.* Tokyo: Kodansha, 1980.

Brown, Peter. *The Cult of Saints: Its Rise and Function in Latin Christianity.* Chicago: University of Chicago Press, 1981.

Bukkyō, tokushū: Sabetsu [Buddhism: Special Issue on Discrimination] 15/4 (1991).

Buruma, Ian. *Inventing Japan, 1853–1964.* New York: Modern Library, 2003.

Buruma, Ian, and Avishai Margalit. *Occidentalism: The West in the Eyes of Its Enemies.* New York: Penguin, 2004.

Cage, John. *Silence: Lectures and Writings.* Middletown, CT: Wesleyan University Press, 1961.

Carroll, Lewis. *Alice's Adventures in Wonderland and Through the Looking-Glass,* ed. Hugh Haughton. New York: Penguin, 1998.

Carse, James P. *Finite and Infinite Games: A Vision of Life as Play and Possibility.* New York: Ballantine, 1986.

Castaneda, Carlos. *The Teachings of Don Juan: A Yaqui Way of Knowledge.* Berkeley: University of California Press, 1968.

Ch'an-men kuei-shih. In *Taishō shinshū daizōkyō,* ed. Takakusu Junjirō and Watanabe Kaigyoku, 100 vols. Tokyo: Taishō issaikyō kankōkai, 1924–1932, 51:250c–251b. Cited in text as CMK.

Chappell, David. "Formless Repentance in Comparative Perspective," in *Report of International Conference on Ch'an Buddhism.* Taiwan: Fo Kuang Shan, 1990, pp. 251–267.

Clarke, J. J. *The Tao of the West: Western Transformations of Taoist Thought.* London: Routledge, 2000.

Cleary, Thomas. *No Barrier: Unlocking the Zen Koan*. New York: Bantam, 1993.

Cleary, Thomas, trans. *Book of Serenity: One Hundred Zen Dialogues*. Hudson, NY: Lindisfarne, 1990.

Cohen, Leonard. "There Is a War," on *New Skin for the Old Ceremony* (1974).

Cole, Alan. *Patriarchs on Paper: The Gradual Birth of Chinese Buddhas in Tang-Era Literature*. Berkeley: University of California Press, forthcoming.

Collcutt, Martin. *Five Mountains: The Rinzai Zen Monastic Institution in Medieval Japan*. Cambridge, MA: Harvard University Press, 1981.

Covell, Stephen G. *Japanese Temple Buddhism: Worldliness in a Religion of Renunciation*. Honolulu: University of Hawaii Press, 2006.

Daiyūzan: Daiyūzan Saijōji kaisō roppyakunen hōzan. Kanagawa-ken, Japan: Daiyūzan Saijōji kaisō roppyakunen hōzan jimuchō, 1994.

Dale, Peter N. *The Myth of Japanese Uniqueness*. New York: St. Martin's, 1986.

Dōgen zenji zenshū, ed. Kawamura Kōdō et al., 7 vols. Tokyo: Shunjūsha, 1988–1993.

Droit, Roger-Pol. *The Cult of Nothingness: The Philosophers and the Buddha*. Chapel Hill: University of North Carolina Press, 2003.

Dumoulin, Heinrich. *A History of Zen Buddhism*. Boston: Beacon, 1963.

———. *Zen Buddhism: A History I (India and China)*. New York: Macmillan, 1987.

———. *Zen Buddhism: A History II (Japan)*. New York: Macmillan, 1990.

Dutt, Sukumar. *Buddhist Monks and Monasteries of India: Their History and Their Contribution to Indian Culture*. Rpt., Delhi: Motilal Banarsidass, 1988.

Eliot, T. S. *The Waste Land and Other Poems*. New York: Barnes & Noble Classics, 2005.

Faure, Bernard. *The Rhetoric of Immediacy*. Princeton, NJ: Princeton University Press, 1991.

———. "Fair and Unfair Language Games in Chan/Zen," in Steven T. Katz, ed., *Mysticism and Language*. New York: Oxford University Press, 1992, pp. 158–180.

———. *Chan Insights and Oversights: An Epistemological Critique of the Chan Tradition*. Princeton, NJ: Princeton University Press, 1993.

———. "The Kyoto School and Reverse Orientalism," in Charles Wei-hsun Fu and Steven Heine, eds., *Japan in Traditional and Postmodern Perspectives*. Albany: State University of New York Press, 1995, pp. 245–281.

———. *Visions of Power: Imagining Medieval Japanese Buddhism*. Princeton, NJ: Princeton University Press, 1996.

———. "Chan and Zen Studies: The State of the Field," in Bernard Faure, ed., *Chan Buddhism in Ritual Context*. London: RoutledgeCurzon, 2003, pp. 1–35.

———. "*Quand l'habit fait le moine*: The Symbolism of the *Kasaya* in Sōtō Zen," in Bernard Faure, ed., *Chan Buddhism in Ritual Context*. London: RoutledgeCurzon, 2003, pp. 211–249.

Foulk, T. Griffith. "Myth, Ritual, and Monastic Practice in Sung Ch'an Buddhism," in Patricia B. Ebrey and Peter N. Gregory, eds., *Religion and Society in T'ang and Sung China*. Honolulu: University of Hawaii Press, 1993, pp. 147–208.

———. "Sung Controversies concerning the 'Separate Transmission' of Ch'an," in Peter N. Gregory and Daniel A. Getz, eds., *Buddhism in the Sung*. Honolulu: University of Hawaii Press, 1999, pp. 220–284.

———. "The Form and Function of Kōan Literature," in Steven Heine and Dale S. Wright, eds., *The Kōan: Texts and Contexts in Zen Buddhism*. New York: Oxford University Press, 2000, pp. 15–45.

———. "The 'Rules of Purity' in Japanese Zen," in Steven Heine and Dale S. Wright, eds., *Zen Classics: Formative Texts in the History of Zen Buddhism*. New York: Oxford University Press, 2005, pp. 137–169.

———. "Ritual in Japanese Zen Buddhism," in Steven Heine and Dale S. Wright, eds., *Zen Ritual*. New York: Oxford University Press, 2007, pp. 21–82.

Foulk, T. Griffith, and Robert H. Sharf. "On the Ritual Use of Ch'an Portraiture in Medieval China," *Cahiers d'Extrême-Asie* 7 (1993–1994): 149–219.

The Funeral, dir. Itami Jūzō (1987).

Goff, Janet. "Foxes in Japanese Culture," *Japan Quarterly* 44/2 (April–June 1997): 67–77.

Goodwin, Janet R. *Alms and Vagabonds: Buddhist Temples and Popular Patronage in Medieval Japan*. Honolulu: University of Hawaii Press, 1994.

Gorai Shigeru, ed. *Inari shinkō no kenkyū*. Tokyo: Sanin shimbunsha, 1985.

Goto, Seiko. *The Japanese Garden: Gateway to the Human Spirit*. New York: Peter Lang, 2003.

Gozan jissatsu zu: Zengaku daijiten. Tokyo: Taishūkan shoten, 1985, first appendix, pp. 10–32. Cited in text as GJZ.

Grapard, Allan. *The Protocol of the Gods: A Study of the Kasuga Cult in Japanese History*. Berkeley: University of California Press, 1992.

Gregory, Peter N. *Tsung-mi and the Sinification of Buddhism*. Rpt., Honolulu: University of Hawaii Press, 2002.

Gurevich, Aron. *Medieval Popular Culture: Problems of Belief and Perception*. Cambridge: Cambridge University Press, 1988.

Hakamaya Noriaki. *Hongaku shisō hihan*. Tokyo: Daizō shuppan, 1989.

———. *Hihan Bukkyō*. Tokyo: Daizō shuppan, 1990.

Hanley, Susan B. *Everyday Things in Premodern Japan: The Hidden Legacy of Material Culture*. Berkeley: University of California Press, 1999.

Heine, Steven. "Postwar Issues in Japanese Buddhism," in Charles W. Fu and Gerhard Spiegler, eds., *Religious Issues and Interreligious Dialogues: An Analysis and Sourcebook of Developments since 1945*. Westport, CT: Greenwood, 1989, pp. 245–276.

———. *Shifting Shape, Shaping Text: Philosophy and Folklore in the Fox Kōan*. Honolulu: University of Hawaii Press, 1999.

———. *Opening a Mountain: Kōans of the Zen Masters*. New York: Oxford University Press, 2002.

———. "Abbreviation or Aberration: The Role of the *Shushōgi* in Modern Sōtō Zen Buddhism," in Steven Heine and Charles S. Prebish, eds., *Buddhism and the Modern World: Adaptations of an Ancient Tradition*. New York: Oxford University Press, 2003, pp. 161–219.

———. "Dōgen and the Precepts, Revisited," in Damien Keown, ed., *Buddhist Studies from India to America: Essays in Honor of Charles S. Prebish*. London: RoutledgeCurzon, 2005, pp. 11–31.

———. *White Collar Zen: Using Zen Principles to Overcome Obstacles and Achieve Your Career Goals*. New York: Oxford University Press, 2005.

———. *Did Dōgen Go to China? What He Wrote and When He Wrote It*. New York: Oxford University Press, 2006.

———. "A Critical Survey of Works on Zen after Yampolsky," *Philosophy East and West* 47/4 (2007): 125–142.

Heine, Steven, trans. "Advice on the Practice of Zazen: Taishō Volume 82, Number 2586," in *Zen Texts* (BDK English Tripitaka 73-III, 98-VIII, 98-IX, 104-I). Berkeley, CA: Numata Center for Buddhist Translation and Research, 2005, pp. 263–275.

———. *The Zen Poetry of Dōgen: Verses from the Mountain of Eternal Peace*. Mt. Tremper, NY: Dharma Communications, 2005.

Heisig, James W., and John C. Maraldo, eds. *Rude Awakenings: Zen, the Kyoto School, & the Question of Nationalism*. Honolulu: University of Hawaii Press, 1995.

Herrigel, Eugen. *Zen in the Art of Archery*. New York: Vintage, 1953.

Herrigel, Gustie. *Zen and the Art of Flower Arrangement*, trans. R. F. C. Hull. Rpt., London: Souvenir, 1999.

Hirose Ryōko. "Sōtō zensō ni okeru shinjin kado-akurei chin'atsu," *Indogaku Bukkyōgaku kenkyū* 21/2 (1983): 233–236.

Hori, Victor Sōgen. "Kōan and *Kenshō* in the Rinzai Zen Curriculum," in Steven Heine and Dale S. Wright, eds., *The Kōan: Texts and Contexts in Zen Buddhism*. New York: Oxford University Press, 2000, pp. 280–315.

———. *Zen Sand: The Book of Capping Phrases for Kōan Practice*. Honolulu: University of Hawaii Press, 2003.

Horio Tsutomu. "The *Chūōkōron* Discussions: Their Background and Meaning," in James W. Heisig and John C. Maraldo, eds., *Rude Awakenings: Zen, the Kyoto School, & the Question of Nationalism*. Honolulu: University of Hawaii Press, 1995, pp. 289–315.

Hu Shih. "Ch'an (Zen) Buddhism in China: Its History and Method," *Philosophy East and West* 3/1 (1953): 3–24.

Hur, Nam-lin. "The Sōtō Sect and Japanese Military Imperialism in Korea," *Japanese Journal of Religious Studies* 26/1–2 (1999): 107–134.

Ichikawa Hakugen. *Bukkyōsha no sensō-sekinin*. Tokyo: Shunjūsha, 1970.

Iriya Yoshitaka, ed. *Baso goroku*. Kyoto: Zen bunka kenkyūjō, 1974.

Iriya Yoshitaka et al., eds. *Hekiganroku*, 3 vols. Tokyo: Iwanami shoten, 1992–1996.

Ishii Shūdō. *Sōdai zenshū shi no kenkyū*. Tokyo: Daitō shuppansha, 1987.

Ishikawa Rikizan. "Chūsei Zenshū to shinbutsu shūgō: Toku ni Sōtōshū no chihōteki tenkai to kirigami shiryō o chūshin ni shite," *Nihon Bukkyō* 60–61 (1984): 41–56.

———. "Transmission of *Kirigami* (Secret Initiation Documents): A Sōtō Practice in Medieval Japan," in Steven Heine and Dale S. Wright, eds., *The Kōan: Texts and Contexts in Zen Buddhism*. New York: Oxford University Press, 2000, pp. 233–243.

Ives, Christopher. *Zen Awakening and Society*. Honolulu: University of Hawaii Press, 1991.

———. "What's Compassion Got to Do with It? Determinants of Zen Social Ethics in Japan," *Journal of Buddhist Ethics* 12 (2005): 37–61.

Jaffe, Richard. *Neither Monks nor Laymen*. Princeton, NJ: Princeton University Press, 2002.

James, Simon P. *Zen Buddhism and Environmental Ethics*. Hampshire, England: Ashgate, 2004.

Jensen, Lin. "An Ear to the Ground: Uncovering the Living Source of Zen Ethics," *Tricycle* 15/4 (2006): 34–37.

Jia, Jinhua. *The Hongzhou School of Chan Buddhism in Eighth- through Tenth-Century China*. Albany: State University of New York Press, 2006.

Kagamishima Genryū, Satō Tatsugen, and Kosaka Kiyū, eds. *Yakuchū Zen'en shingi*. Tokyo: Sōtōshū shūmuchō, 1972.

Kasahara, Kazuo, ed. *A History of Japanese Religion*. Tokyo: Kosei, 2001.

Kasulis, Thomas. "Researching the Strata of the Japanese Self," in Roger T. Ames and Wimal Dissanayake, eds., *Self as Person in Asian Theory and Practice*. Albany: State University of New York Press, 1994, pp. 87–106.

Katz, Steven. *Mysticism and Philosophical Analysis*. New York: Oxford University Press, 1978.

Kelsey, Michael. "Salvation of the Snake, the Snake of Salvation: Buddhist-Shinto Conflict and Resolution," *Japanese Journal of Religious Studies* 8/1–2 (1981): 83–113.

Kim, Hee-Jin. "The Reason of Words and Letters: Dōgen and *Kōan* Language," in William R. LaFleur, ed., *Dōgen Studies*. Honolulu: University of Hawaii Press, 1985, pp. 54–82.

King, Sallie. *Buddha Nature*. Albany: State University of New York Press, 1991.

Kirita Kiyohide. "D. T. Suzuki on Society and the State," in James W. Heisig and John C. Maraldo, eds., *Rude Awakenings: Zen, the Kyoto School, & the Question of Nationalism*. Honolulu: University of Hawaii Press, 1995, pp. 52–76.

Koestler, Arthur. "The Lotus and the Robot," *Encounter* 15 (1959): 13–32.

———. *The Lotus and the Robot*. New York: Harper Colophon, 1960.

———. "Neither Lotus nor Robot," *Encounter* 16 (1960): 58–59.

Koizuka Minoru. *Kitsune monogatari*. Tokyo: Sanichi shobō, 1982.

Kraft, Kenneth. *Eloquent Zen: Daitō and Early Japanese Zen*. Honolulu: University of Hawaii Press, 1992.

Lai, Whalen. "The *Chan-ch'a ching*: Religion and Magic in Medieval China," in Robert Buswell, ed., *Chinese Buddhist Apocrypha*. Honolulu: University of Hawaii Press, 1990, pp. 175–206.

Lehmann, John F. *Lewis Carroll and the Spirit of Nonsense*. Nottingham, England: University of Nottingham Press, 1972.

Leighton, Taigen Dan, and Shohaku Okumura, trans. *Dōgen's Extended Record: A Translation of the Eihei Kōroku*. Boston: Wisdom, 2004.

Leven, Laura Victoria. "Introduction," in Robert Louis Stevenson, *Dr. Jekyll and Mr. Hyde*. New York: Barnes and Noble, 2001, pp. vii–xv.

Life of Oharu, dir. Mizoguchi Kenji (1964).

Little, Stephen, with Shawn Eichman, eds. *Taoism and the Arts of China*. Chicago: Art Institute of Chicago, 2000.

Lindemans, Micha F. "Janus," available at http://www.pantheon.org/articles/j/janus.html (accessed August 28, 2006).

Lopez, Donald. *Prisoners of Shangri-la: Tibetan Buddhism and the West*. Chicago: University of Chicago Press, 1999.

Lost in Translation, dir. Sofia Coppola (2003).

MacKenzie, John. *Orientalism: History, Theory and the Arts*. Manchester, England: Manchester University Press, 1995.

Mahbubani, Kishore. *Can Asians Think? Understanding the Divide between East and West*. London: Steerforth, 2002.

Matsuo Kenji. "What Is Kamakura New Buddhism? Official Monks and Reclusive Monks," *Japanese Journal of Religious Studies* 24/1–2 (1997): 179–189.

McFarland, H. Neill. *Daruma: The Founder of Zen in Japanese Popular Culture*. Tokyo: Kodansha, 1987.

McRae, John R. *The Northern School and the Formation of Early Ch'an Buddhism*. Honolulu: University of Hawaii Press, 1986.

———. "Yanagida Seizan's Landmark Work on Chinese Ch'an," *Cahiers d'Extrême-Asie* 7 (1993–1994): 51–103.

———. *Seeing through Zen: Encounter, Transformation, and Genealogy in Chinese Chan Buddhism*. Berkeley: University of California Press, 2003.

Menand, Louis. *The Metaphysical Club: A Story of Ideas in America*. New York: Farrar, Straus and Giroux, 2001.

Miller, Alan L. "Religions of Japan," in *Religions of the World*. New York: St. Martin's, 1983.

Mishima Yukio. *Temple of the Golden Pavilion*. New York: Perigee, 1959.

Mitchell, Donald, ed. *Masao Abe: A Zen Life of Dialogue*. New York: Tuttle, 1998.

Moon, Susan, ed. *Not Turning Away: The Practice of Engaged Buddhism*. Boston: Shambhala, 2004.

Nagahara Keiji. "The Medieval Origins of the Eta-Hinin," *Journal of Japanese Studies* 5/2 (1979): 385–403.

Nakamura, Kyoko Motomichi, trans. *Miraculous Stories from the Japanese Buddhist Tradition: The Nihon Ryōiki of the Monk Kyōkai*. Cambridge, MA: Harvard University Press, 1971.

Nakao Shunbaku. *Bukkyō to sabetsu* [Buddhism and Discrimination]. Kyoto: Nagata bunshodō, 1985.

Nara, Yasuaki. "May the Deceased Get Enlightenment! An Aspect of the Enculturation of Buddhism in Japan," *Buddhist-Christian Studies* 15 (1995): 19–42.

———. "The Sōtō Zen School in Modern Japan," paper presented at Dōgen Zen and Its Relevance for Our Time. Symposium at Stanford University, October 1999.

Available at http://www.stanford.edu/group/scbs/calendar/1999–00/dogen_
zen/papers/nara.html

Nisbett, Richard E. *The Geography of Thought: How Asians and Westerners Think Differently... and Why.* New York: Free Press, 2003.

Nishimura Eshin, ed. *Mumonkan.* Tokyo: Iwanami bunko, 1994.

Nishitani Keiji. *Religion and Nothingness,* trans. Jan Van Bragt. Berkeley: University of California Press, 1982.

———. "Science and Zen," in Frederick Franck, ed., *The Buddha Eye: An Anthology of the Kyoto School.* New York: Crossroad, 1982, pp. 107–136.

Noma Hiroshi, and Okiura Kazuteru. *Sei to sen* [Sacred and Profane], 4 vols., *Ajia, Nihon no chūsei, kinsei, kindai.* Tokyo: Ninbun shoin, 1983–1986.

Nozaki, Kiyoshi. *Kitsune: Japan's Fox of Mystery, Romance and Humor.* Tokyo: Hokuseido, 1961.

Odin, Steve. *The Social Self in Zen and American Pragmatism.* Albany: State University of New York Press, 1996.

Ōgawa Takashi. "*Hekiganroku zōkō* (5)," *Zen bunka* 179 (2003): 23–31.

Orwell, George. *1984.* New York: Signet, 1949.

Ōtani Teppu, ed. "Daijōji hihon 'Tōkokuki,'" *Shūgaku kenkyū* 16 (1974): 231–248.

Parkes, Graham. "The Putative Fascism of the Kyoto School and the Political Correctness of the Modern Academy," *Philosophy East and West* 47/3 (1997): 305–336.

Poceski, Mario. *The Hongzhou School and the Development of Tang Dynasty Chan.* New York: Oxford University Press, 2007.

Pye, Michael, trans. *Emerging from Meditation.* Honolulu: University of Hawaii Press, 1990.

Reader, Ian. "Zazenless Zen? The Position of Zazen in Institutional Zen Buddhism," *Japanese Religions* 14/3 (1986): 7–27.

Reader, Ian, and George J. Tanabe, Jr. *Practically Religious: Worldly Benefits and the Common Religion of Japan.* Honolulu: University of Hawaii Press, 1998.

Reeve, C. D. C., ed. *The Trials of Socrates.* Indianapolis, IN: Hackett, 2002.

Reps, Paul, and Nyogen Senzaki, comps. *Zen Flesh, Zen Bones: A Collection of Zen and Pre-Zen Writings.* Boston: Tuttle, 1957; rpt., 1998.

Rowe, Mark. "Stickers for Nails: The Ongoing Transformation of Roles, Rites, and Symbols in Japanese Funerals," *Japanese Journal of Religious Studies* 27/3–4 (2000): 353–378.

———. "Where the Action Is: Sites of Contemporary Sōtō Buddhism," *Japanese Journal of Religious Studies* 31/2 (2004): 357–388.

Ruf, Henry. *Postmodern Rationality, Social Criticism, and Religion.* St. Paul, MN: Paragon, 2005.

Said, Edward. *Orientalism.* New York: Vintage, 1979.

———. *The Zen Monastic Experience.* Princeton, NJ: Princeton University Press, 1992.

Schlütter, Morten. "'Before the Empty Eon' versus 'A Dog Has No Buddha-nature': Kung-an Use in the Ts'ao-tung Tradition and Ta-hui's Kung-an Introspection

Ch'an," in Steven Heine and Dale S. Wright, eds., *The Kōan: Texts and Contexts in Zen Buddhism*. New York: Oxford University Press, 2000, pp. 168–199.

Schmid, Randolph. "Asian, Westerners See World Differently: When Shown a Photo, Chinese Pay More Attention to the Background," available at http://www.chron .com/cs/CDA/ssistory.mpl/nation/3320805.

Schmitt, Jean-Claude. *The Holy Greyhound: Guinefort, Healer of Children since the Thirteenth Century*, trans. Martin Thom. Cambridge: Cambridge University Press, 1979.

Schopen, Gregory. *Bones, Stones and Buddhist Monks: Collected Papers on the Archaeology, Epigraphy and Texts of Monastic Buddhism in India*. Honolulu: University of Hawaii Press, 1997.

Schumacher, E. F. *Small Is Beautiful: Economics as if People Mattered*. Rpt., New York: Harper, 1989.

Sekida, Katsuki, trans. *Two Zen Classics: Mumonkan and Hekiganroku*. New York: Weatherhill, 1977.

"Sendara mondai senmon i'inkai hokoku" [Report of the Research Group on the Problem of Candala], no. 10, ed. Eiheiji Sendara Mondai Senmon I'inkai, *Sanshō* 606 (1994): 8–31.

Sharf, Robert H. "The Idolization of Enlightenment: On the Mummification of Ch'an Masters in Medieval China," *History of Religions* 32/1 (1992): 1–31.

———. "Buddhist Modernism and the Rhetoric of Meditative Experience," *Numen* 42/3 (1995): 228–283.

———. "Sanbōkyōdan: Zen and the Way of the New Religions," *Japanese Journal of Religious Studies* 22/3–4 (1995): 417–458.

———. "Whose Zen? Zen Nationalism Revisited," in James W. Heisig and John C. Maraldo, eds., *Rude Awakenings: Zen, the Kyoto School, & the Question of Nationalism*. Honolulu: University of Hawaii Press, 1995, pp. 40–51.

———. "The Zen of Japanese Nationalism," in Donald S. Lopez, ed., *Curators of the Buddha: The Study of Buddhism under Colonialism*. Chicago: University of Chicago Press, 1995, pp. 107–160.

Shibayama, Zenkei. *Zen Comments on the Mumonkan*. New York: Mentor, 1974.

Shimada Hiromi. *Kaimyō: Naze shigo ni namae o kaeru no ka* [Posthumous Initiation Names: Why Are Names Changed Posthumously?]. Kyoto: Hōzōkan, 1991.

Smyers, Karen. "The Jewel and the Fox: A Study of Shared and Private Meanings in *Inari* Worship." Ph.D. diss., Princeton University, 1993.

———. *The Fox and the Jewel: Shared and Private Meanings in Contemporary Japanese Inari Worship*. Honolulu: University of Hawaii Press, 1998.

Spence, Jonathan. *The Chan's Great Continent: China in Western Minds*. New York: Norton, 1997.

Steinhardt, Nancy Shatzman. *Chinese Imperial City Planning*. Honolulu: University of Hawaii Press, 1990.

Steinhardt, Nancy Shatzman, ed. *Chinese Architecture*. New Haven, CT, and London: Yale University Press, 2002.

Stevenson, Daniel. "The Four Kinds of Samadhi in Early T'ien-t'ai Buddhism," in
Peter N. Gregory, ed., *Traditions of Meditation in Chinese Buddhism*. Honolulu:
University of Hawaii Press, 1986, pp. 45–97.

Stone, Jacqueline. *Original Enlightenment and the Transformation of Medieval Japanese
Buddhism*. Honolulu: University of Hawaii Press, 1999.

Suzuki, Daisetz Teitaro. "Zen: A Reply to Hu Shih," *Philosophy East and West* 3/1
(1953): 25–46.

————. *Introduction to Zen Buddhism*. Rpt., New York: Grove, 1964.

Swanson, Paul L., and Jamie Hubbard, eds. *Pruning the Bodhi Tree: The Storm over
Critical Buddhism*. Honolulu: University of Hawaii Press, 1997.

Taishō shinshū daizōkyō, ed. Takakusu Junjirō and Watanabe Kaigyoku, 100 vols.
Tokyo: Taishō issaikyō kankōkai, 1924–1932. Cited in text as *Taishō*.

Takeuchi Yoshimi. *What Is Modernity? Writings of Takeuchi Yoshimi*, ed. and trans.
Richard F. Calichman. New York: Columbia University Press, 2005.

Takuan Sōhō. *The Unfettered Mind Writings of the Zen Master to the Sword Master*,
trans. William Scott Wilson. New York: Kodansha, 1986.

Tamamuro Taijō. *Sōshiki Bukkyō*. Tokyo: Daihōrinkaku, 1963.

Tanabe, Hajime. *Philosophy as Metanoetics*, trans. Takeuchi Yoshinori. Berkeley:
University of California Press, 1990.

Tanahashi, Kazuaki, ed. *Moon in a Dewdrop: Writings of Zen Master Dōgen*. New York:
North Point, 1985.

Taylor, Mark C. *Erring: A Postmodern A/theology*. Chicago: University of Chicago Press,
1987.

Tillich, Paul, and Hisamatsu Shin'ichi. "Dialogues, East and West: Paul Tillich and
Hisamatsu Shin'ichi (Part One)," *Eastern Buddhist* 4/2 (1971): 89–107.

————. "Dialogues, East and West: Paul Tillich and Hisamatsu Shin'ichi (Part Two),"
Eastern Buddhist 5/2 (1972): 107–128.

Tough, Paul. "What It Takes to Make a Student," *New York Times Sunday Magazine*
(November 26, 2006).

Toyokawa Inari: Myōgonji ni tsutaerareta shinkō, NHK documentary (1993).

Tsunoda, Ryusaku, Wm. Theodore de Bary, and Donald Keene, comps. *Sources of
Japanese Tradition*, 2 vols. New York: Columbia University Press, 1964.

Tucker, Mary Evelyn, and Duncan Ryūken Williams, eds. *Buddhism and Ecology: The
Interconnection of Dharma and Deeds*. Cambridge, MA: Harvard Center for World
Religions, 1998.

Tyler, Royall, trans. *Japanese Tales*. New York: Pantheon, 1988.

Ueda Shizuteru. "Nishida, Nationalism, and the War in Question," in James W.
Heisig and John C. Maraldo, eds., *Rude Awakenings: Zen, the Kyoto School, & the
Question of Nationalism*. Honolulu: University of Hawaii Press, 1995, pp. 77–106.

Umehara Takeshi. *Rakan: Hotoke to hito no aida*. Tokyo: Kodansha, 1977.

Victoria, Brian (Daizen). "Japanese Corporate Zen," in E. Patricia Tsurumi, ed., *The
Other Japan: Postwar Realities*. Armonk, NY: Sharpe, 1988, pp. 131–138.

————. *Zen at War*. New York: Weatherhill, 1997.

————. *Zen War Stories*. London: RoutledgeCurzon, 2003.

Watson, Burton, trans. *Basic Writings of Mo-tzu, Hsun-Tzu, Han Fei-tzu*. New York: Columbia University Press, 1967.

———. *The Complete Works of Chuang Tzu*. New York: Columbia University Press, 1968.

Weigel, George. "Pope Places Large Questions on Our Agenda," *Miami Herald* (September 24, 2006).

Welter, Albert. "Mahakasyapa's Smile: Silent Transmission and the Kung-an (Kōan) Tradition," in Steven Heine and Dale S. Wright, eds., *The Kōan: Texts and Contexts in Zen Buddhism*. New York: Oxford University Press, 2000, pp. 75–109.

———. *Monks, Rulers, and Literati: The Political Ascendancy of Chan Buddhism*. New York: Oxford University Press, 2006.

Williams, Duncan Ryūken. *The Other Side of Zen: A Social History of Sōtō Zen Buddhism in Tokugawa Japan*. Princeton, NJ: Princeton University Press, 2005.

Wittgenstein, Ludwig. *Tractatus Logico-Philosophicus*, trans. D. F. Pears and B. E. McGuinness. New York: Humanities, 1961, no. 6.54.

Wright, Dale S. *Philosophical Meditations on Zen Buddhism*. New York: Cambridge University Press, 1998.

Wu, John C. H. *The Golden Age of Zen*. Taipei: United Publishing Center, 1975.

Wu, Pei-yi. "Self-Examination and Confession of Sins in Traditional China," *Harvard Journal of Asiatic Studies* 39/1 (1978): 5–38.

Wullschlager, Jackie. *Inventing Neverland: The Lives and Fantasies of Lewis Carroll, Edward Lear, J. M. Barrie, Kenneth Grahame and A. A. Milne*. New York: Free Press, 1995.

Yamada Shōji. "The Myth of Zen in the Art of Archery," *Japanese Journal of Religious Studies* 28/1–2 (2001): 1–30.

Yamada Yoshino et al., eds. *Nihon koten bungaku taikei*. Tokyo: Iwanami shoten, 1961–1963.

Yamaoka Takaaki. "Daiyūzan Saijōji ni okeru Bukkyōteki fukugō ni tsuite," *Shūgaku kenkyū* 25 (1983): 115–136.

Yampolsky, Philip B., trans. *The Platform Sutra of the Sixth Patriarch: The Text of the Tun-Huang Manuscript*. New York: Columbia University Press, 1967.

Yanagida Seizan. *Shoki zenshū shisho no kenkyū*. Kyoto: Hōzōkan, 1967.

Yifa. *The Origins of Buddhist Monastic Codes in China: An Annotated Translation and Study of the Chanyuan Qinggui*. Honolulu: University of Hawaii Press, 2002.

Yü, Chün-fang. *The Renewal of Buddhism in China: Chu-hung and the Late Ming Synthesis*. New York: Columbia University Press, 1990.

Yusa, Michiko. *Zen & Philosophy: An Intellectual Biography of Nishida Kitarō*. Honolulu: University of Hawaii Press, 2002.

Zengaku daijiten. Tokyo: Taishūkan shoten, 1985.

Zhang Longxi. *The Tao and the Logos: Literary Hermeneutics, East and West*. Durham, NC: Duke University Press, 1992.

Index

Abe, Masao, 130–131
Aitken, Robert, 16, 67–68
Awa Kenzō, 19–21, 27

Bashō, 103–104
Blue Cliff Record. See *Pi-yen lu*
Bodhidharma, 6–7, 22–25, 34,
   40, 58, 74
The Book of Serenity.
   See *Tsung-jung lu*

Cage, John, 52, 54
Carroll, Lewis, 13, 53
   and *Alice and Wonderland*,
      29, 40, 53
      Humpty Dumpty in, 53–54
   and *The Hunting of the
      Snark*, 53
Carse, James P., 12
Ch'an-men kuei-shih (CMK), 31–36,
      42–47, 71, 73, 77–80,
      120–121, 123–126, 162–163,
      179n.66
Ch'an-yüan ch'ing-kuei, 7, 44,
      121–122, 124–126, 141
Ching-te chuan-teng lu, 22–25, 40
Chuan fa-pao chi, 38, 50

Chuang-tzu, 38, 51, 56
Cohen, Leonard, 5–7, 157

Dadaism, 52–53
Daitokuji temple, 74, 105
Dōgen, 13–14, 22, 25, 44–45, 74, 81,
      167–168
   and *Eihei kōroku*, 44, 151
   and Genjōkōan, 104, 189n.55
   and *Kana Shōbōgenzō*,
      "Kattō," 22
   and *Mana Shōbōgenzō*, 22
   and *Shōbōgenzō*, 69, 165
      "Immo," 27–28
      "Keisei-sanshoku," 164
      "Raihaitokuzui," 106–107
      "Sanjigo," 164
   and *Shōbōgenzō zuimonki*, 164
   and *Tenzokyōkun*, 126, 138
   use of the kōan by, 183n.41
Dumoulin, Heinrich, 16, 19–20, 41,
      86, 105–106

Eiheiji temple, 45, 47, 74, 105,
      148, 159
Eliot, T. S., 29, 40, 54
Enni Ben'en, 45, 120

Fa-hua san-mei ch'an-i, 161
Five Mountains, 33, 45, 121
Fushimi Inari, 100

Gasan Jōseki, 86
    and "five ranks" (*go-i*), 86
Gennō Shinshō, 103–104
Gozan jissatsu zu (GJZ), 31–36, 44–47,
    77–80

Hakamaya Noriaki, 140, 148, 151, 168.
    See also under Zen Rights, Critical
    Buddhism
Harada Sōgaku, 116, 148
Heidegger, Martin, 26, 118, 132
Herrigel, Eugen, 4–5, 13, 18–21, 26–28,
    118, 178n.55
    and "It shoots," 19–21, 27–28
Hie Sannō Jinja, 97
Hisamatsu Shin'ichi, 131–132
Historical and Cultural Criticism (HCC),
    8–13, 28–31, 33–34, 39–41, 47,
    56–57, 73–79, 105–106, 113–114,
    166–120, 128, 139–147, 155–158,
    167–168
"Honored One" (*zon*), 77
Hsüeh-feng, 41, 67–68
Huang-po, 14, 32, 43, 49
Hu Shih, 17–18
Hui-k'o, 6, 22–25, 56
Hui-neng, 6, 24, 50, 116
Hung-chih, 15
Hung-chou school, 32, 39, 58, 162–163

Ichikawa Hakugen, 140, 144–147, 164
Ikkyū, 10–11, 128, 143–144, 164

James, William, 118, 171–172
Jochū Tengin, 86

Kannon, 75, 89–90
Keizan, 85–89
    Zazenyōjinki, 85
Kenchōji temple, 45–46
Kenninji temple, 74
Knitter, Paul, 130–131

Kōan. *See under* Zen Writes
Koestler, Arthur, 5–6, 9, 18–20, 157,
    175n.20, 176n.25
Kōganji temple, 75, 87, 94, 96
Konjaku monogatari, 102
Kuei-shan, 60, 63–65

Li-tai fa-pao chi, 23

Mahakasyapa, 26, 40
Maruyama Masao, 136, 140
Ma-tsu, 32, 58–59, 130, 162.
    See also Hung-chou School
Matsumoto Shirō, 140, 148, 151.
    See also under Zen Rights, Critical
    Buddhism
Mishima Yukio, 16, 19, 49–50,
    140
Mt. A-yü-wang, 79, 81
Mt. Ching, 45
Mt. Hakusan, 81, 83
Mt. T'ien-t'ung, 45
Mujaku Dōchū, 31
Myōgonji temple, 87, 96–101.
    See also Toyokawa Inari
Myōshinji temple, 74, 77, 105, 131

Nihonjinron, 5, 152
Nikujiki saitai, 165
Nishida Kitarō, 118, 136, 145,
    155–156
Nishitani Keiji, 119, 131–134, 144–145
    and *Religion and Nothingness (Shūkyō
    to wa nanika)*, 131–132
    and "Science and Zen," 133–134
Noma Hiroshi, 150–151
Northern school, 50

Ōmori Sōgen, 147
Orientalism, 3–6
    Post-Orientalism, 5, 174n.12
    Reverse Orientalism, 4–6, 49–50
Outcasts. *See under* Zen Rights,
    Burakumin
"Overcoming Modernity" Symposium,
    141

Pai-chang, 7, 31–32, 58–59, 64–65, 77,
88–89, 124. *See also Ch'an-men
kuei-shih*
and geomancer/wizard Ssu-ma, 64
Pi-yen lu (Hekiganroku), 34, 41, 57,
59, 66
Case 4 in, 66–67
Cases 1 in, 73, and 93, 106
Cases 51 and 66 in, 68
Platform Sutra, 116, 160–163, 165–166,
169, 171

Repentance, 45, 127, 160–172
"Formless repentance," 127, 160–166
and *jiko hihan,* 30, 170
and *zangedō,* 30, 155–156, 170–172
and *zange metsuzai,* 165–166, 170–171
Reps, Paul, 16, 26
Rinzai school, 105, 129, 148, 163
Rude Awakenings, 11, 118, 137
Ryōan Emmyō, 86, 89

Saijōji temple, 75, 88–94, 105
Sakyamuni, 26, 37, 40, 42, 73, 80,
85, 130
Schumacher, E. F., 137, 175n.22
Senzaki, Nyogen, 16, 26
Shichidō garan. See under Temple
grounds, Seven-Hall Monastery
Shōbai hanjō, 75
Shōbōgenzō. See under Dōgen
Shushōgi, 165–166, 170
"Skin, Flesh, Bones, Marrow," 6, 13–14,
22–26, 119
Sōjiji temple, 74, 85–89, 100
Sōtō school, 74, 84–85, 96, 105, 148, 159,
163, 197n.10
and "Green Plan," 193n.37
and role of women, 190n.1
Stevenson, Robert Louis, 158–159
Sugamo, 94–96
Suzuki, D.T., 13, 15, 17–18, 118–119, 148

Ta-hui, 15
Takuan Sōhō, 116, 164
Tanabe Hajime, 140, 155–156

Tao-yü, 22–24
Tao Yuan-ming, 51–52, 137, 174n.9
and "Peach Blossom Spring," 137,
174n.9
Te-mizu, 75
Temple grounds, 31–32, 73–83, 179n.68,
181n.19, 184n.57, 184n.1
Abbot's Quarters (*hōjō*), 34–35, 43–45,
77–78
entering the, 43–44
as a "ten-foot square hut," 44
Ancestors Hall *See* Patriarchs Hall
Bathhouse (*yokushitsu*), 32
Buddha Hall (*butsudō*), 32, 34–36,
43–44, 47, 77–78, 81, 84
Cloud Hall (*undō*), 122
Dharma Hall (*hondō/hattō*), 32, 34–36,
43–47, 70, 77–78, 84, 88, 91, 100,
121, 141
Earth Deity Hall, 80–84
Founder's Hall (*daisodō*), 88
Guardian Deity Hall, 81
Main Hall. *See* Dharma Hall
Monks Hall. *See* Samgha Hall
Mountain Gate (*sanmon*), 75
Patriarchs Hall (*soshidō*), 80–84
Repentance Hall (*gokudō*), 93
Samgha Hall (*sōdō*), 32, 34–36, 47,
78, 87–88, 91, 120–123, 137,
141–142
Scripture Hall (*shoin*), 91
Seven Hall Monastery (*shichidō garan*),
7, 29, 75
White Cloud Pavilion (*hakuunkaku*), 91
Temple of the Golden Pavillion, 16, 50, 135,
172. *See also* Mishima Yukio
Father Zenkai in, 50–51
Ten Oxherding Pictures, 7, 135,
145–146
Te-shan, 6, 61, 65–71, 107. *See also under*
Zen Writes, Kōan
T'ien-sheng kuang-teng lu, 24, 40, 55
T'ien-t'ai school, 127, 161–162
Tōfukuji temple, 45, 120, 122
Toyokawa Inari, 96–101, 105, 113.
See also Myōgonji temple

Traditional Zen Narrative (TZN), 6–13,
    28–31, 33–34, 38–39, 41, 49, 52,
    55–56, 63, 73–77, 106–107,
    113–114, 116–120, 128–130, 137,
    139, 155–158, 166–168
Tsung-chih, 22–24
Tsung-jung lu (Shōyōroku), 41, 48, 65–70,
    84, 106. See under Zen Writes,
    Kōan
Tsung-mi, 14, 24, 162–163
    and Chung-hua ch'uan-hsin-ti
    ch'an-men shih-tzu ch'eng-hsi
    t'u, 24
Tung-shan Liang-chieh, 68, 86

Uchiyama Gudō, 159
Ueda Shizuteru, 140–141
Uposatha (Buddhist Sabbath), 127

Victoria, Brian (Daizen), 140–141,
    147–148, 157, 167
    Zen at War, 11, 140, 167
    Zen War Stories, 140, 147, 167
Vimalakirti Sutra, 38, 44
Vinaya school, 33

Watts, Alan, 16–17, 54
Wieger, Leon, 49, 57
Wittgenstein, Ludwig, 51
Wu-men kuan, 6, 27, 41, 55, 62, 65–71,
    106, 116. See also under Zen
    Writes, Kōan

Yamabushi, 86
Yamada Shōji, 20–21, 23
Yasutani Haku'un, 147–148
Yen-t'ou, 65, 68–70
Yojimbo, 16
Yōkōji temple, 86
Yüan-wu, 68
Yün-men, 39, 59, 67–68

Zen
    Communal labor in, 123
    History of, 175n.17
    Rector, 125

Self-power in, 128
Zen Rights
    and burakumin, 9, 115, 150–151,
        159–160
    and Critical Buddhism (hihan Bukkyō),
        148, 151–153, 164, 167–168
    and F.A.S Society, 131–132
    and "Imperial Way Zen" (kōdō Zen),
        115, 141, 147
    and Kyoto School philosophers,
        139–141, 144–146, 191n.4
    and Pratimoksha, 127, 163
    and Pravanana, 127
    and the precepts, 124, 192n.15
    and sabetsu mondai, 115
    and sōshiki Bukkyō, 9, 139
    and Suiheisha Movement, 169
Zen Rites
    and Abbot's staff, 125
    and avatars of Buddha. See Gongen,
        Chinju
    and Benzaiten, 85, 99
    and ceremonial fly whisk in, 47, 82
    and chinju, 83–84, 96, 111
    and Dakini-shinten, 75, 97–101
    and "divided spirit sites"
        (bunreisho), 96
    and Dōryōzon, 89
    and the "Eclipse of Buddha," 77,
        104–106, 108–110
    and ema, 75
    and exorcism (oharai/tsuina) in, 109
    and folk religions, 75–77, 83–111,
        187n.40
    and garanjin. See chinju
    and genze riyaku in, 9, 75
    and gongen, 30, 75, 96
    and honji suijaku, 105, 111
    and honzon, 96, 111
    and Inari, 75, 83, 98–102, 108–109,
        188n.4
    and Jizō, 75
        Togenuki Jizō, 94, 113–114
    use of kaimyō (posthumous initiation
        names) in, 9, 115, 140, 149–150,
        159

and the "Killing Stone" (*sesshō seki*), 103
and *kitō jiin*, 10, 29, 73
and Kitsune, 75, 98–99, 102–103, 108–109. *See also* Inari
and *Kojiki/Nihongi* fertility gods, 99
and *Obaachan no Harajuku* ("granny's Harajuku"), 94
and *o-mikuji*, 75
and the "One-strike Stone" (*ittekiseki*), 93
and *onryō* (conflictive) spirits, 109
and *shinbutsu bunri*, 99
and *shinkō*, 99–100
and stylized portraits of abbots. See *Chinsō*
and supernormal powers in, 82
and Tengu, 75, 89–90, 108–109
and the "Zazen Stone" (*zazen seki*), 92
Zen Writes
and Abbot entering the Dharma Hall, 43
and *chinsō*, 82, 149
and encounter dialogues in, 39, 60–62
extraordinary words and strange deeds (*kigen kikō*), 60
and *kirigami*, 149–150
Kōan in, 39, 41, 56–60
"Kicking Over the Water Pitcher" (*Wu-men kuan* 40), 62–65

"Ma-tsu's Four Affirmations and Hundred Negations" (*Pi-yen lu* 73), 57–59
"Nan-ch'üan Kills the Cat," 50
"The Sound of the Bell and the 7-Piece Robe" (*Wu-men kuan* 16), 179n.64
"Te-shan Carries His Bowl" (*Wu-men kuan* 13 and *Tsung-jung lu* 55), 41, 65–71
Tsung-jung lu case 10, 83, 112
Tsung-jung lu case 14, 68
"White and Black" (*Tsung jung lu* 40), 59, 71
"Wild Fox" (*Wu-men kuan* 2 and *Tsung-jung lu* 8), 69
Wu-men kuan case 4/*Tsung-jung lu* case 8, 116
Wu-men kuan case 23, 116
Wu-men kuan case 28, 66–67
"Wu-tsu's Buffalo Passes through the Window" (*Wu-men kuan* 38), 130
and "large convocation[s]" (*daisan*), 44
"Living words and dead words" in, 39
and puns and wordplay, 198n.16
and *shōmono*, 39
and "small convocation[s]" (*shōsan*), 44